SILK

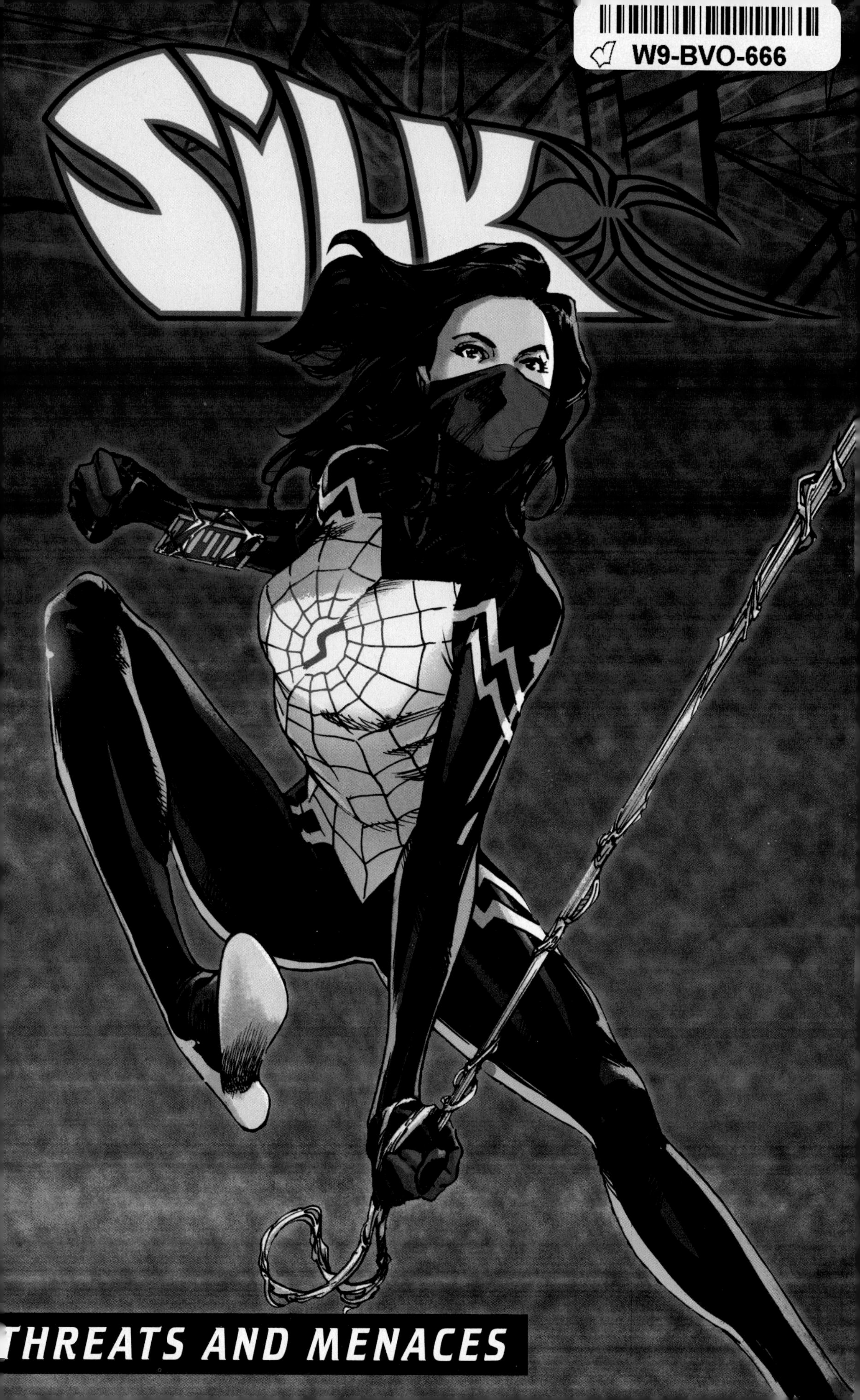

THREATS AND MENACES

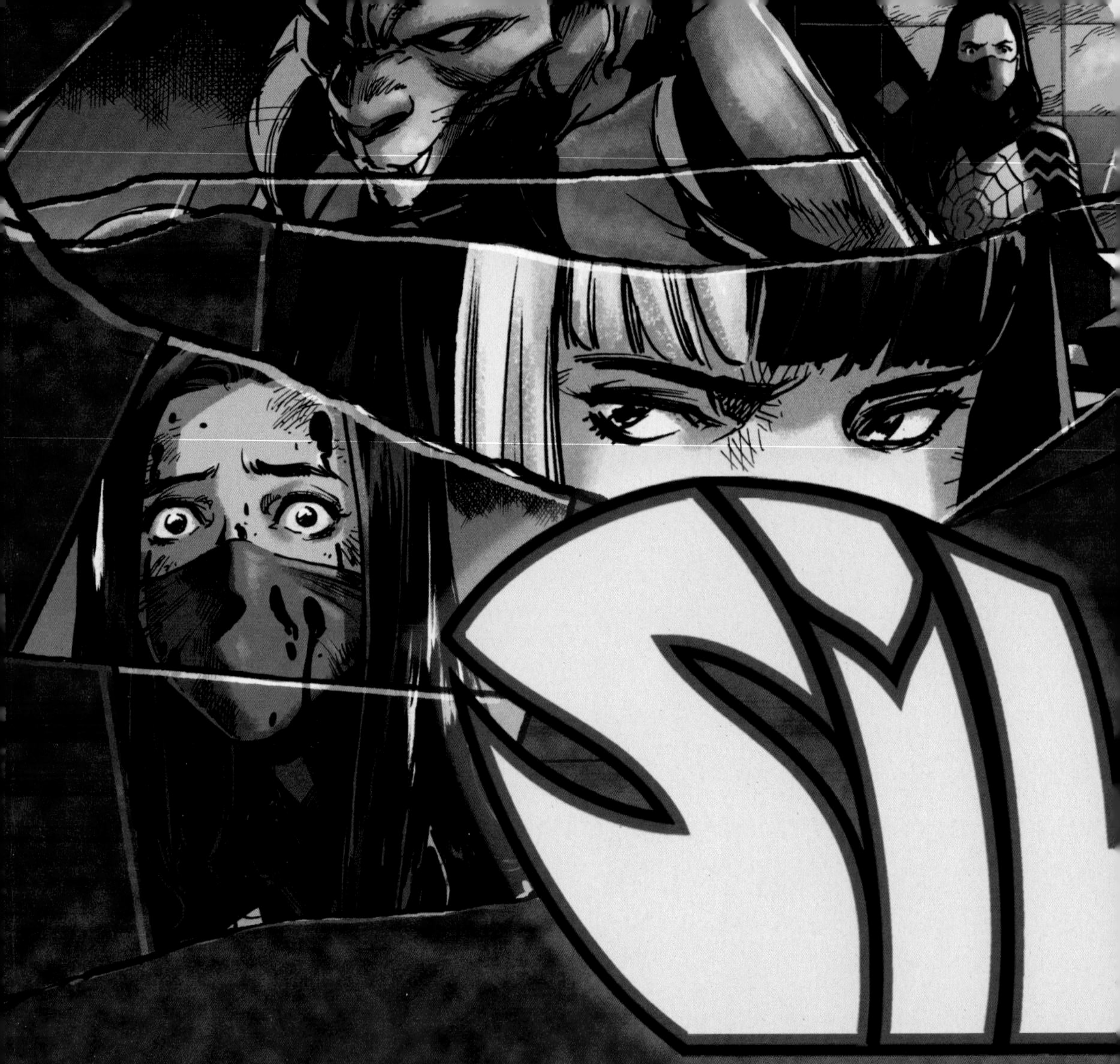

AS A TEENAGER, CINDY MOON WAS BITTEN BY THE SAME SPIDER THAT BIT PETER PARKER, GIVING HER POWERS SIMILAR TO THOSE OF THE AMAZING SPIDER-MAN: ADHESION AND A PRECOGNITIVE AWARENESS OF DANGER. UNLIKE SPIDEY, SHE SHOOTS VERSATILE WEBS OUT OF HER FINGERTIPS! TARGETED BY DANGEROUS PEOPLE FOR HER POWERS, SHE WAS LOCKED IN A BUNKER FOR OVER A DECADE.

SINCE REJOINING THE WORLD, SHE FOUND HER MISSING PARENTS, RESCUED HER LITTLE BROTHER AND SAVED THE MULTIVERSE. SHE'S BEEN A DOUBLE AGENT, A NEW AGENT OF ATLAS AND A COFOUNDER OF THE ORDER OF THE WEB. BUT MOST JUST KNOW HER AS THE WEB-SPINNING SUPER HERO...

SILK VOL. 1: THREATS AND MENACES. Contains material originally published in magazine form as SILK (2021) #1-5. First printing 2021. ISBN 978-1-302-92439-3. Published by MARVEL WORLDWIDE, INC., a subsidiary of MARVEL ENTERTAINMENT, LLC. OFFICE OF PUBLICATION: 1290 Avenue of the Americas, New York, NY 10104. © 2021 MARVEL No similarity between any of the names, characters, persons, and/or institutions in this magazine with those of any living or dead person or institution is intended, and any such similarity which may exist is purely coincidental. **Printed in Canada.** KEVIN FEIGE, Chief Creative Officer; DAN BUCKLEY, President, Marvel Entertainment; JOE QUESADA, EVP & Creative Director; DAVID BOGART, Associate Publisher & SVP of Talent Affairs; TOM BREVOORT, VP, Executive Editor; NICK LOWE, Executive Editor, VP of Content, Digital Publishing; DAVID GABRIEL, VP of Print & Digital Publishing; JEFF YOUNGQUIST, VP of Production & Special Projects; ALEX MORALES, Director of Publishing Operations; DAN EDINGTON, Managing Editor; RICKEY PURDIN, Director of Talent Relations; JENNIFER GRÜNWALD, Senior Editor, Special Projects; SUSAN CRESPI, Production Manager; STAN LEE, Chairman Emeritus. For information regarding advertising in Marvel Comics or on Marvel.com, please contact Vit DeBellis, Custom Solutions & Integrated Advertising Manager, at vdebellis@marvel.com. For Marvel subscription inquiries, please call 888-511-5480. **Manufactured between 9/10/2021 and 10/12/2021 by SOLISCO PRINTERS, SCOTT, QC, CANADA.**

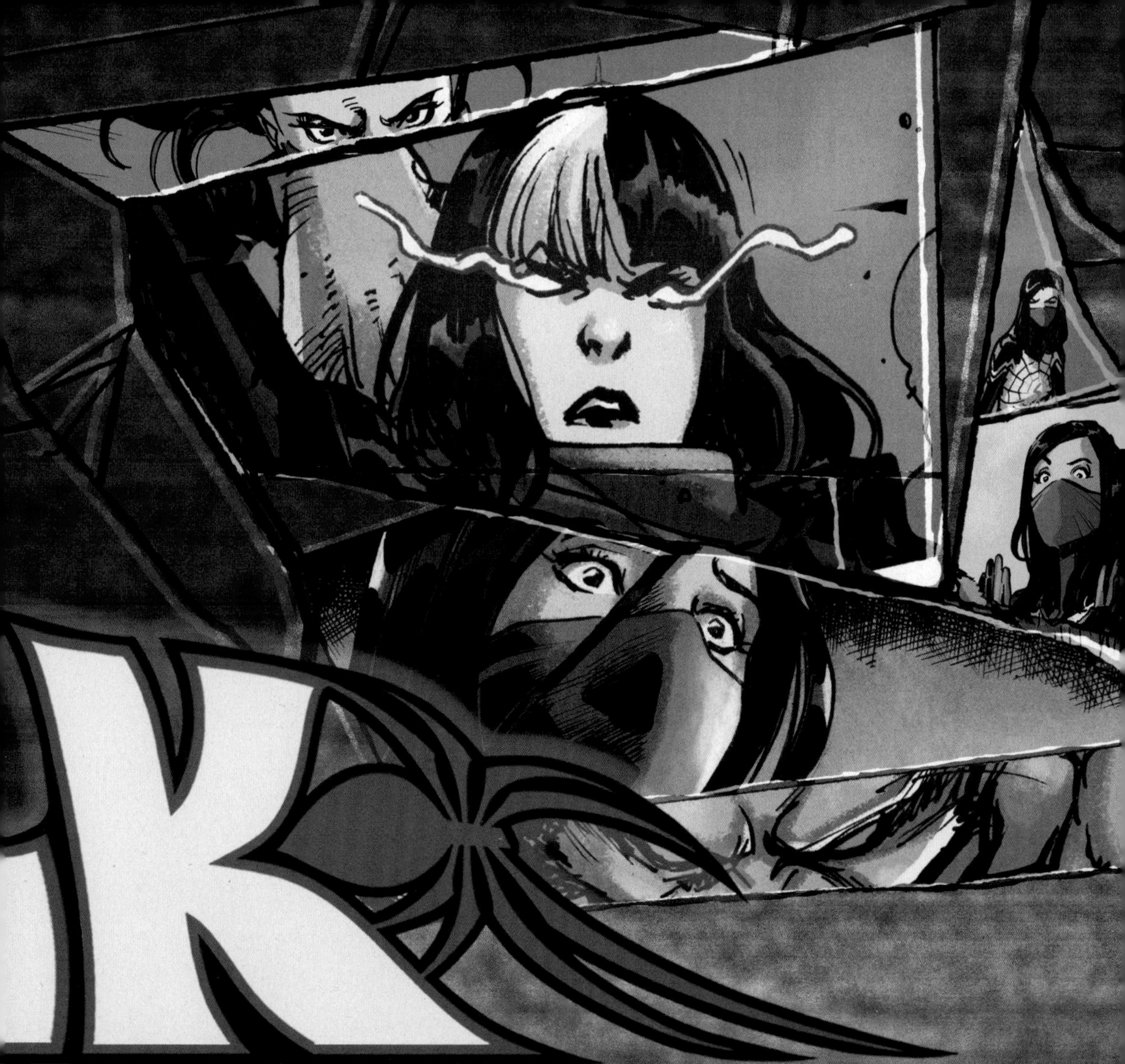

writer — MAURENE GOO
artist — TAKESHI MIYAZAWA
color artist — IAN HERRING
letterer — VC's ARIANA MAHER
cover art — STONEHOUSE (#1), INHYUK LEE (#2), WOO-CHUL LEE (#3), PYEONG-JUN PARK (#4) & RICO (#5)

editors — LINDSEY COHICK & JAKE THOMAS
executive editor — NICK LOWE

collection editor — JENNIFER GRÜNWALD
assistant editor — DANIEL KIRCHHOFFER
assistant managing editor — MAIA LOY
assistant managing editor — LISA MONTALBANO
vp production & special projects — JEFF YOUNGQUIST
book designer — SARAH SPADACCINI
editor in chief — C.B. CEBULSKI

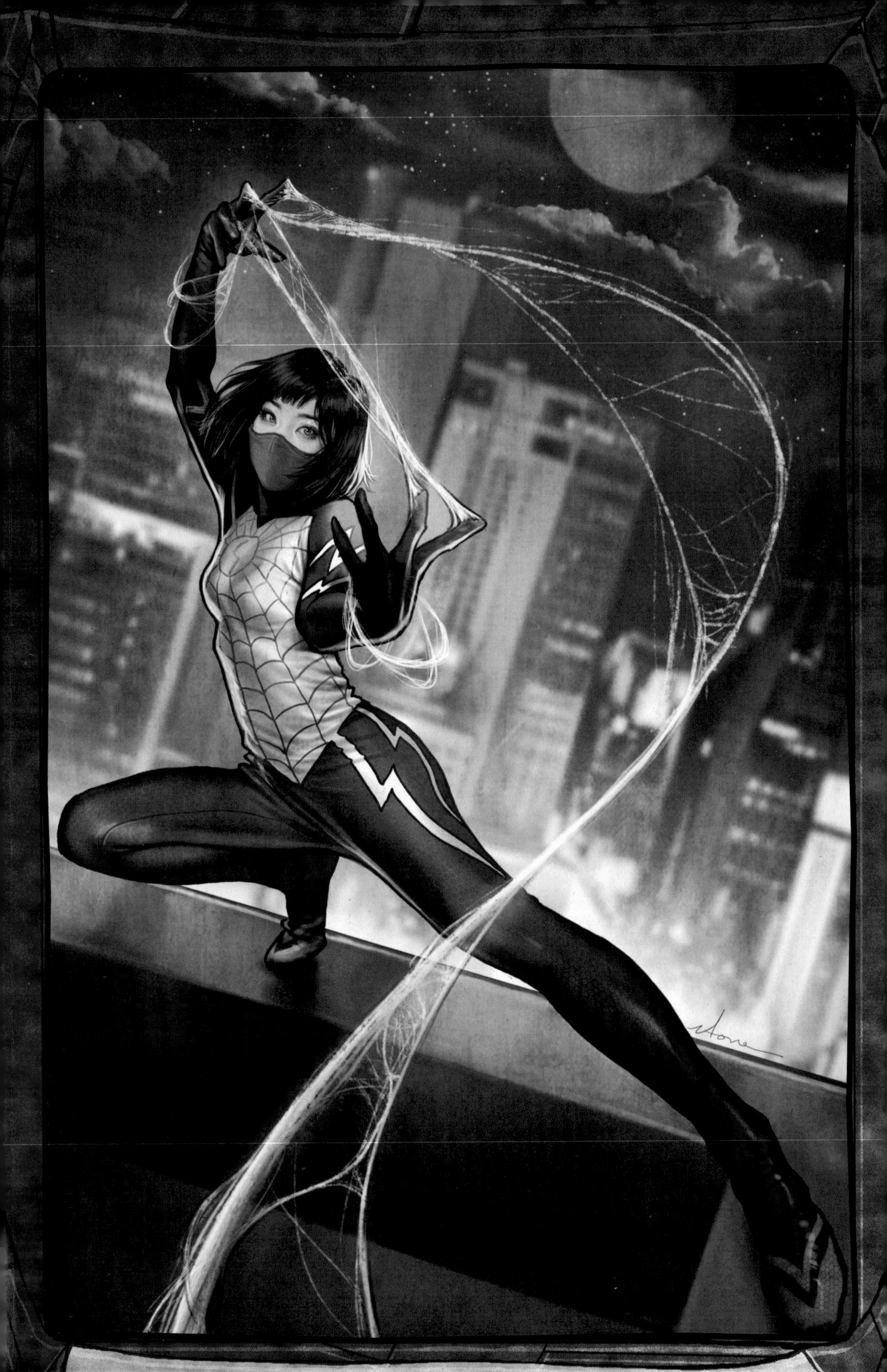

SILK #1

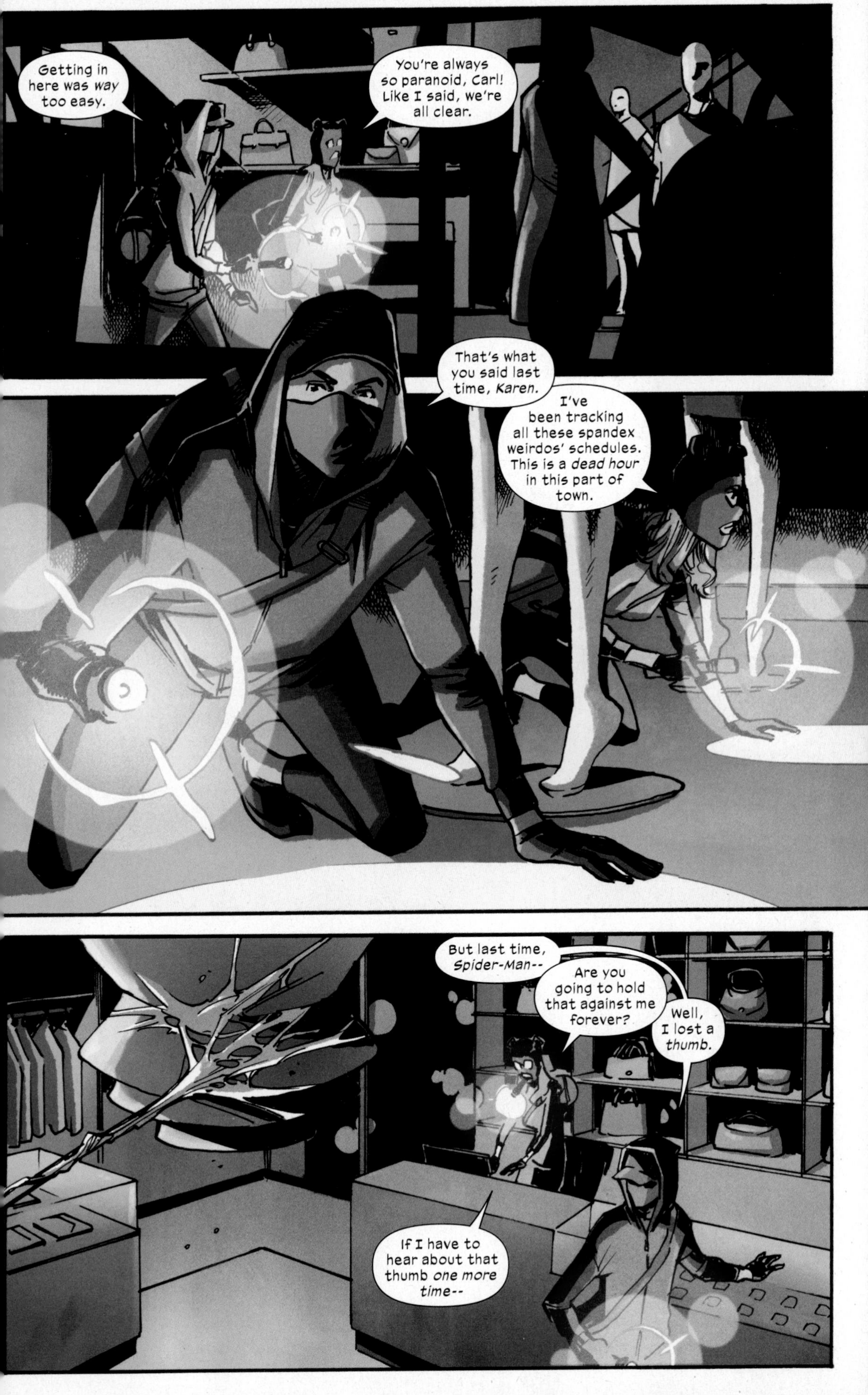
Getting in here was *way* too easy.
You're always so paranoid, Carl! Like I said, we're all clear.
That's what you said last time, *Karen*.
I've been tracking all these spandex weirdos' schedules. This is a *dead hour* in this part of town.
But last time, *Spider-Man*--
Are you going to hold that against me forever?
Well, I lost a *thumb*.
If I have to hear about that thumb *one more time*--

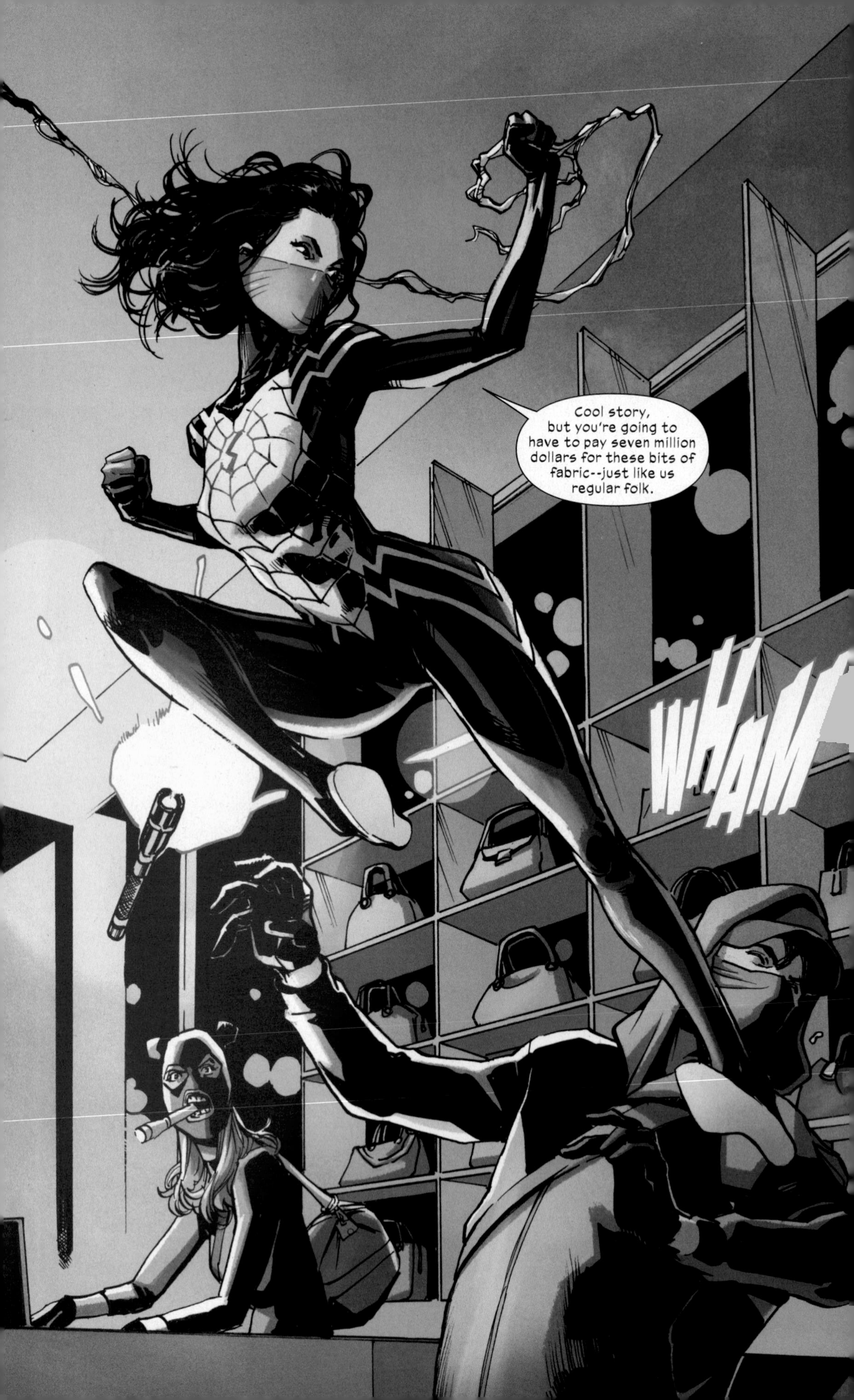
Cool story, but you're going to have to pay seven million dollars for these bits of fabric--just like us regular folk.
WHAM

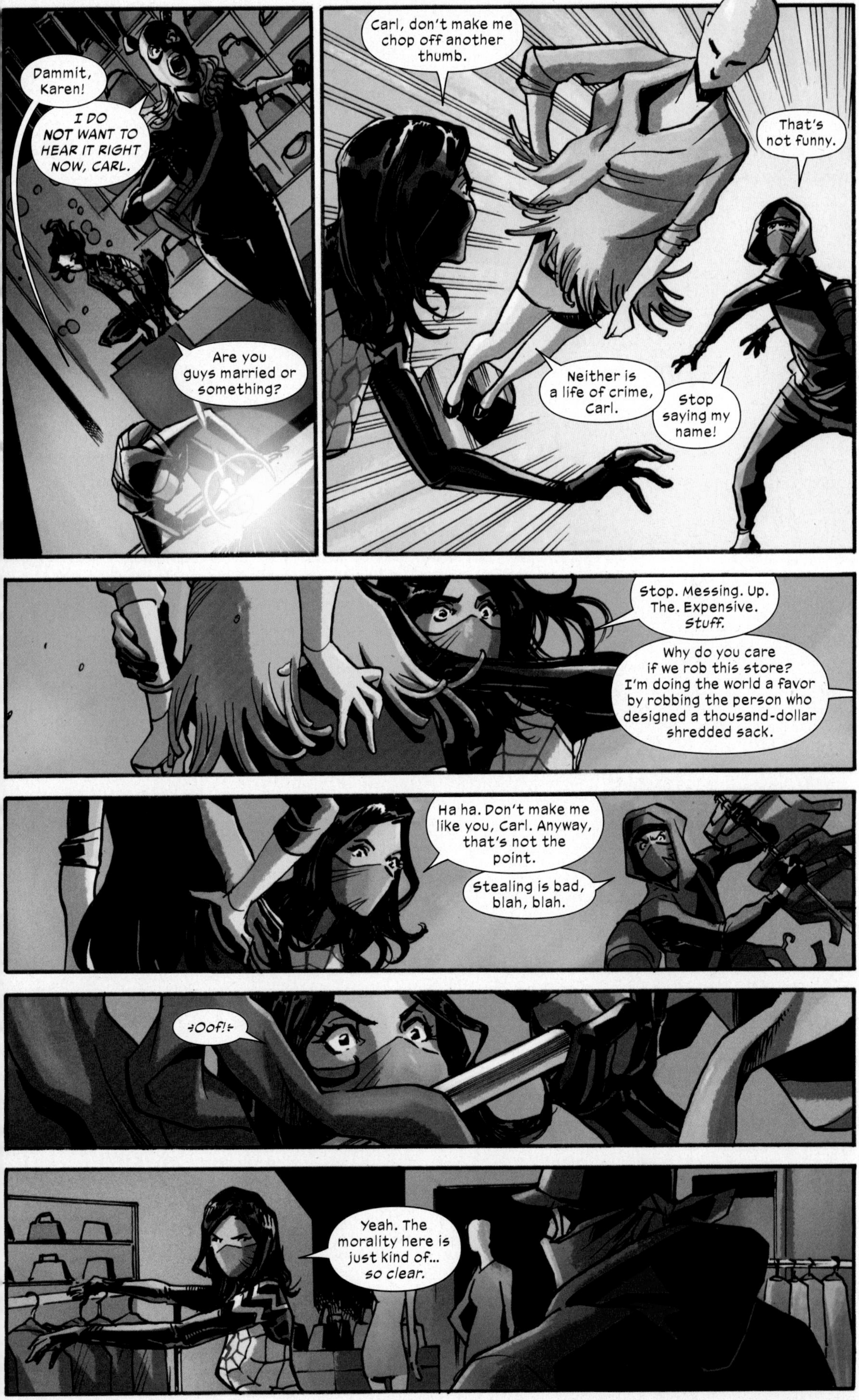
Dammit, Karen!
I DO NOT WANT TO HEAR IT RIGHT NOW, CARL.
Are you guys married or something?
Carl, don't make me chop off another thumb.
That's not funny.
Neither is a life of crime, Carl.
Stop saying my name!
Stop. Messing. Up. The. Expensive. Stuff.
Why do you care if we rob this store? I'm doing the world a favor by robbing the person who designed a thousand-dollar shredded sack.
Ha ha. Don't make me like you, Carl. Anyway, that's not the point.
Stealing is bad, blah, blah.
Oof!
Yeah. The morality here is just kind of... so clear.

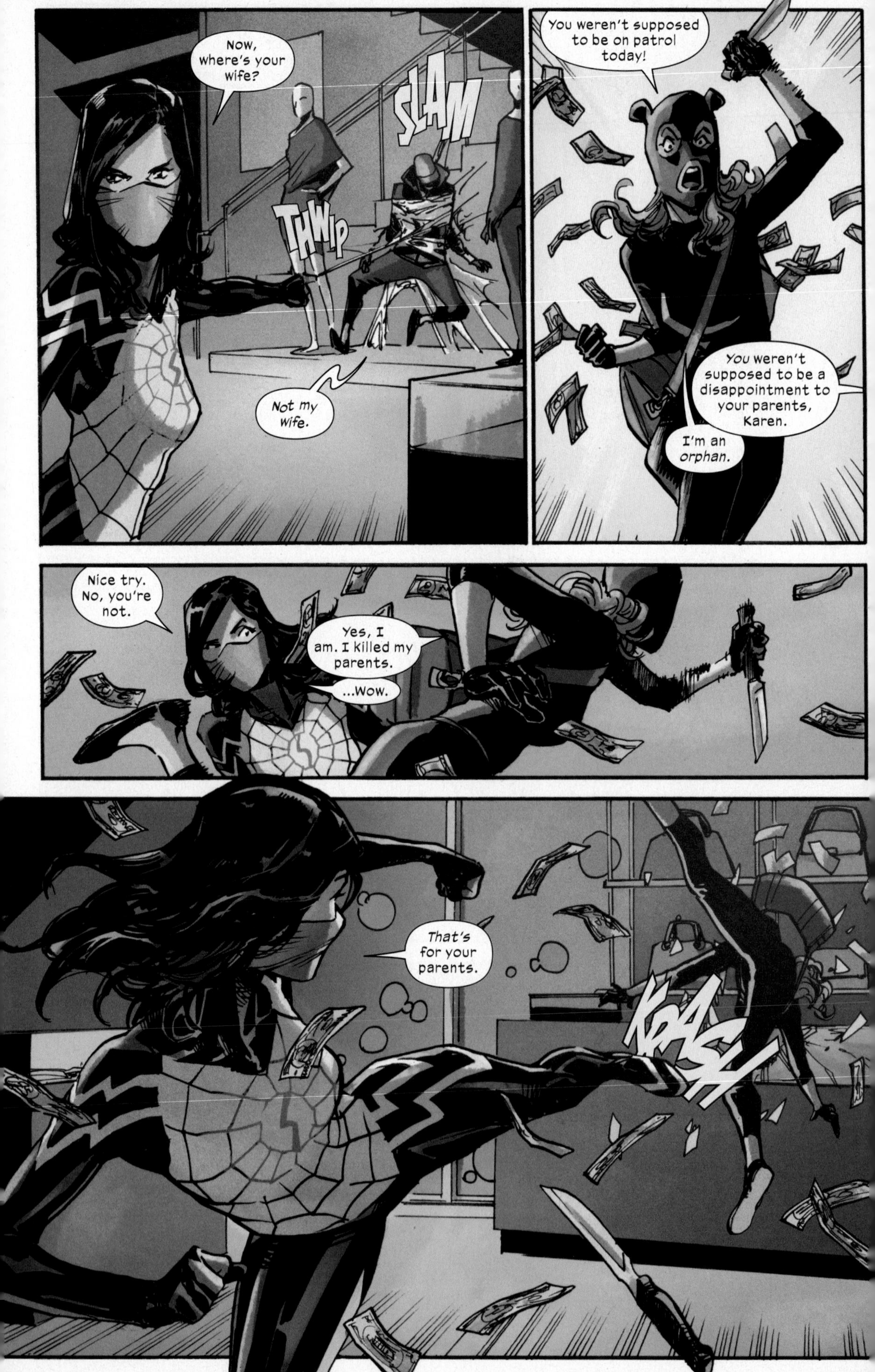
Now, where's your wife?
SLAM
THWIP
Not my wife.
You weren't supposed to be on patrol today!
You weren't supposed to be a disappointment to your parents, Karen.
I'm an orphan.
Nice try. No, you're not.
Yes, I am. I killed my parents.
...Wow.
That's for your parents.
KRASH

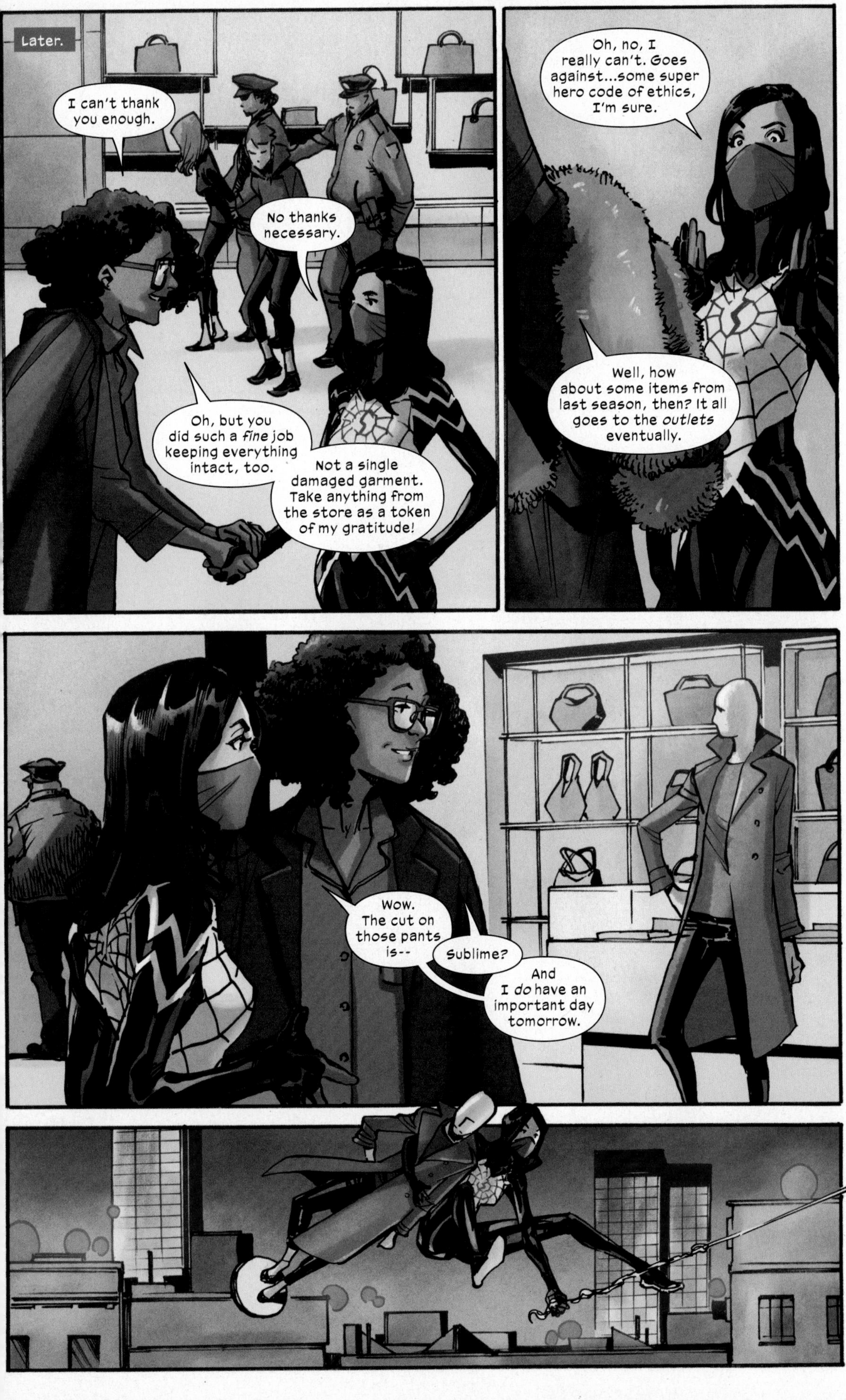
Later.
I can't thank you enough.
No thanks necessary.
Oh, but you did such a *fine* job keeping everything intact, too.
Not a single damaged garment. Take anything from the store as a token of my gratitude!
Oh, no, I really can't. Goes against...some super hero code of ethics, I'm sure.
Well, how about some items from last season, then? It all goes to the *outlets* eventually.
Wow. The cut on those pants is--
Sublime?
And I *do* have an important day tomorrow.

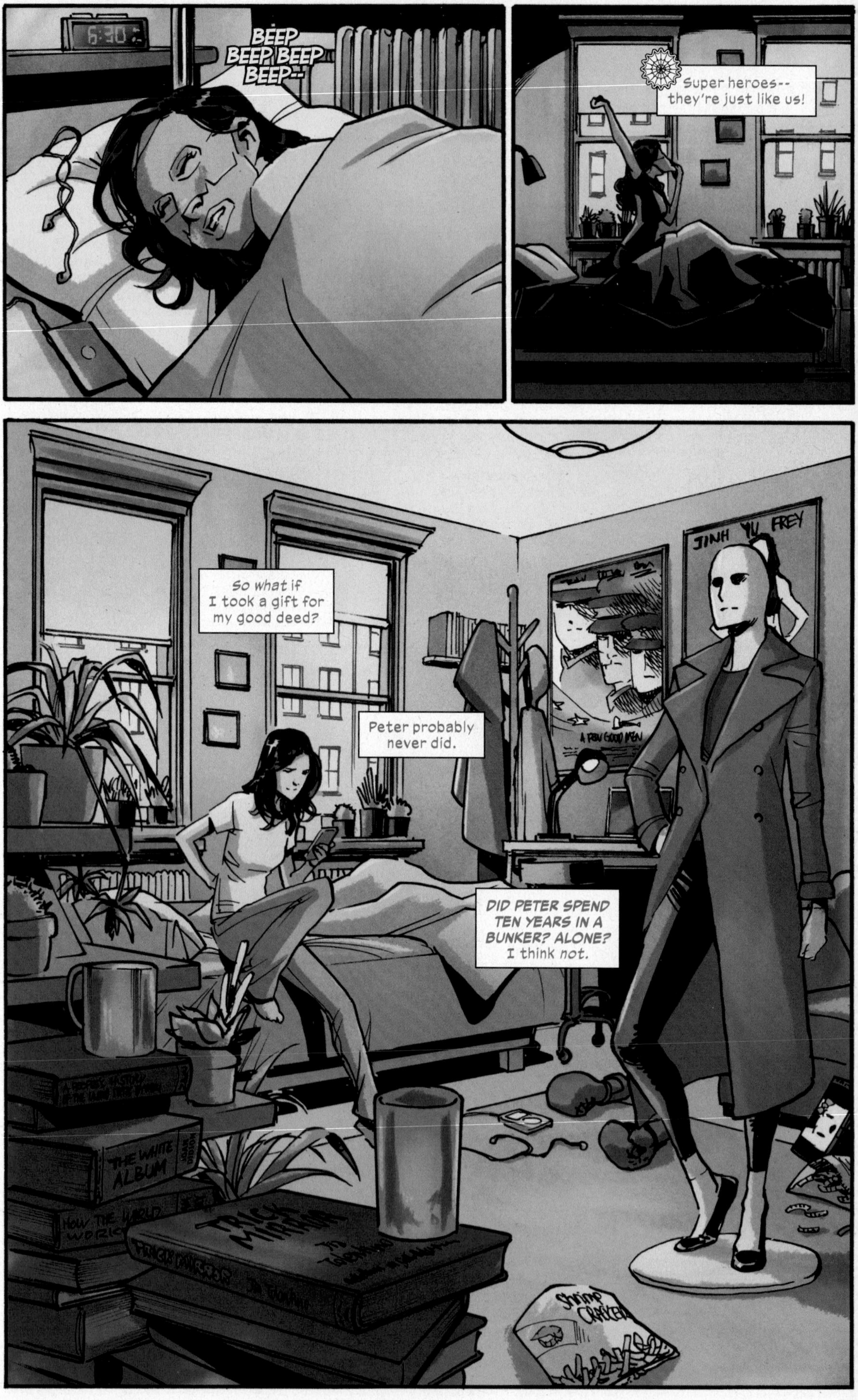
BEEP BEEP BEEP BEEP--
Super heroes-- they're just like us!
So what if I took a gift for my good deed?
Peter probably never did.
JINH YU FREY
A FEW GOOD MEN
DID PETER SPEND TEN YEARS IN A BUNKER? ALONE? I think not.
THE WHITE ALBUM
TRICK MIRROR
SHRIMP CRACKERS

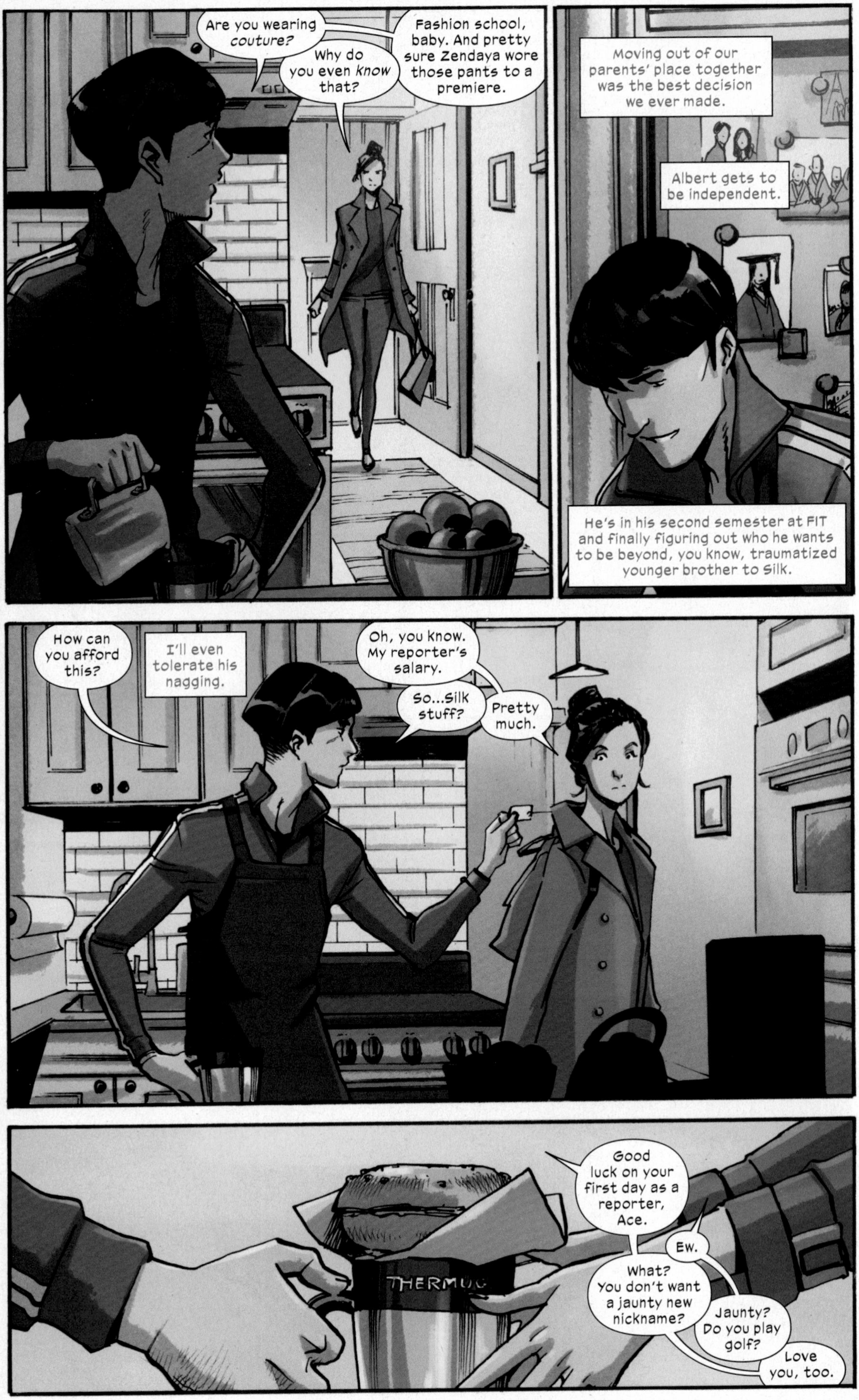

Are you wearing *couture?*
Fashion school, baby. And pretty sure Zendaya wore those pants to a premiere.
Why do you even *know* that?
Moving out of our parents' place together was the best decision we ever made.
Albert gets to be independent.
He's in his second semester at FIT and finally figuring out who he wants to be beyond, you know, traumatized younger brother to Silk.
How can you afford this?
I'll even tolerate his nagging.
Oh, you know. My reporter's salary.
So...Silk stuff?
Pretty much.
Good luck on your first day as a reporter, Ace.
Ew.
What? You don't want a jaunty new nickname?
Jaunty? Do you play golf?
Love you, too.
THERMUG

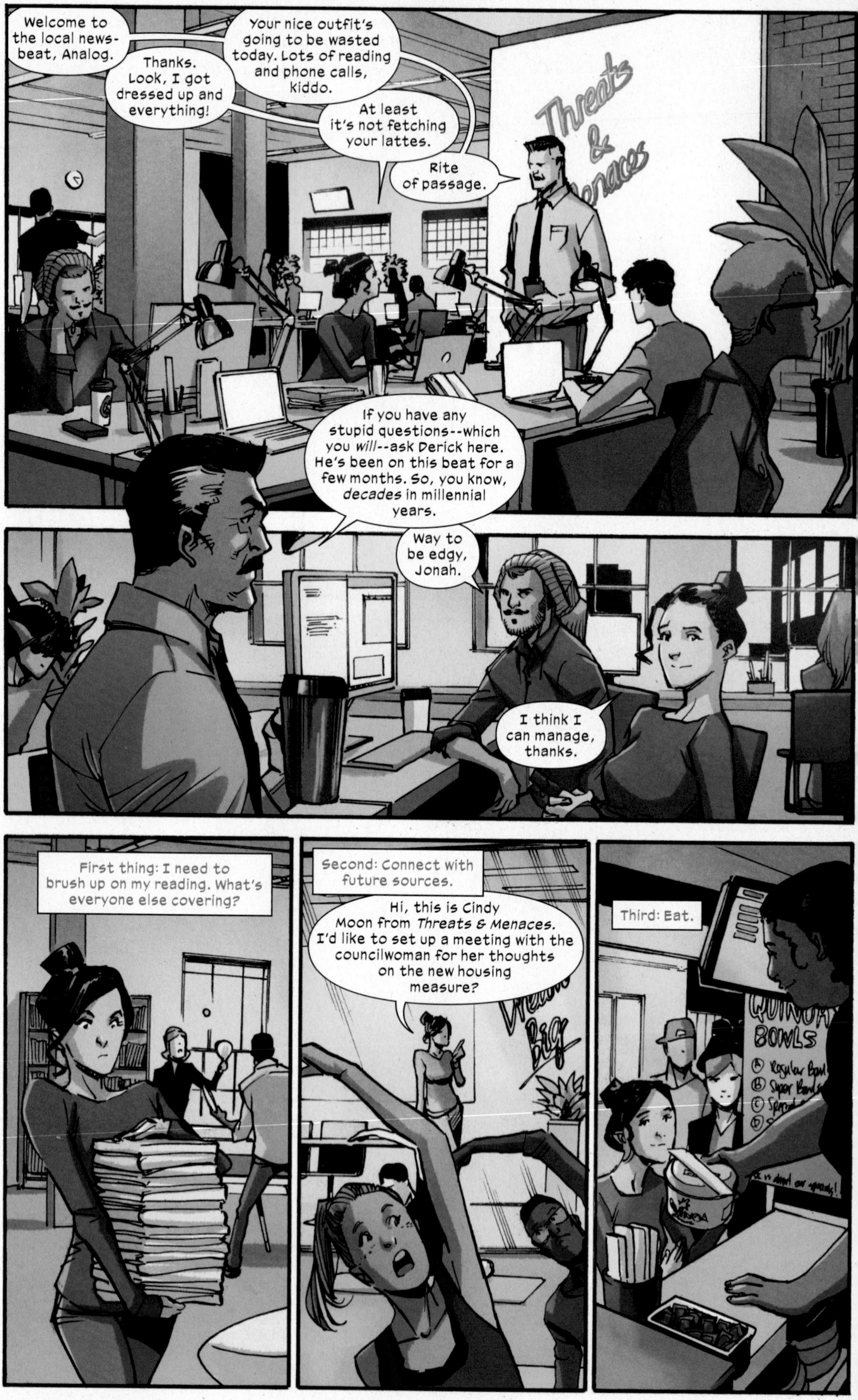
Welcome to the local news-beat, Analog.
Thanks. Look, I got dressed up and everything!
Your nice outfit's going to be wasted today. Lots of reading and phone calls, kiddo.
At least it's not fetching your lattes.
Rite of passage.
Threats & Menaces
If you have any stupid questions--which you *will*--ask Derick here. He's been on this beat for a few months. So, you know, *decades* in millennial years.
Way to be edgy, Jonah.
I think I can manage, thanks.
First thing: I need to brush up on my reading. What's everyone else covering?
Second: Connect with future sources.
Hi, this is Cindy Moon from *Threats & Menaces*. I'd like to set up a meeting with the councilwoman for her thoughts on the new housing measure?
Third: Eat.

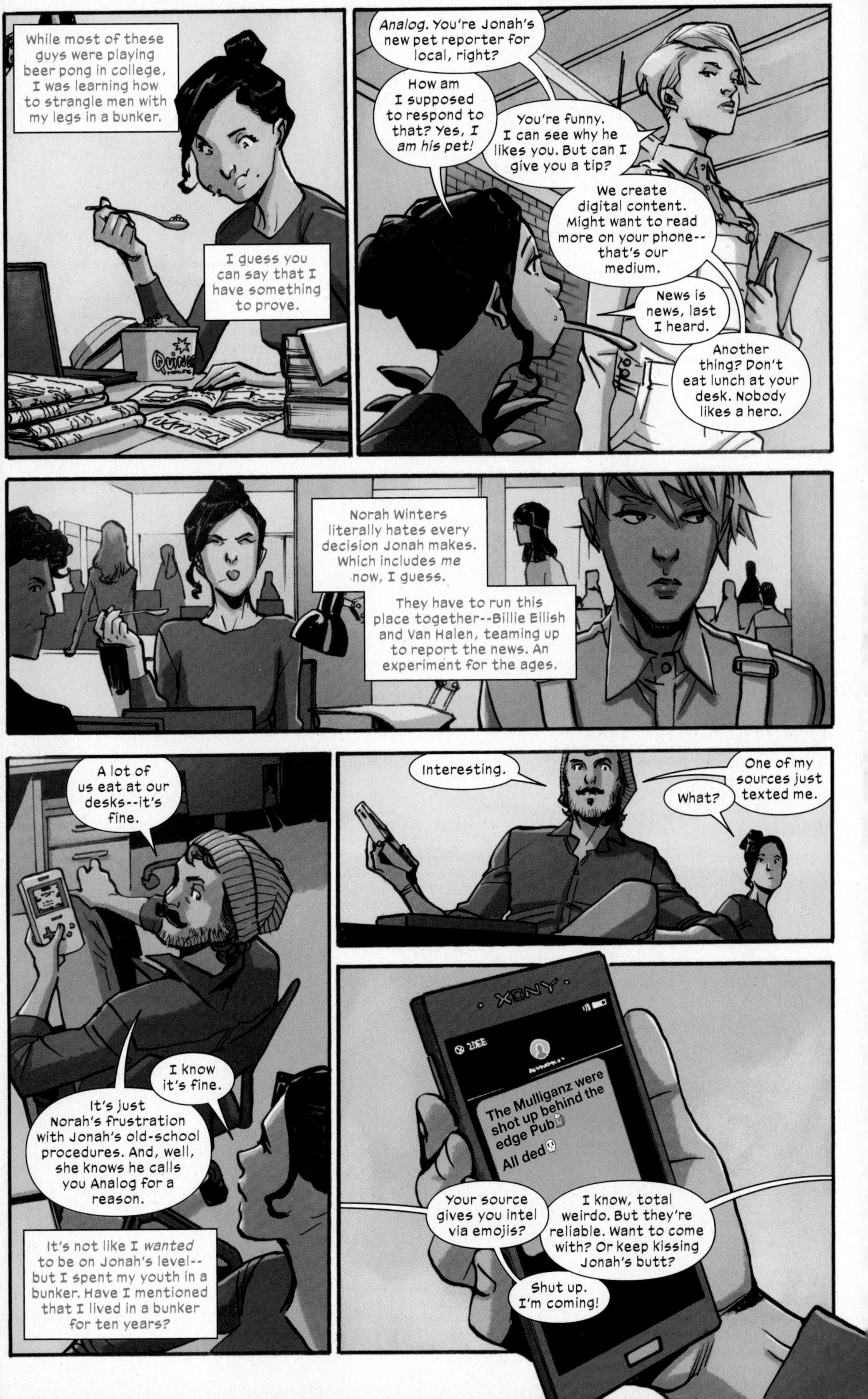

While most of these guys were playing beer pong in college, I was learning how to strangle men with my legs in a bunker.
I guess you can say that I have something to prove.
Analog. You're Jonah's new pet reporter for local, right?
How am I supposed to respond to that? Yes, I am his pet!
You're funny. I can see why he likes you. But can I give you a tip?
We create digital content. Might want to read more on your phone--that's our medium.
News is news, last I heard.
Another thing? Don't eat lunch at your desk. Nobody likes a hero.
Norah Winters literally hates every decision Jonah makes. Which includes me now, I guess.
They have to run this place together--Billie Eilish and Van Halen, teaming up to report the news. An experiment for the ages.
A lot of us eat at our desks--it's fine.
I know it's fine.
It's just Norah's frustration with Jonah's old-school procedures. And, well, she knows he calls you Analog for a reason.
It's not like I wanted to be on Jonah's level--but I spent my youth in a bunker. Have I mentioned that I lived in a bunker for ten years?
Interesting.
One of my sources just texted me.
What?
XONY
The Mulliganz were shot up behind the edge Pub
All ded
Your source gives you intel via emojis?
I know, total weirdo. But they're reliable. Want to come with? Or keep kissing Jonah's butt?
Shut up. I'm coming!

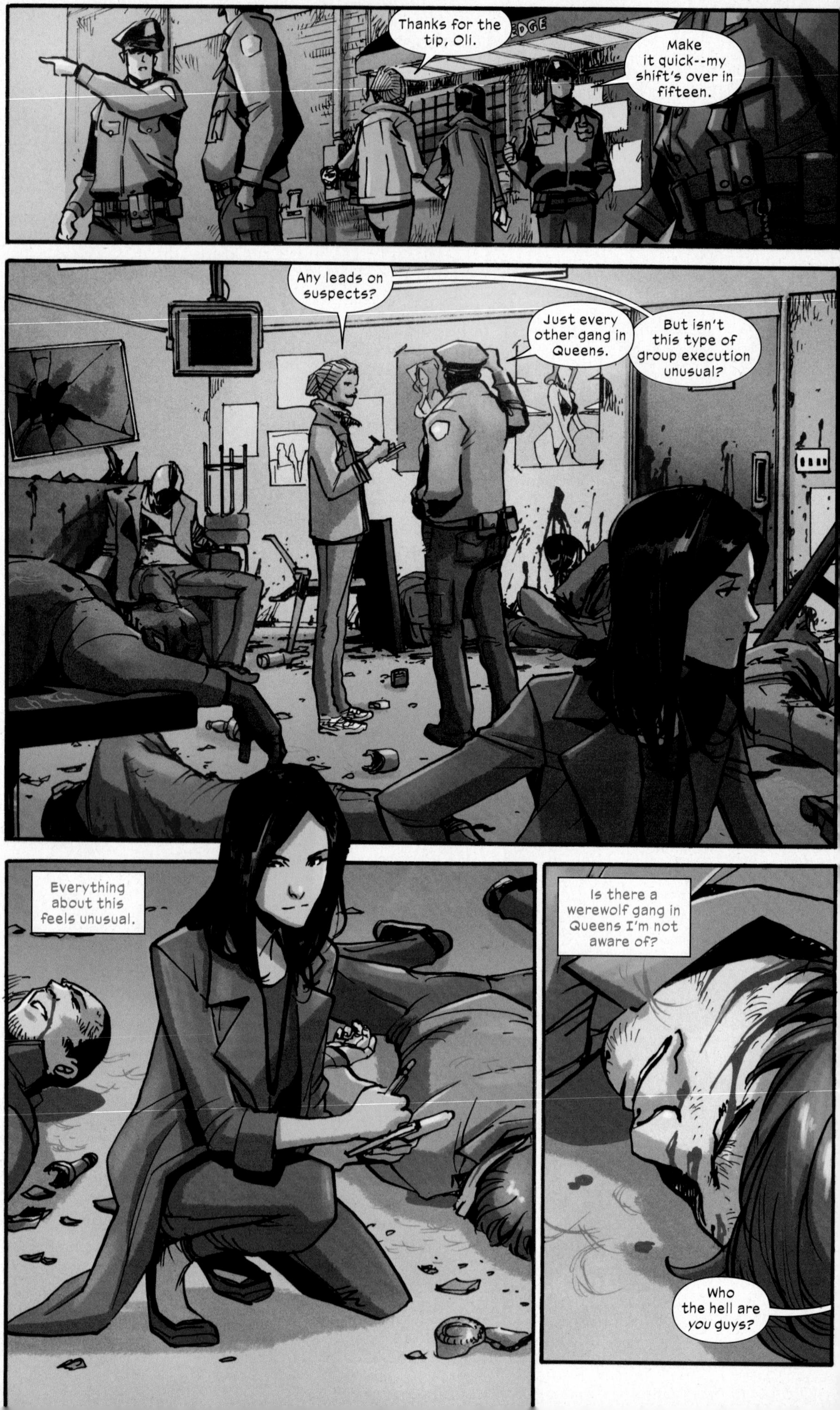
Thanks for the tip, Oli.
Make it quick--my shift's over in fifteen.
Any leads on suspects?
Just every other gang in Queens.
But isn't this type of group execution unusual?
Everything about this feels unusual.
Is there a werewolf gang in Queens I'm not aware of?
Who the hell are *you guys?*

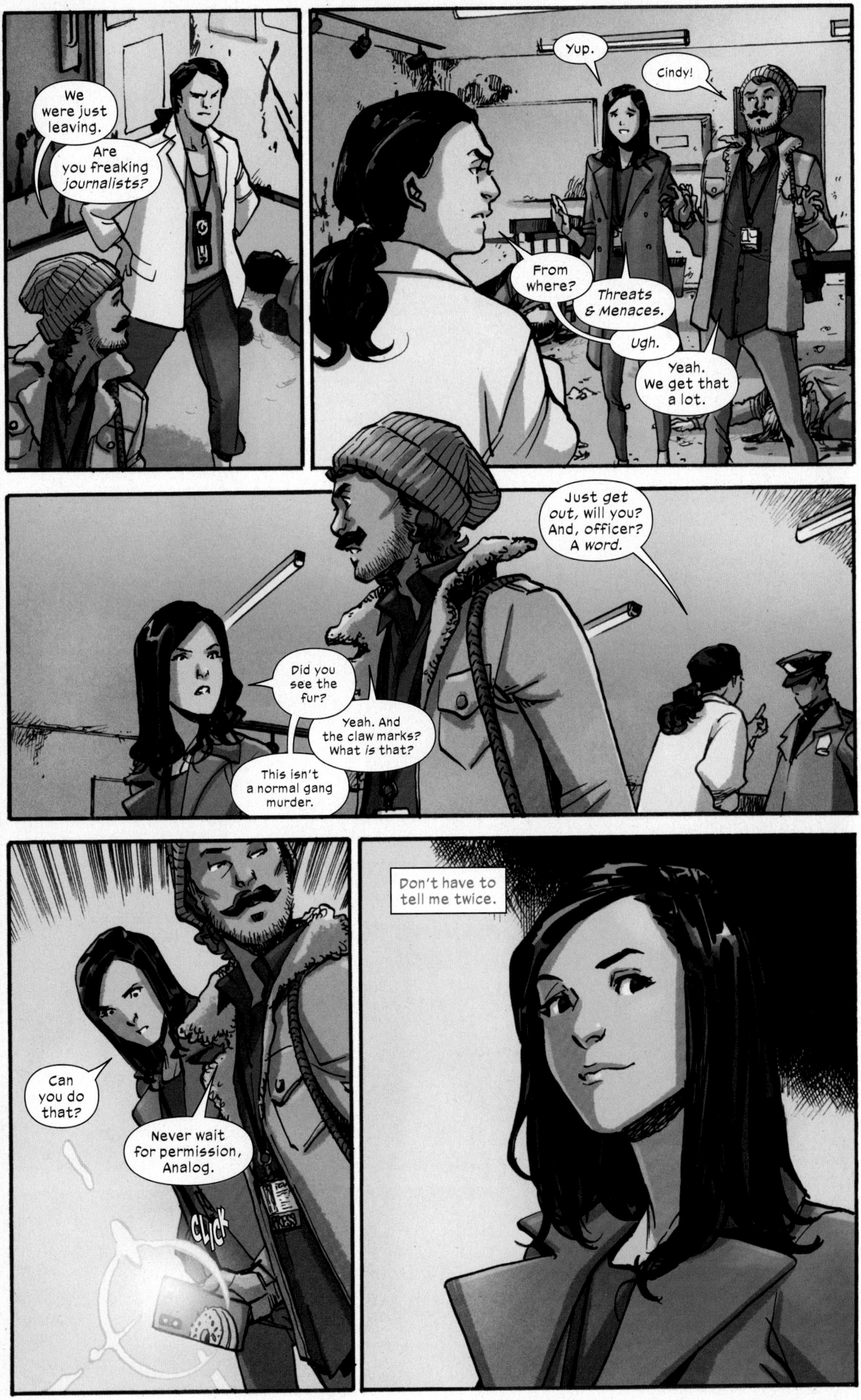
We were just leaving.
Are you freaking *journalists?*
Yup.
Cindy!
From where?
Threats & Menaces.
Ugh.
Yeah. We get that a lot.
Just *get out,* will you? And, officer? A *word.*
Did you see the fur?
Yeah. And the claw marks? What *is* that?
This isn't a normal gang murder.
Can you do that?
Never wait for permission, Analog.
CLICK
Don't have to tell me twice.

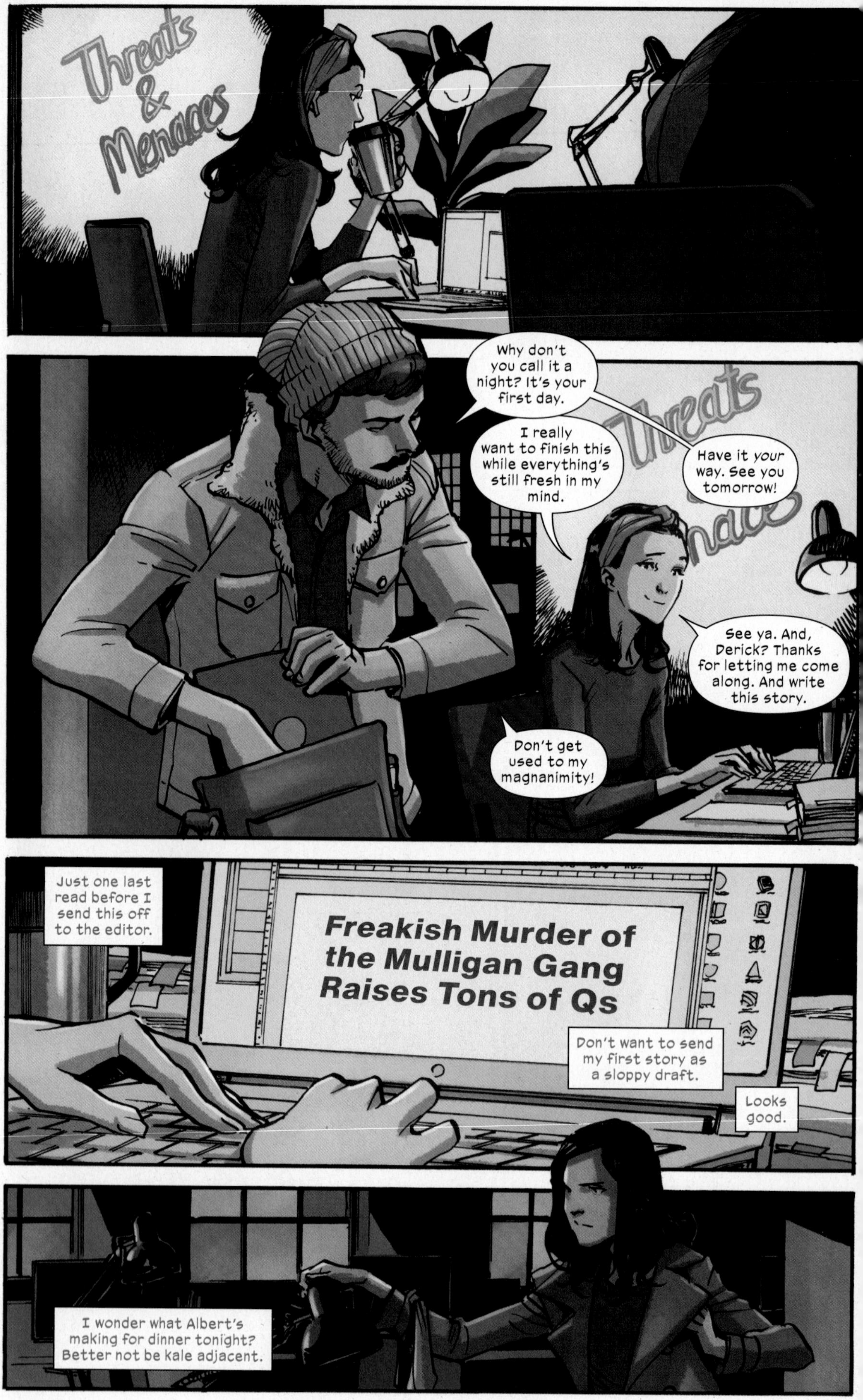
Threats & Menaces
Why don't you call it a night? It's your first day.
I really want to finish this while everything's still fresh in my mind.
Have it *your* way. See you tomorrow!
See ya. And, Derick? Thanks for letting me come along. And write this story.
Don't get used to my magnanimity!
Just one last read before I send this off to the editor.
Freakish Murder of the Mulligan Gang Raises Tons of Qs
Don't want to send my first story as a sloppy draft.
Looks good.
I wonder what Albert's making for dinner tonight? Better not be kale adjacent.

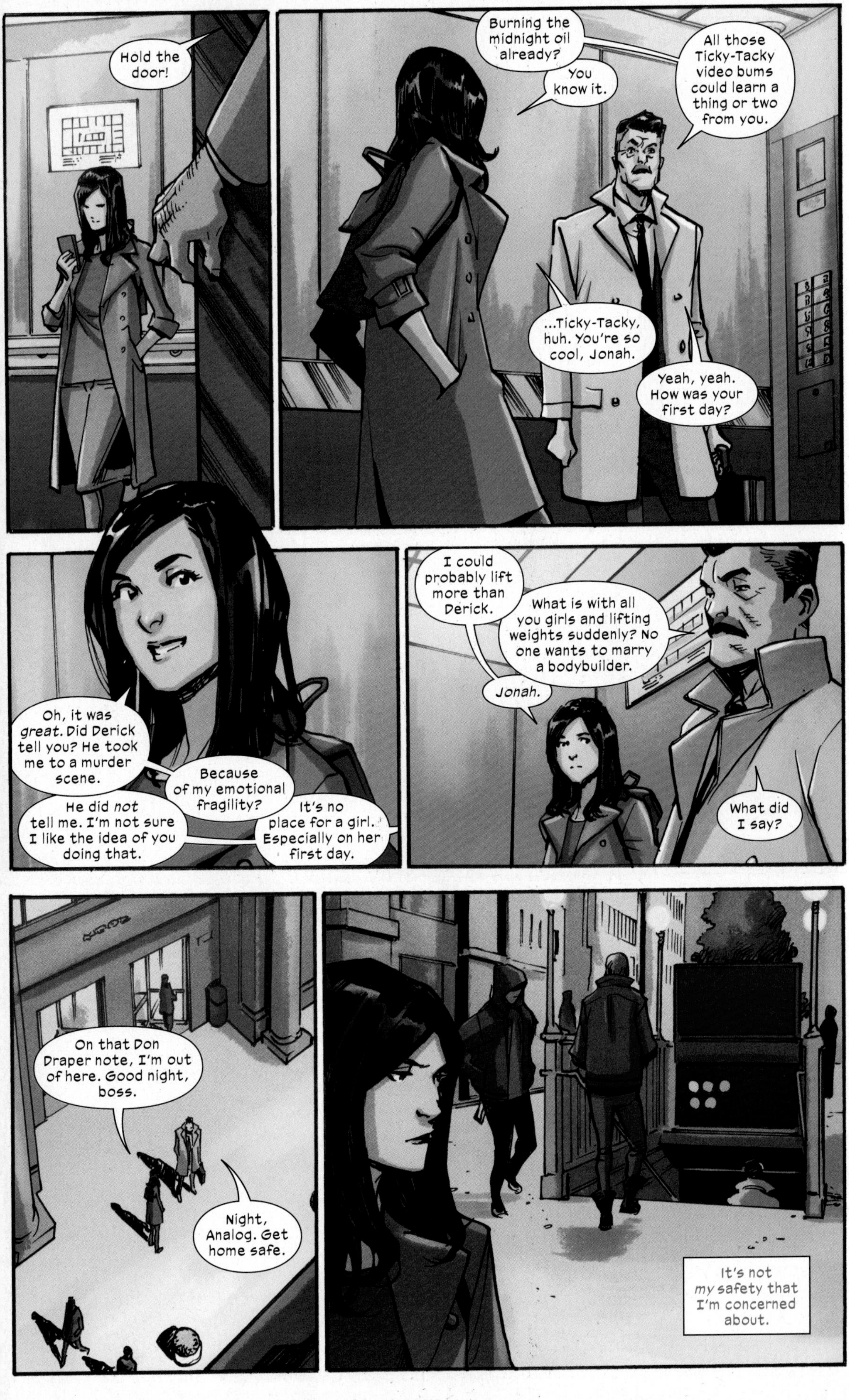
Hold the door!
Burning the midnight oil already?
You know it.
All those Ticky-Tacky video bums could learn a thing or two from you.
...Ticky-Tacky, huh. You're so cool, Jonah.
Yeah, yeah. How was your first day?
Oh, it was *great*. Did Derick tell you? He took me to a murder scene.
He did *not* tell me. I'm not sure I like the idea of you doing that.
Because of my emotional fragility?
It's no place for a girl. Especially on her first day.
I could probably lift more than Derick.
What is with all you girls and lifting weights suddenly? No one wants to marry a bodybuilder.
Jonah.
What did I say?
On that Don Draper note, I'm out of here. Good night, boss.
Night, Analog. Get home safe.
It's not *my* safety that I'm concerned about.

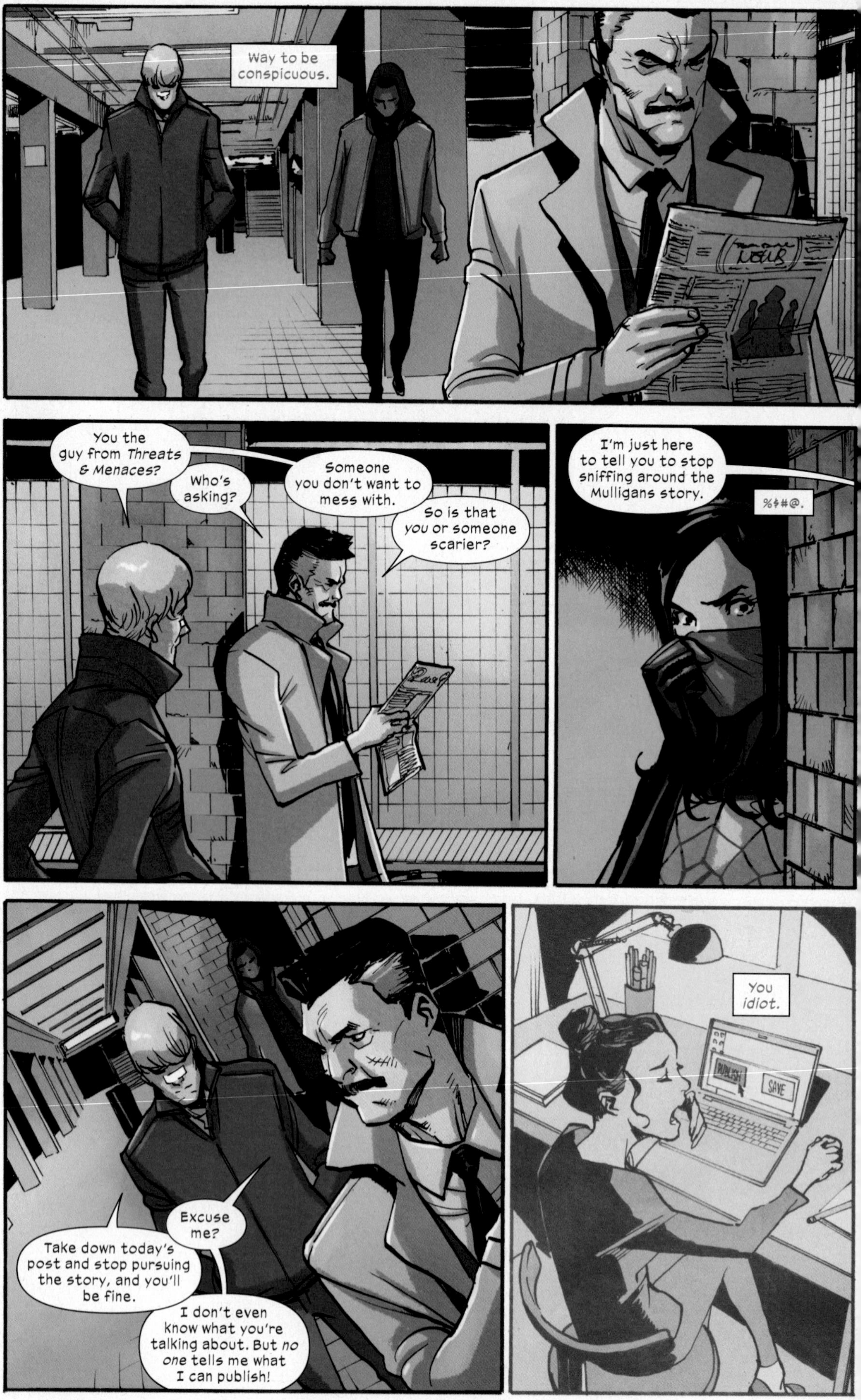

Way to be conspicuous.
You the guy from *Threats & Menaces?*
Who's asking?
Someone you don't want to mess with.
So is that *you* or someone scarier?
I'm just here to tell you to stop sniffing around the Mulligans story.
%$#@.
Excuse me?
Take down today's post and stop pursuing the story, and you'll be fine.
I don't even know what you're talking about. But *no one* tells me what I can publish!
You *idiot.*
PUBLISH
SAVE

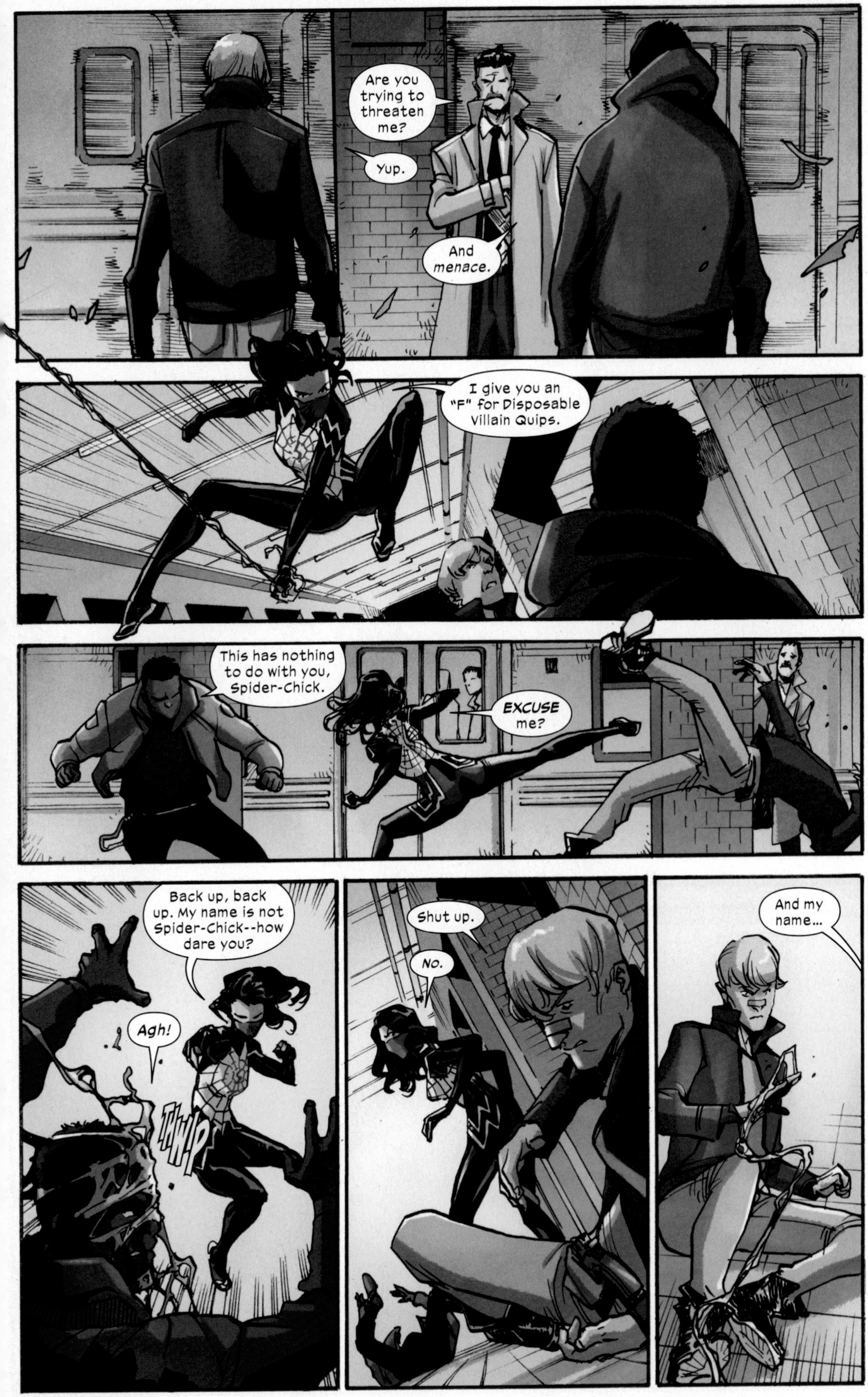

Are you trying to threaten me?
Yup.
And menace.
I give you an "F" for Disposable Villain Quips.
This has nothing to do with you, Spider-Chick.
EXCUSE me?
Back up, back up. My name is not Spider-Chick--how dare you?
Agh!
THWIP
Shut up.
No.
And my name...

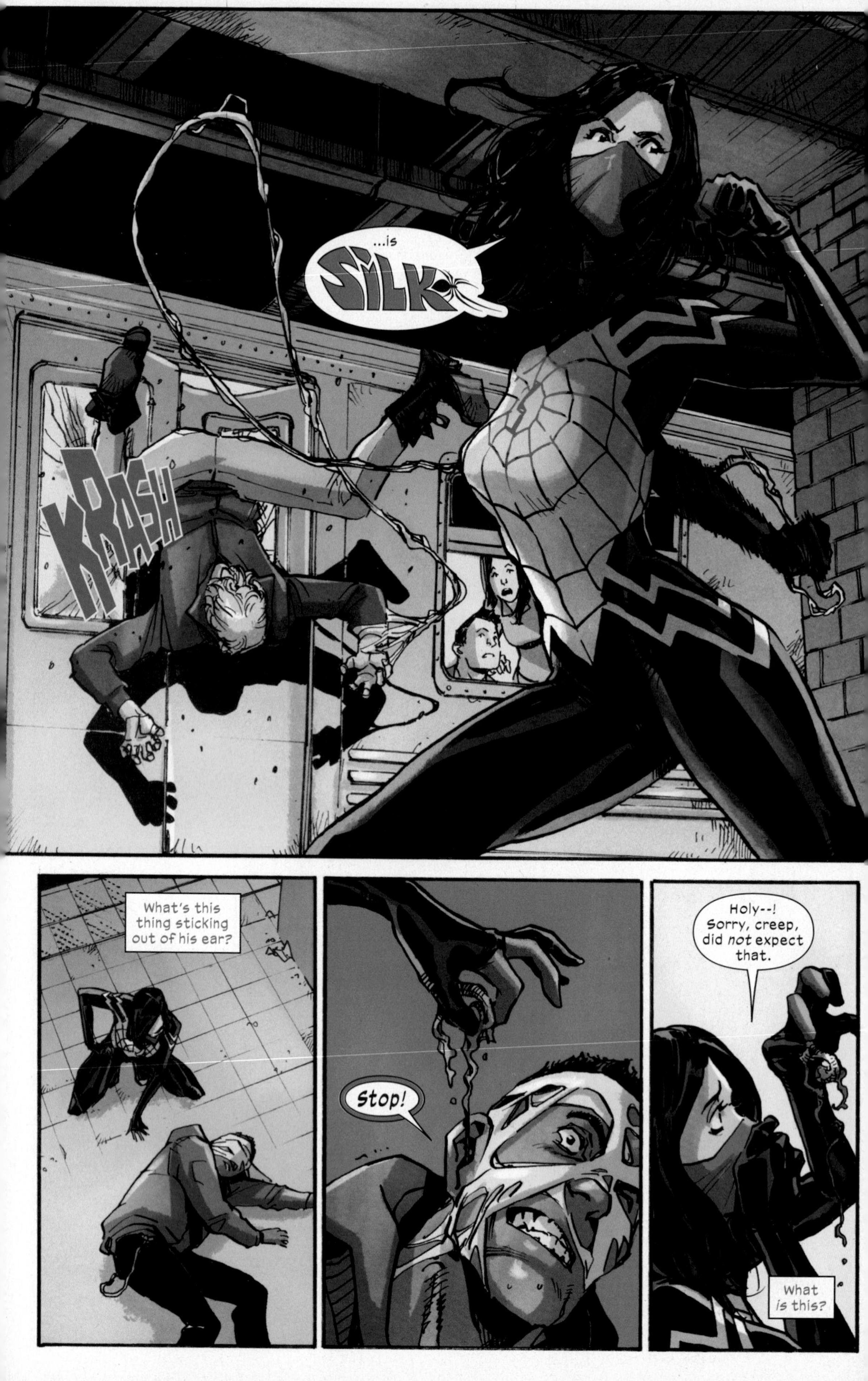
...is
SILK
KRASH
What's this thing sticking out of his ear?
Stop!
Holy--! Sorry, creep, did *not* expect that.
What *is* this?

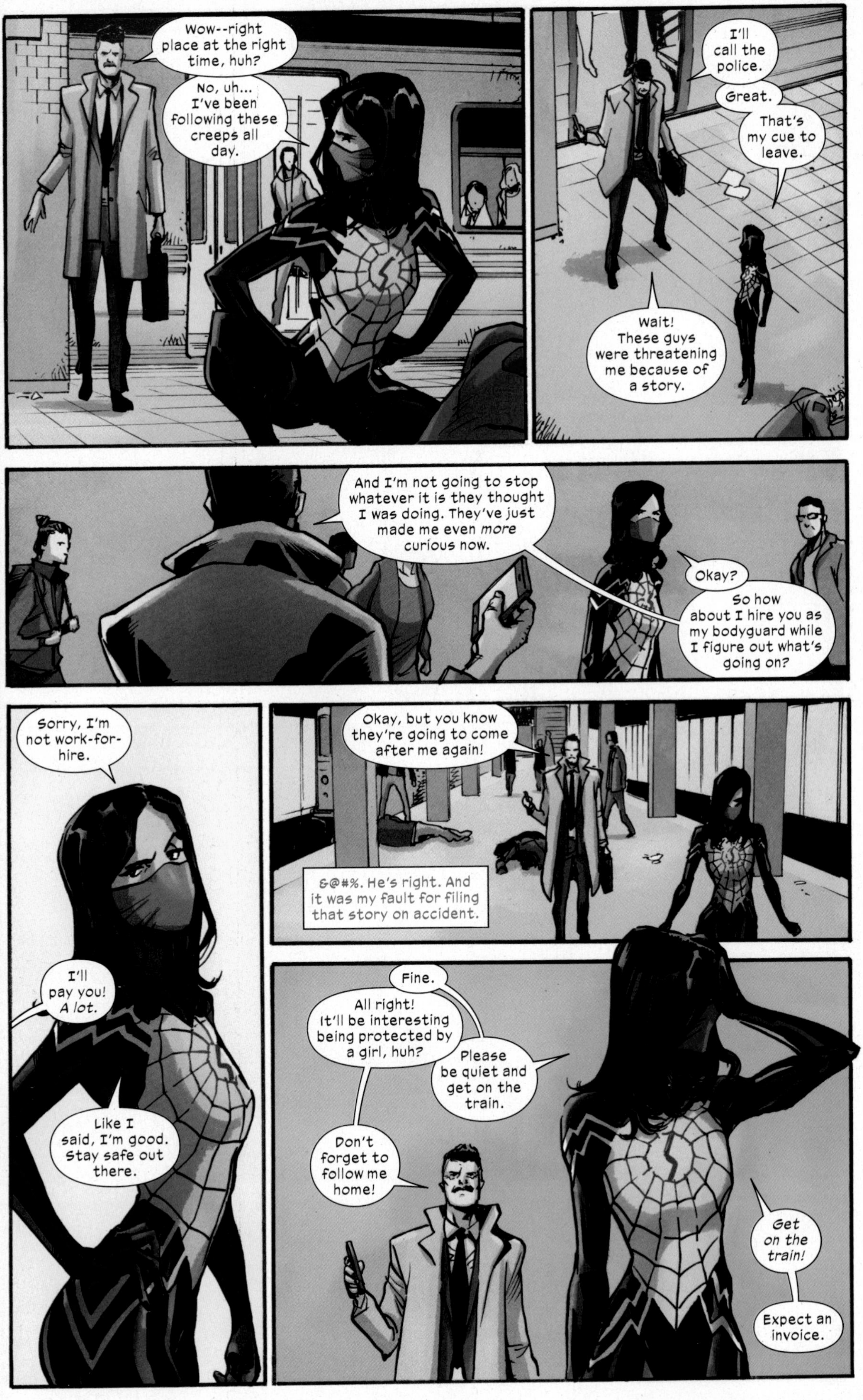
Wow--right place at the right time, huh?
No, uh... I've been following these creeps all day.
I'll call the police.
Great.
That's my cue to leave.
Wait! These guys were threatening me because of a story.
And I'm not going to stop whatever it is they thought I was doing. They've just made me even *more* curious now.
Okay?
So how about I hire you as my bodyguard while I figure out what's going on?
Sorry, I'm not work-for-hire.
I'll pay you! *A lot.*
Like I said, I'm good. Stay safe out there.
Okay, but you know they're going to come after me again!
&@#%. He's right. And it was my fault for filing that story on accident.
Fine.
All right! It'll be interesting being protected by a girl, huh?
Please be quiet and get on the train.
Don't forget to follow me home!
Get on the train!
Expect an invoice.

This thing looks like it's from the U.S.S. Enterprise.

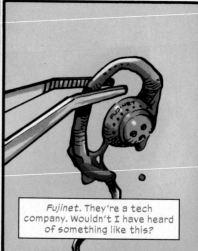

Fujinet. They're a tech company. Wouldn't I have heard of something like this?

Nothing even close to this tech.

FUJINET

ABOUT

Company tech

TECH FOR THE FUTURE

COMPANY HISTORY

Fujinet was founded in 1983 by Matsuko Ishii. What started off as a small, family-run electronics store quickly became a player in manufacturing. By the early nineties, Fujinet was a household name, their stereos and disc players outselling all the competition.

Matsuko Ishii

What are they up to nowadays?

I don't see Fujinet being a competitor with Apple.

FEW GOOD MEN

FU

Saya Ishii

Fujinet looks to the future with Saya Ishii, the daughter of founder Matsuko Ishii. "The future is about connection, and that's what Fujinet aims to do—on a global scale. We look to empathy, and not power, to make the world a better place."

So why are you guys making scary tech that embeds into people's brains, huh? *Empathy?*

Dinner's ready, fool!

COMING!

SLAM

Maybe this Saya trust fund kid has the answers.

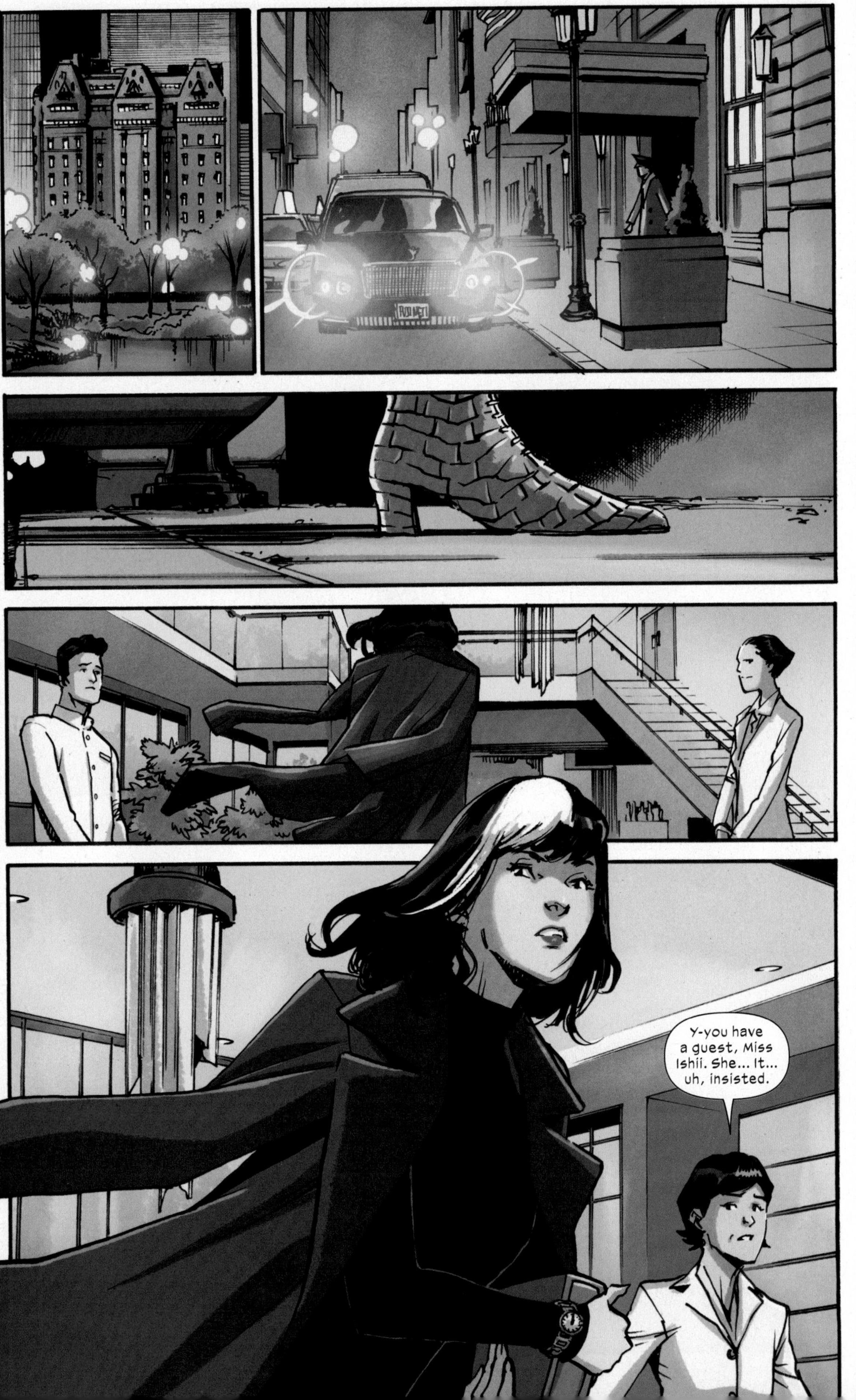
Y-you have a guest, Miss Ishii. She... It... uh, insisted.

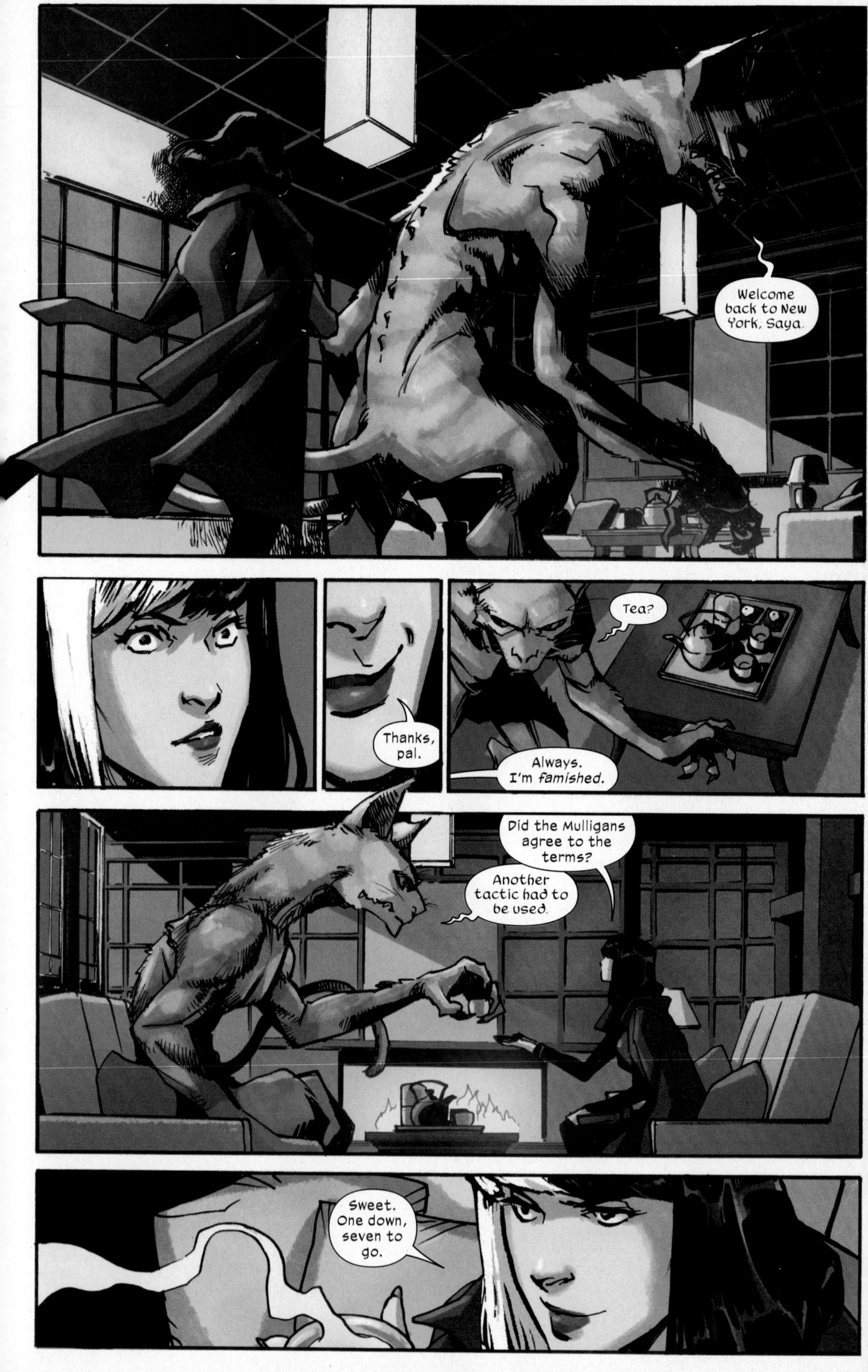

Welcome back to New York, Saya.
Thanks, pal.
Tea?
Always. I'm famished.
Did the Mulligans agree to the terms?
Another tactic had to be used.
Sweet. One down, seven to go.

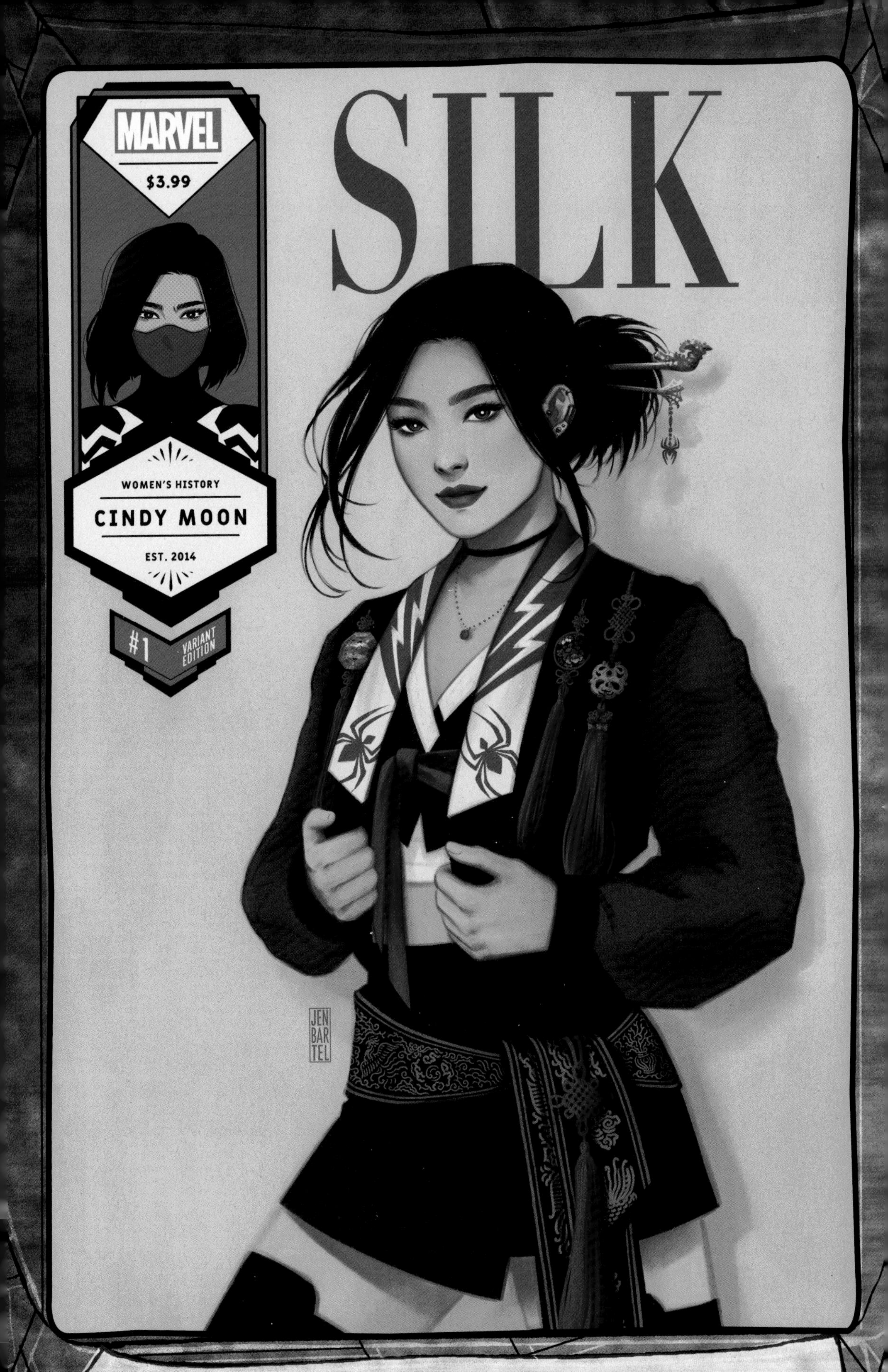
MARVEL
$3.99
SILK
WOMEN'S HISTORY
CINDY MOON
EST. 2014
#1
VARIANT EDITION
JEN BARTEL

#1 WOMEN'S HISTORY MONTH VARIANT by Jen Bartel

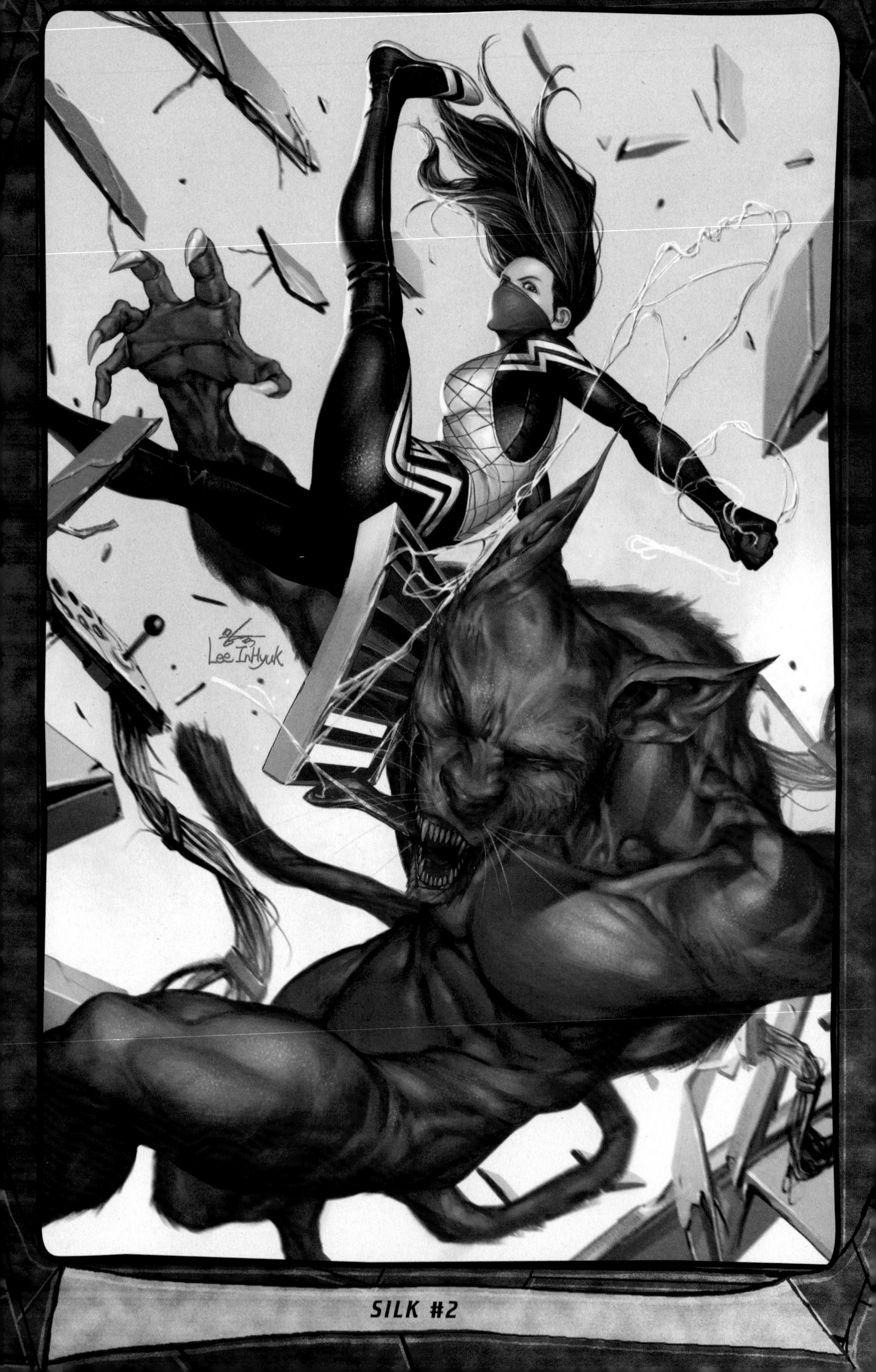
Lee InHyuk

SILK #2

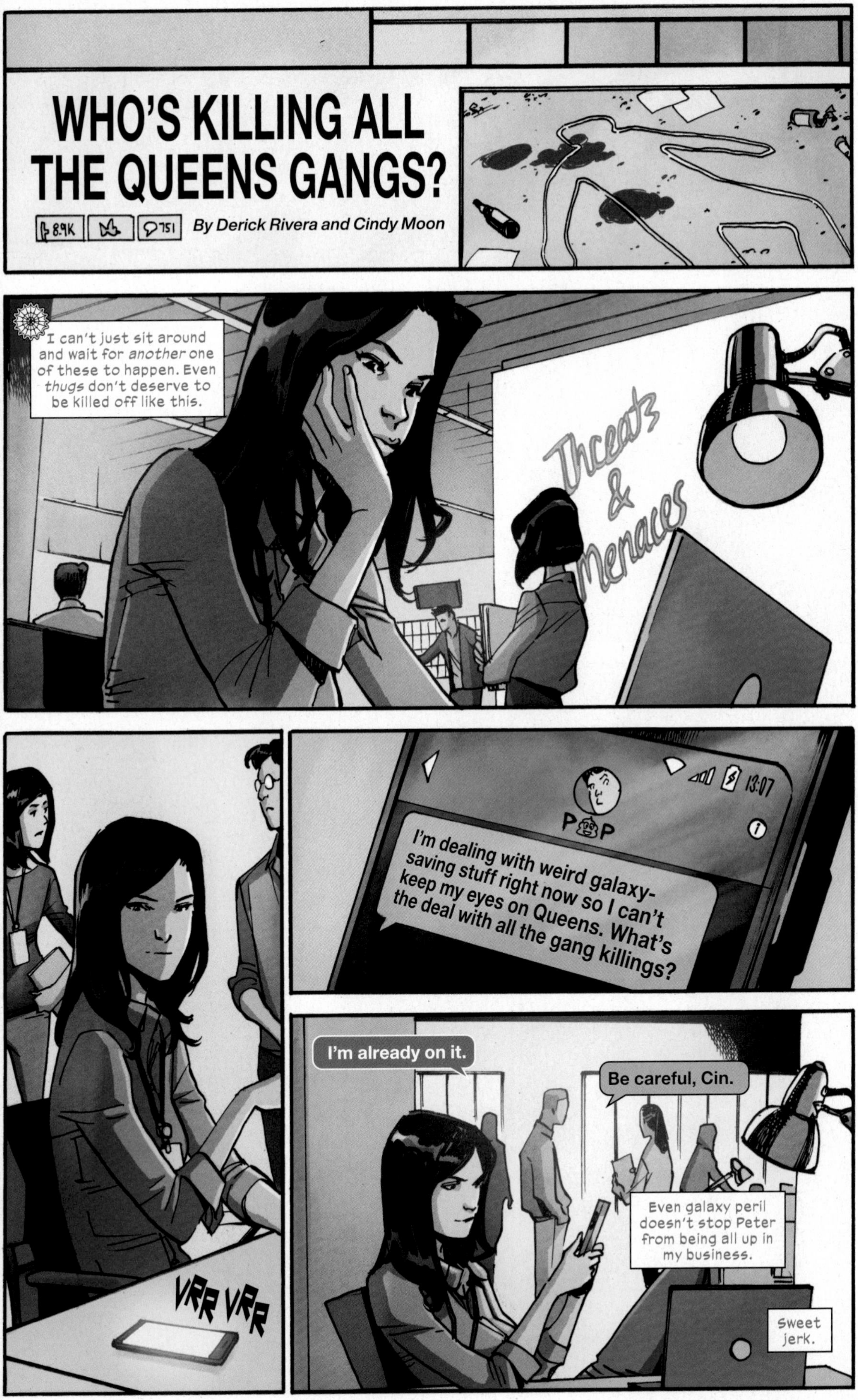
WHO'S KILLING ALL THE QUEENS GANGS?
8.9K
751
By Derick Rivera and Cindy Moon
I can't just sit around and wait for another one of these to happen. Even thugs don't deserve to be killed off like this.
Threats & Menaces
VRR VRR
13:07
P P
I'm dealing with weird galaxy-saving stuff right now so I can't keep my eyes on Queens. What's the deal with all the gang killings?
I'm already on it.
Be careful, Cin.
Even galaxy peril doesn't stop Peter from being all up in my business.
Sweet jerk.

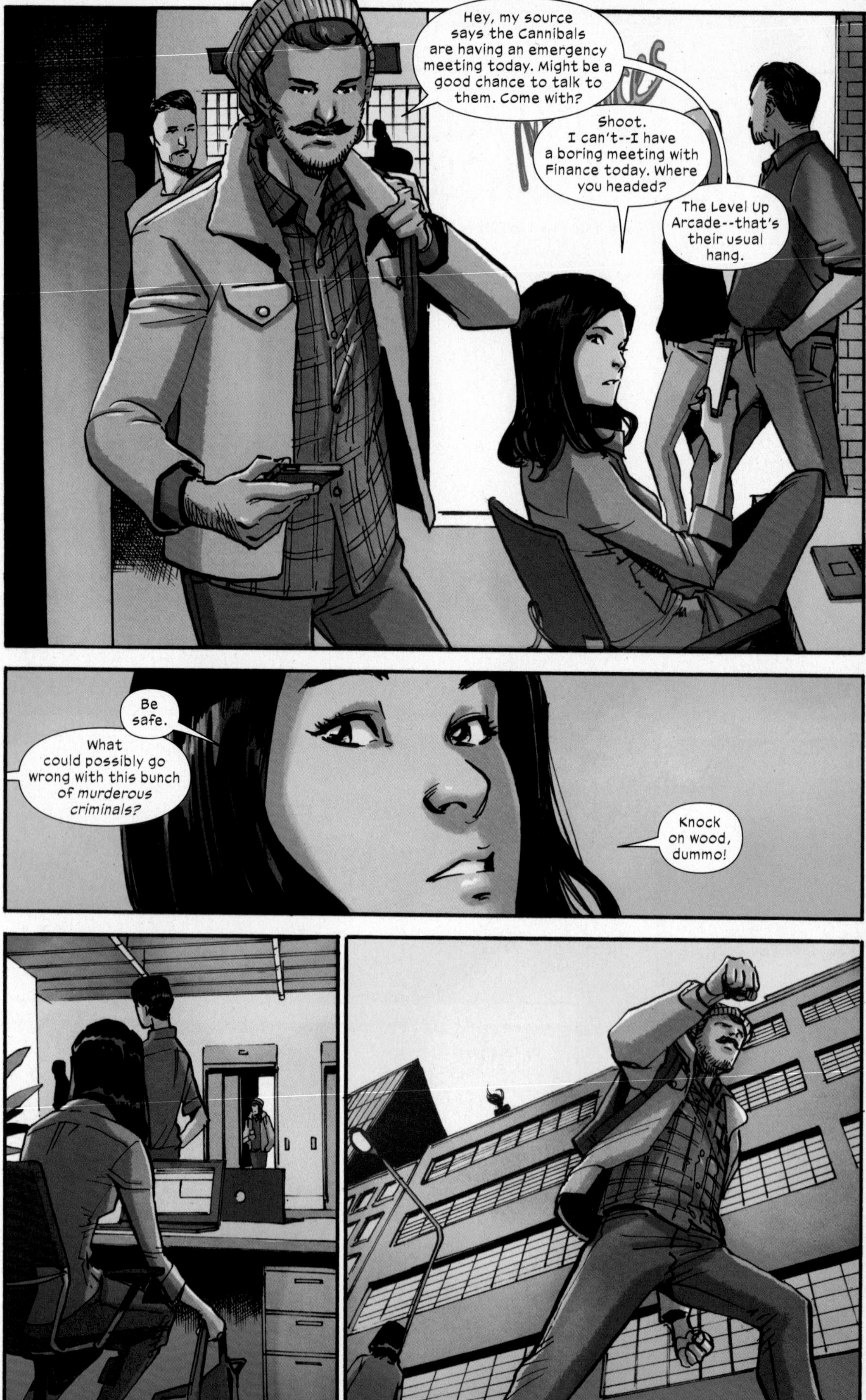
Hey, my source says the Cannibals are having an emergency meeting today. Might be a good chance to talk to them. Come with?
Shoot. I can't--I have a boring meeting with Finance today. Where you headed?
The Level Up Arcade--that's their usual hang.
Be safe.
What could possibly go wrong with this bunch of *murderous criminals?*
Knock on wood, dummo!

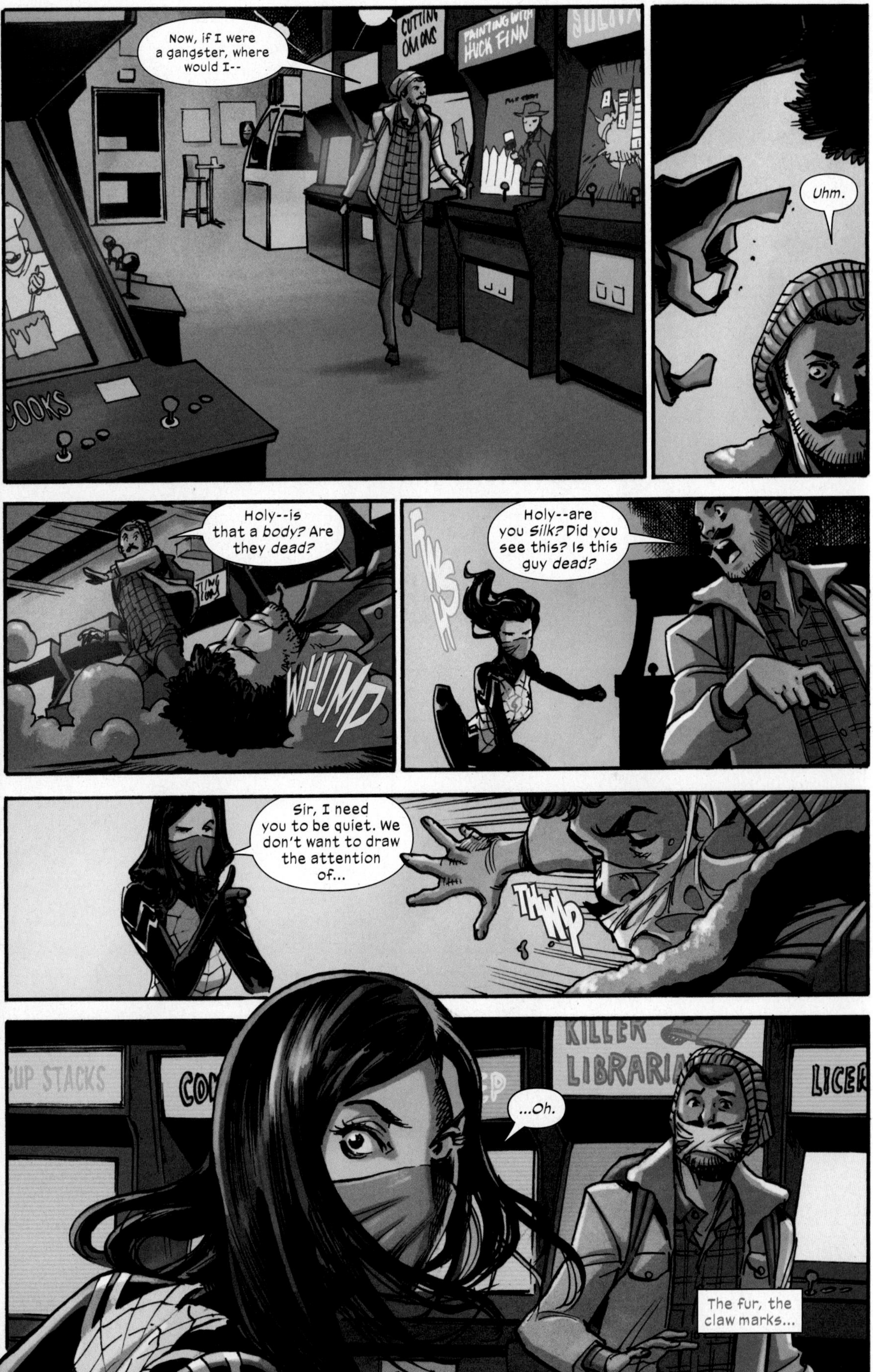
CUTTING ONIONS
PAINTING WITH HUCK FINN
Now, if I were a gangster, where would I--
COOKS
Uhm.
Holy--is that a *body?* Are they *dead?*
WHUMP
FWSHH
Holy--are you *Silk?* Did you see this? Is this guy *dead?*
Sir, I need you to be quiet. We don't want to draw the attention of...
THWMP
KILLER LIBRARIA
CUP STACKS
...Oh.
The fur, the claw marks...

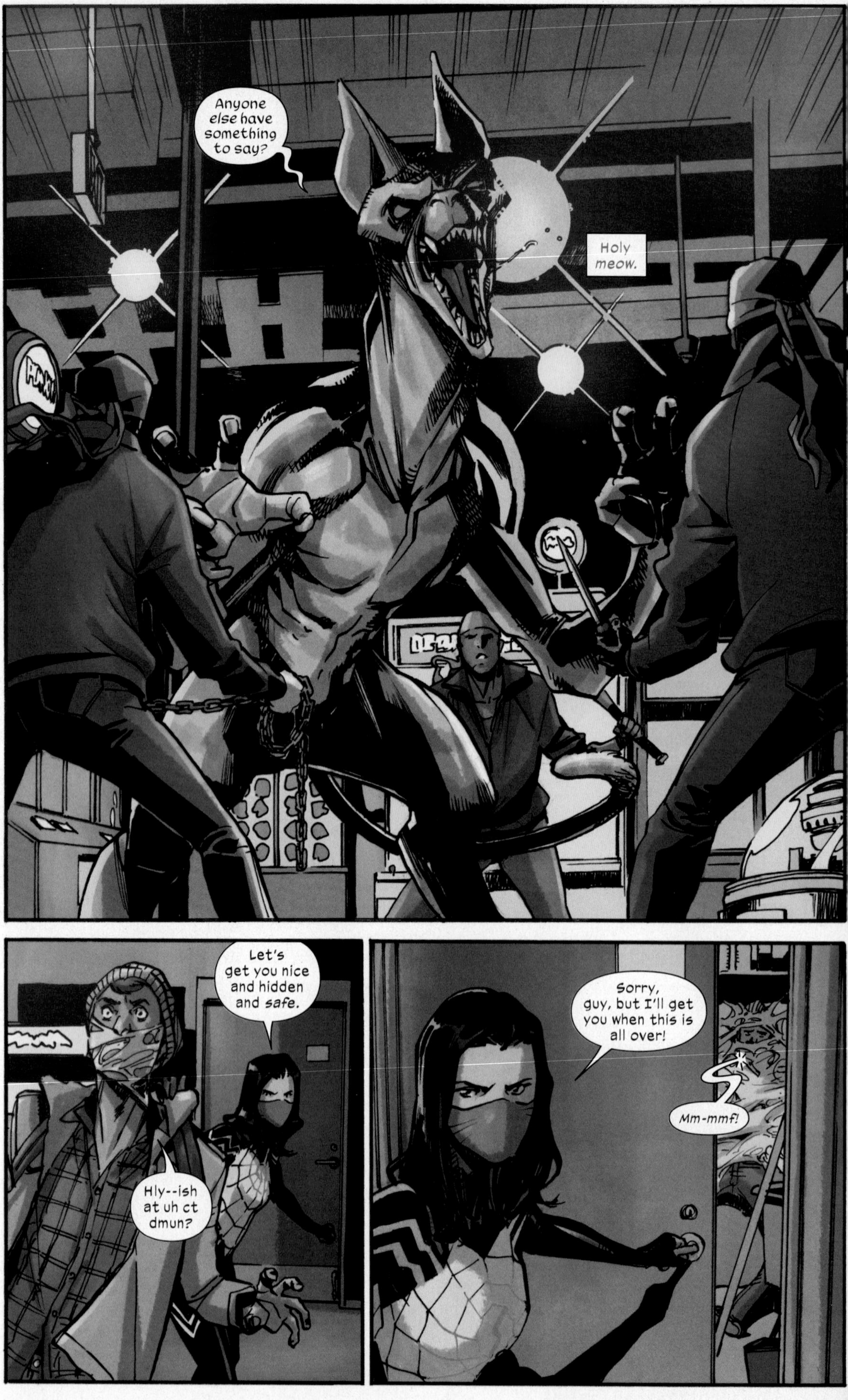
Anyone else have something to say?
Holy meow.
Let's get you nice and hidden and safe.
Hly--ish at uh ct dmun?
Sorry, guy, but I'll get you when this is all over!
Mm-mmf!

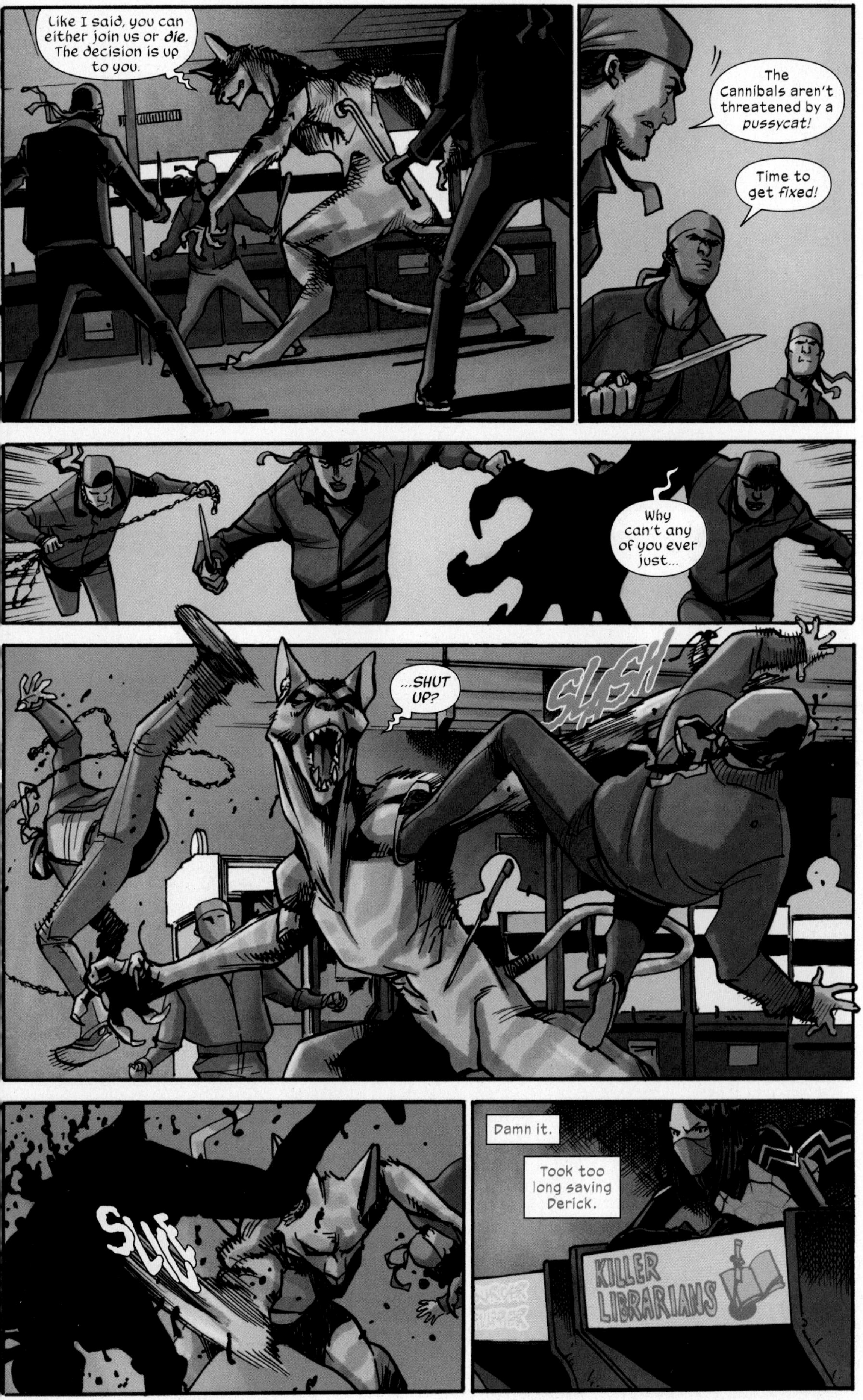
Like I said, you can either join us or *die*. The decision is up to you.
The Cannibals aren't threatened by a *pussycat!*
Time to get *fixed!*
Why can't any of you ever just...
...SHUT UP?
SLASH
Damn it.
Took too long saving Derick.
KILLER LIBRARIANS

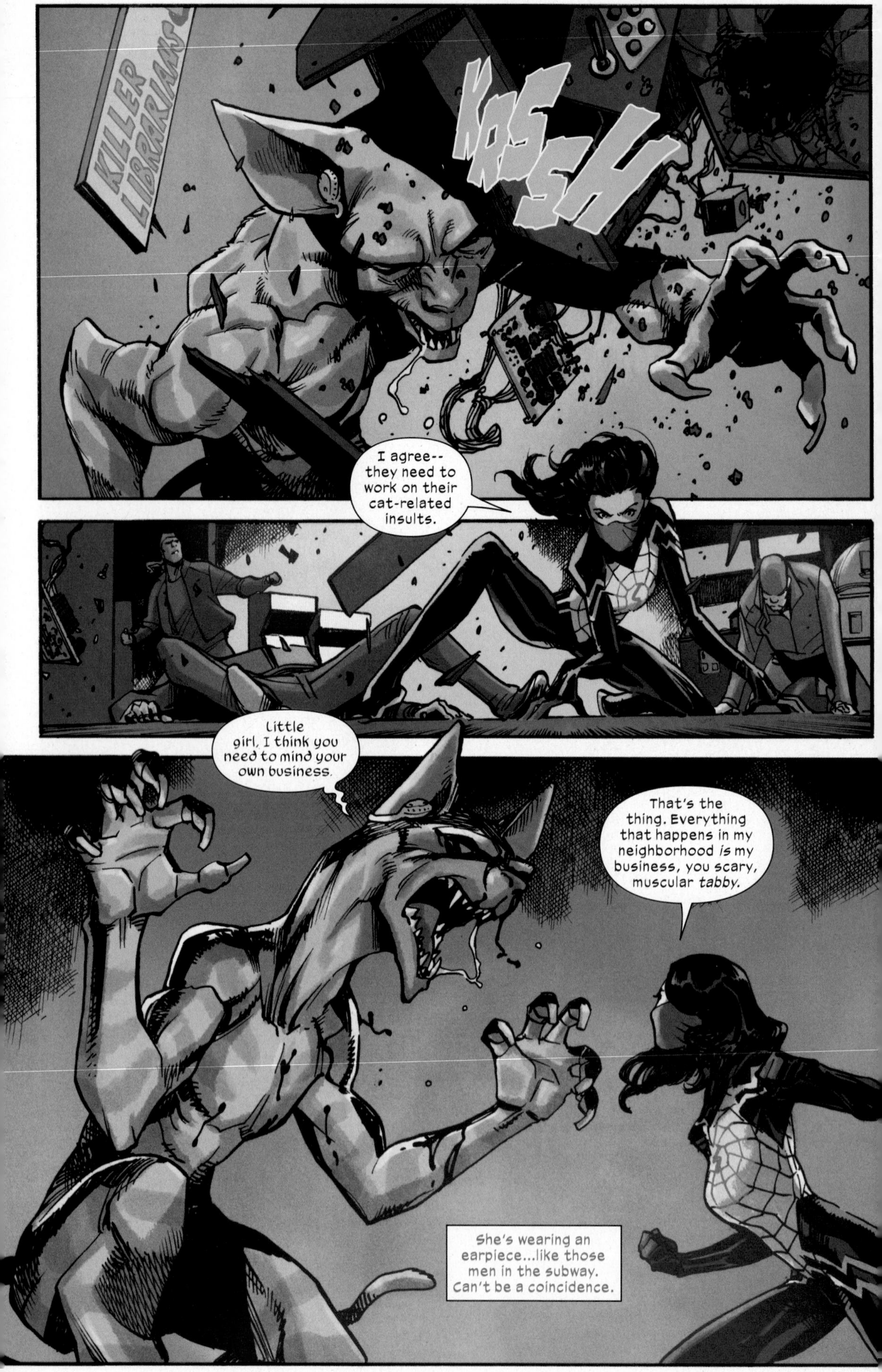
KILLER LIBRARIANS
KRSSH
I agree-- they need to work on their cat-related insults.
Little girl, I think you need to mind your own business.
That's the thing. Everything that happens in my neighborhood *is* my business, you scary, muscular *tabby.*
She's wearing an earpiece...like those men in the subway. Can't be a coincidence.

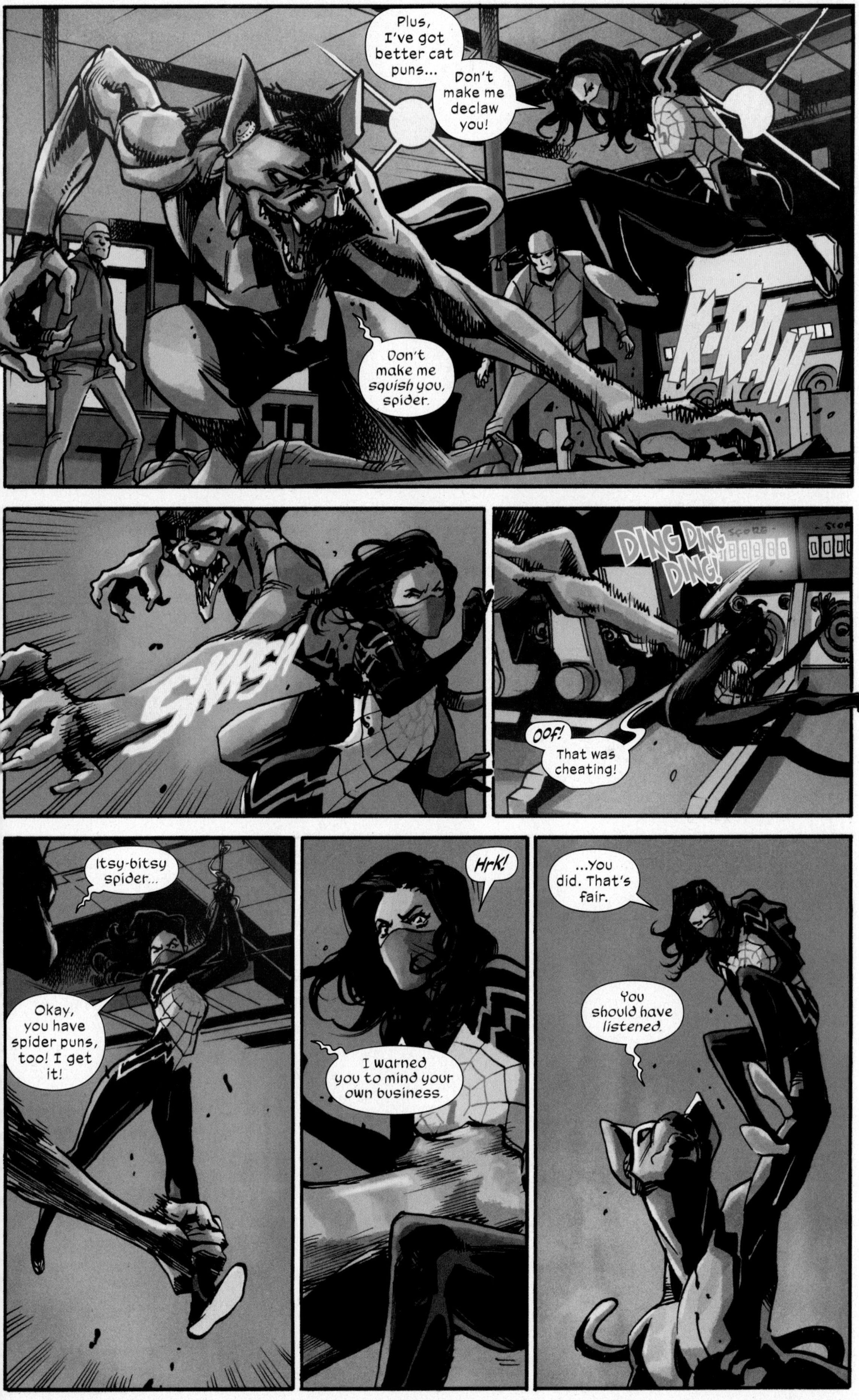
Plus, I've got better cat puns...
Don't make me declaw you!
Don't make me squish you, spider.
K-RAM
SKRSH
DING DING DING!
OOF! That was cheating!
Itsy-bitsy spider...
Okay, you have spider puns, too! I get it!
Hrk!
I warned you to mind your own business.
...You did. That's fair.
You should have listened.

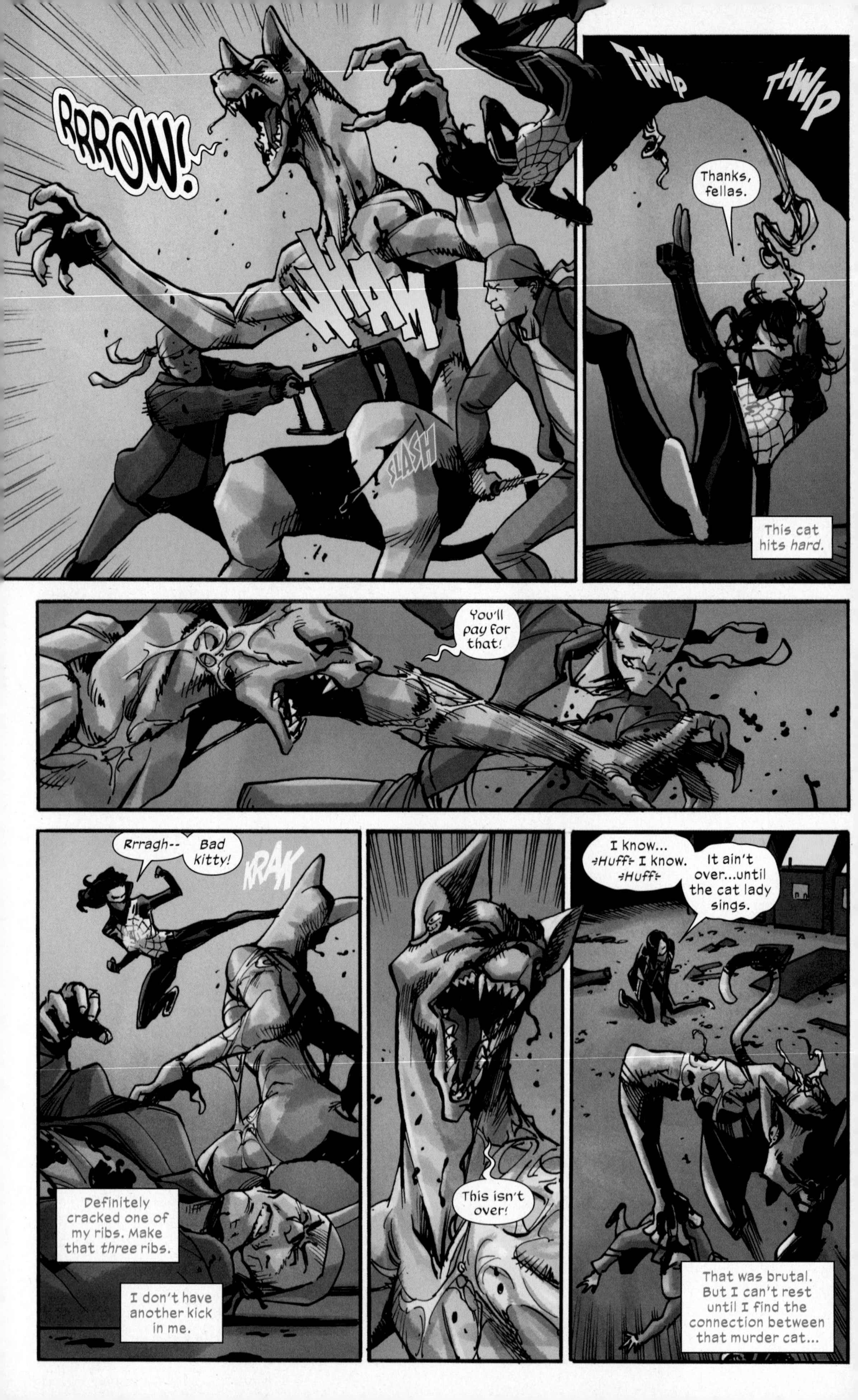

RRROW!
WHAM
SLASH
THWIP
THWIP
Thanks, fellas.
This cat hits *hard.*
You'll pay for that!
Rrragh--
Bad kitty!
KRAK
Definitely cracked one of my ribs. Make that *three* ribs.
I don't have another kick in me.
This isn't over!
I know... *Huff* I know. *Huff*
It ain't over...until the cat lady sings.
That was brutal. But I can't rest until I find the connection between that murder cat...

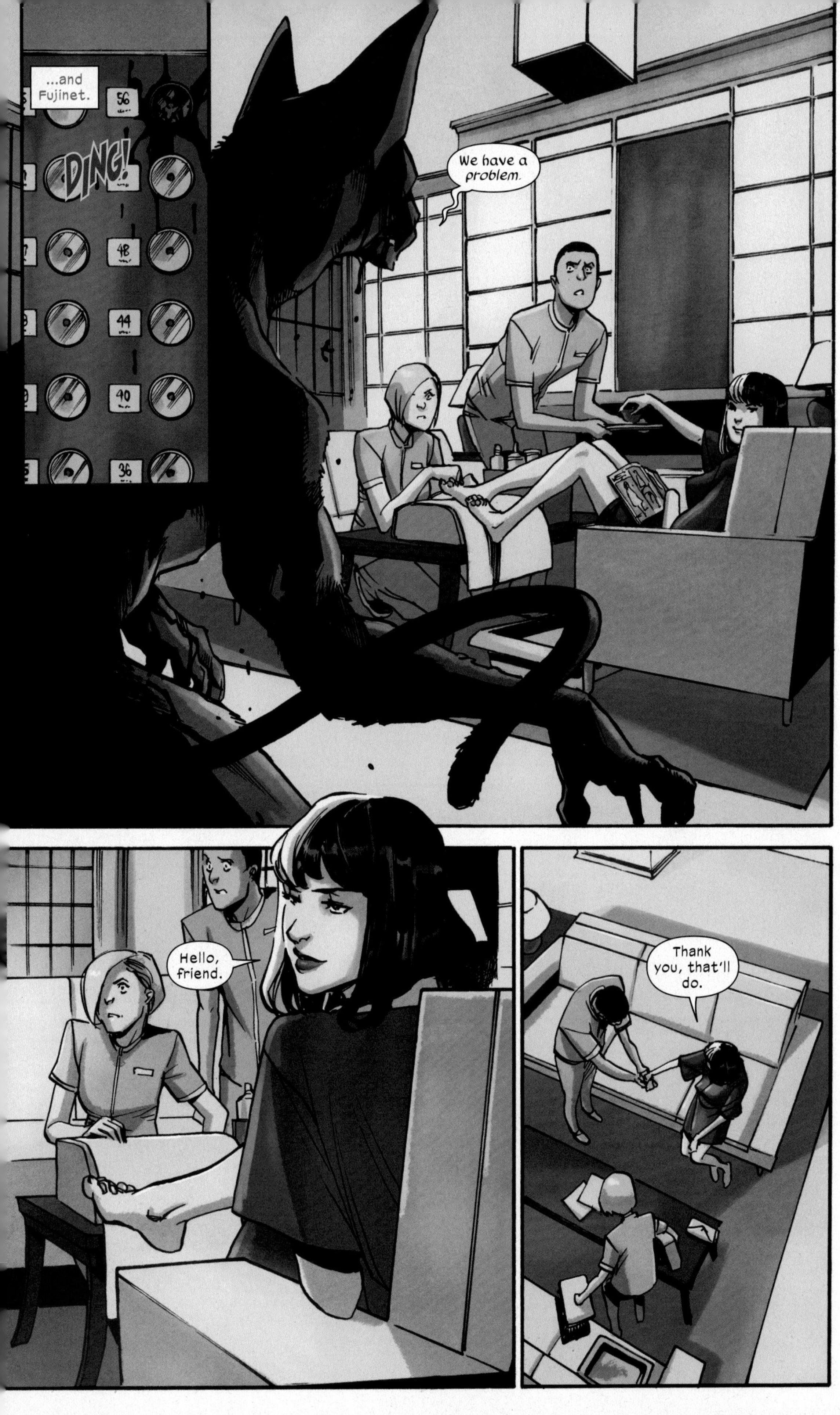
...and Fujinet.
DING!
We have a problem.
Hello, friend.
Thank you, that'll do.

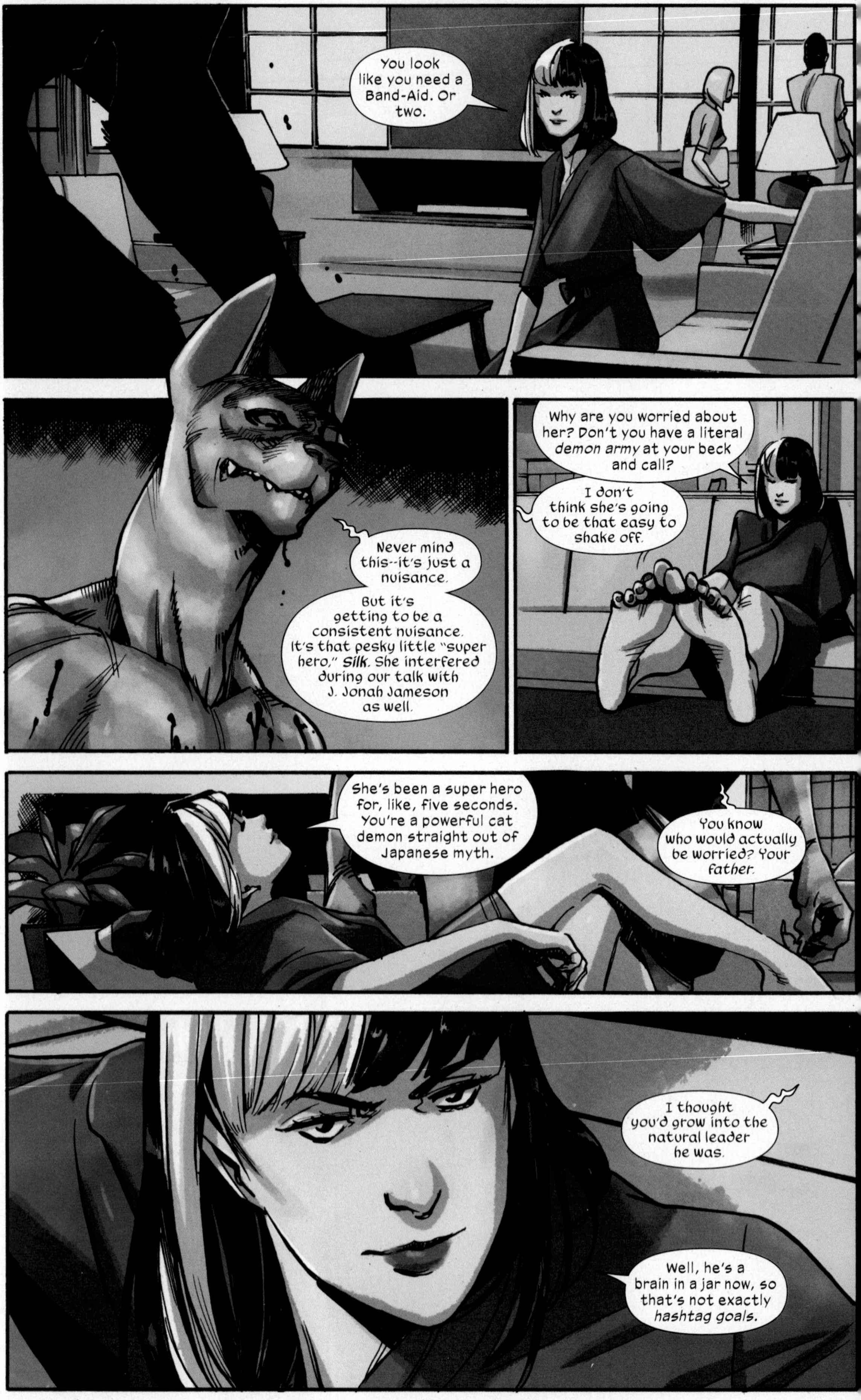
You look like you need a Band-Aid. Or two.
Never mind this--it's just a nuisance.
But it's getting to be a consistent nuisance. It's that pesky little "super hero," *Silk*. She interfered during our talk with J. Jonah Jameson as well.
Why are you worried about her? Don't you have a literal *demon army* at your beck and call?
I don't think she's going to be that easy to shake off.
She's been a super hero for, like, five seconds. You're a powerful cat demon straight out of Japanese myth.
You know who would actually be worried? Your *father*.
I thought you'd grow into the natural leader he was.
Well, he's a brain in a jar now, so that's not exactly *hashtag goals*.

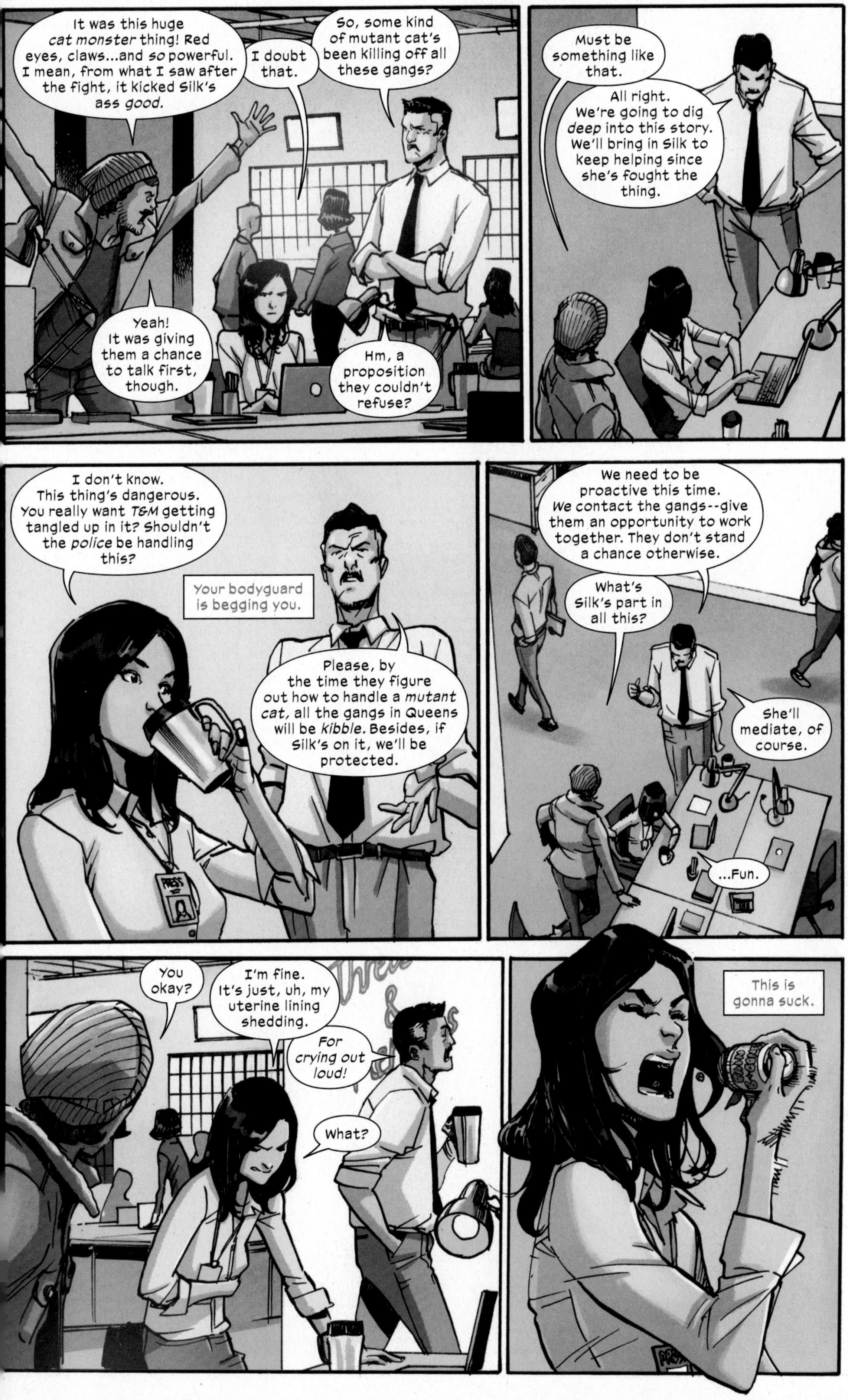
It was this huge *cat monster* thing! Red eyes, claws...and *so* powerful. I mean, from what I saw after the fight, it kicked Silk's ass *good.*
I doubt that.
So, some kind of mutant cat's been killing off all these gangs?
Yeah! It was giving them a chance to talk first, though.
Hm, a proposition they couldn't refuse?
Must be something like that.
All right. We're going to dig *deep* into this story. We'll bring in Silk to keep helping since she's fought the thing.
I don't know. This thing's dangerous. You really want *T&M* getting tangled up in it? Shouldn't the *police* be handling this?
Your bodyguard is begging you.
Please, by the time they figure out how to handle a *mutant cat,* all the gangs in Queens will be *kibble.* Besides, if Silk's on it, we'll be protected.
We need to be proactive this time. *We* contact the gangs--give them an opportunity to work together. They don't stand a chance otherwise.
What's Silk's part in all this?
She'll mediate, of course.
...Fun.
You okay?
I'm fine. It's just, uh, my uterine lining shedding.
For crying out loud!
What?
This is gonna suck.

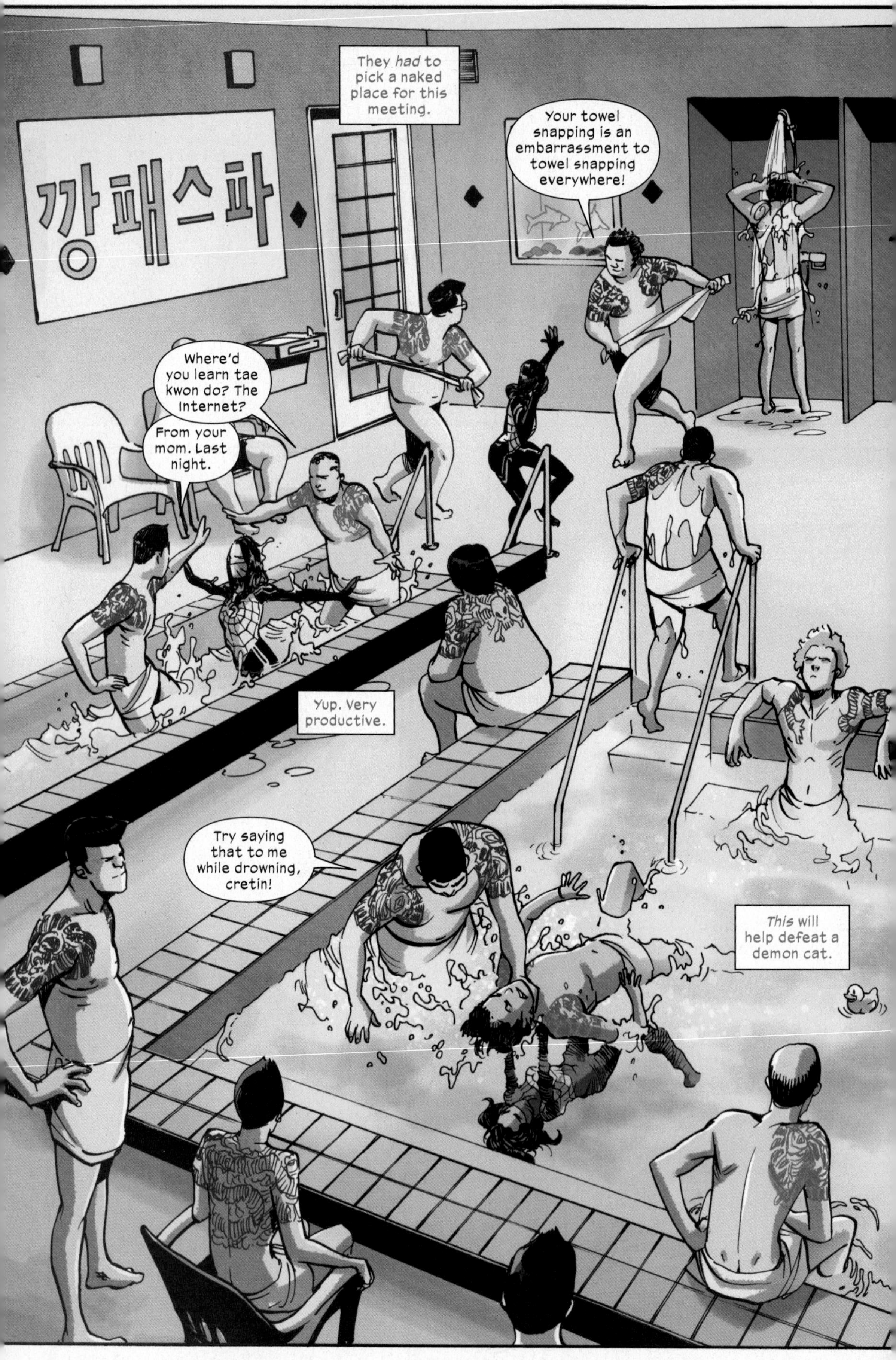

깡패스파
They *had* to pick a naked place for this meeting.
Your towel snapping is an embarrassment to towel snapping everywhere!
Where'd you learn tae kwon do? The Internet?
From your mom. Last night.
Yup. Very productive.
Try saying that to me while drowning, cretin!
This will help defeat a demon cat.

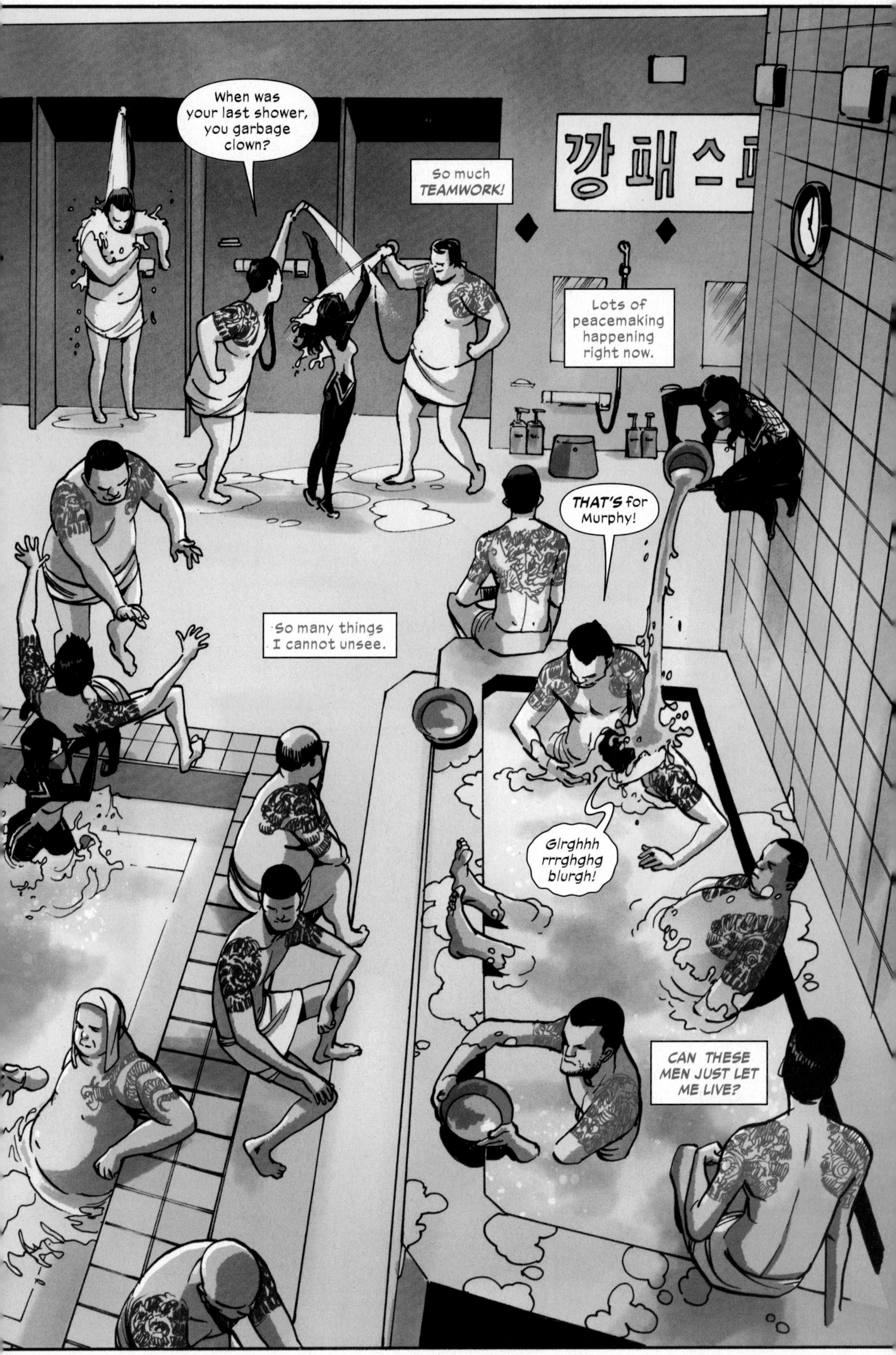

When was your last shower, you garbage clown?
So much *TEAMWORK!*
깡패스
Lots of peacemaking happening right now.
THAT'S for Murphy!
So many things I cannot unsee.
Glrghhh rrrghghg blurgh!
CAN THESE MEN JUST LET ME LIVE?

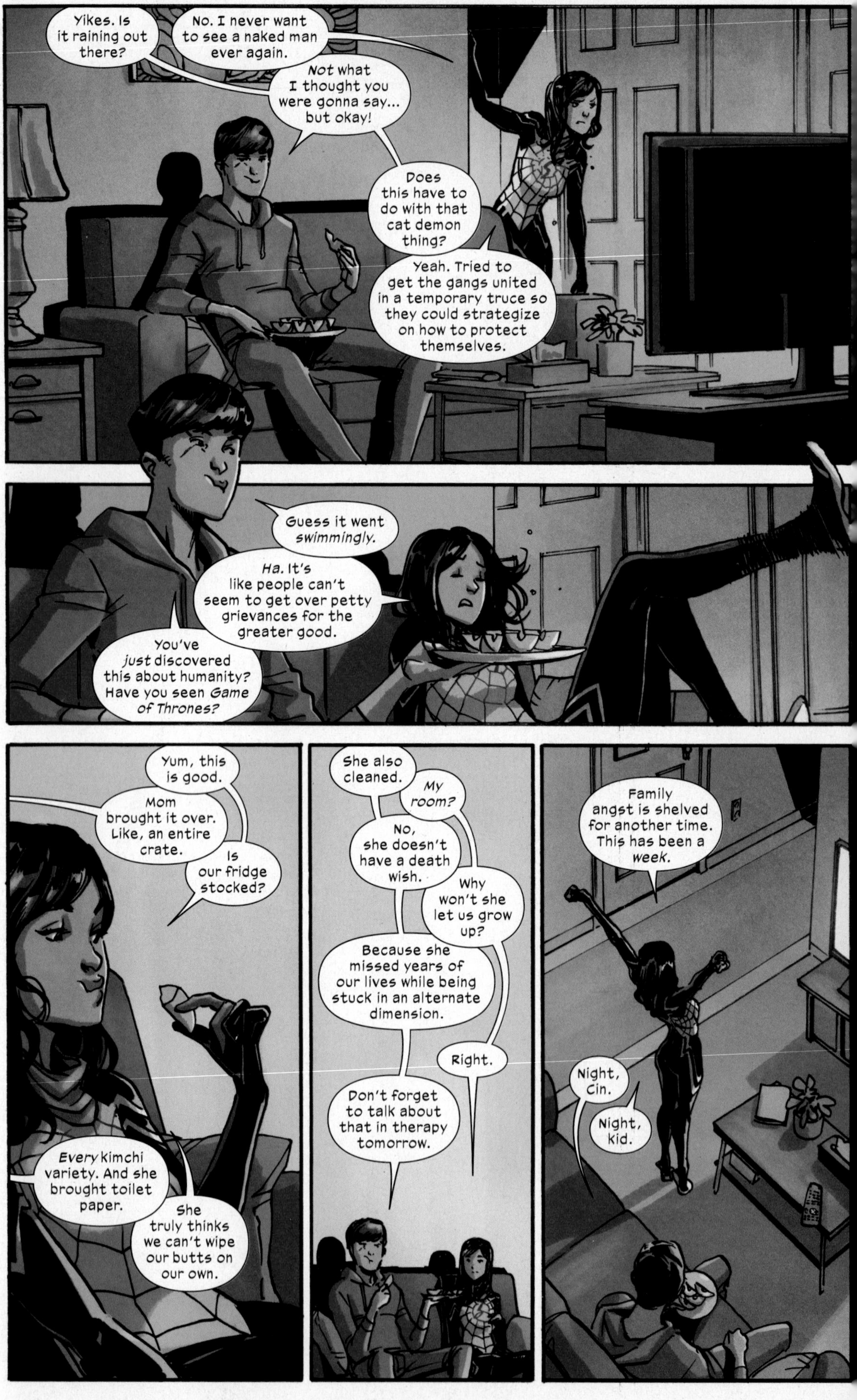
Yikes. Is it raining out there?
No. I never want to see a naked man ever again.
Not what I thought you were gonna say... but okay!
Does this have to do with that cat demon thing?
Yeah. Tried to get the gangs united in a temporary truce so they could strategize on how to protect themselves.
Guess it went swimmingly.
Ha. It's like people can't seem to get over petty grievances for the greater good.
You've just discovered this about humanity? Have you seen Game of Thrones?
Yum, this is good.
Mom brought it over. Like, an entire crate.
Is our fridge stocked?
Every kimchi variety. And she brought toilet paper.
She truly thinks we can't wipe our butts on our own.
She also cleaned.
My room?
No, she doesn't have a death wish.
Why won't she let us grow up?
Because she missed years of our lives while being stuck in an alternate dimension.
Right.
Don't forget to talk about that in therapy tomorrow.
Family angst is shelved for another time. This has been a week.
Night, Cin.
Night, kid.

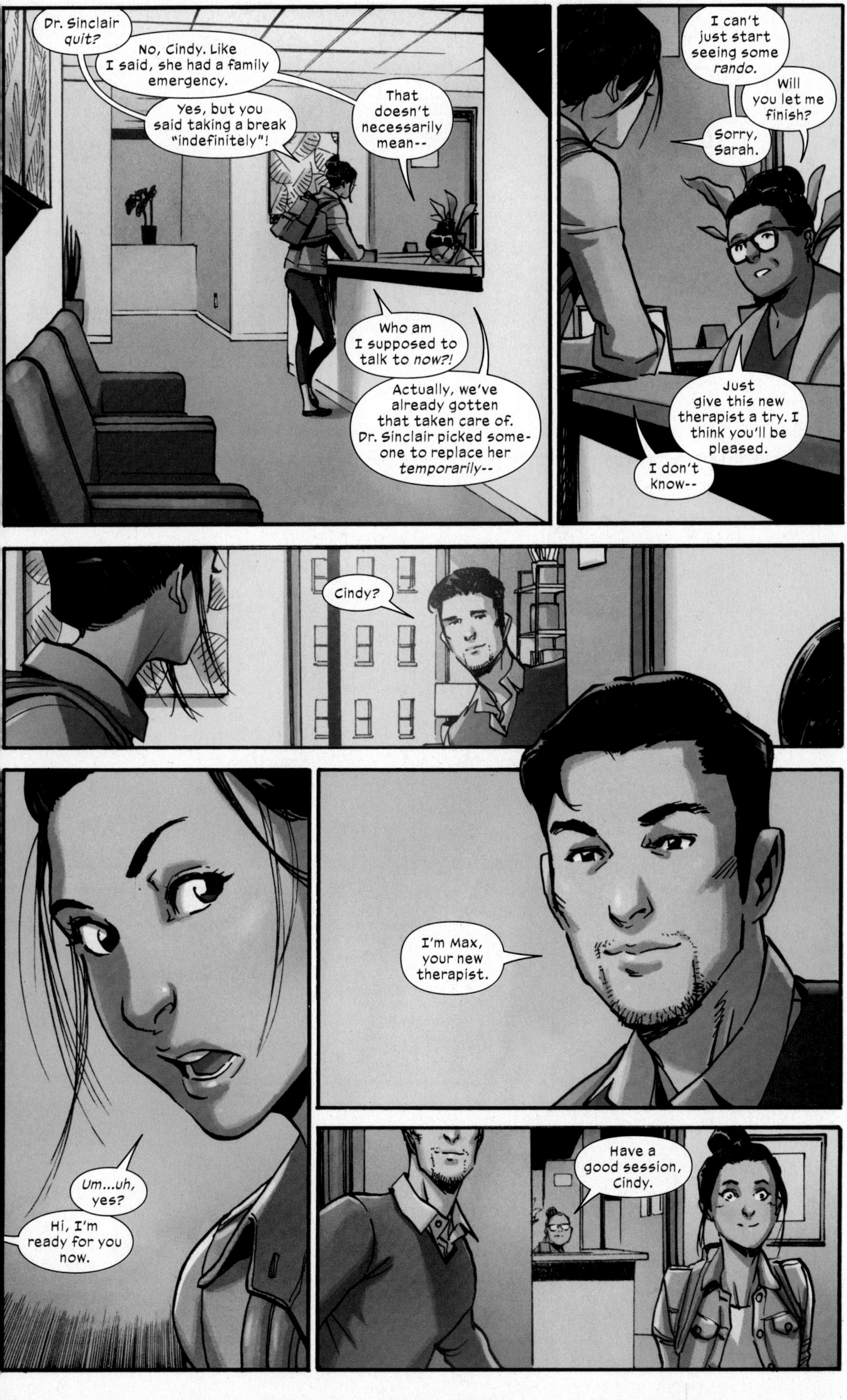
Dr. Sinclair *quit?*
No, Cindy. Like I said, she had a family emergency.
Yes, but you said taking a break "indefinitely"!
That doesn't necessarily mean--
Who am I supposed to talk to *now?!*
Actually, we've already gotten that taken care of. Dr. Sinclair picked someone to replace her *temporarily*--
I can't just start seeing some *rando.*
Will you let me finish?
Sorry, Sarah.
Just give this new therapist a try. I think you'll be pleased.
I don't know--
Cindy?
Um...uh, yes?
Hi, I'm ready for you now.
I'm Max, your new therapist.
Have a good session, Cindy.

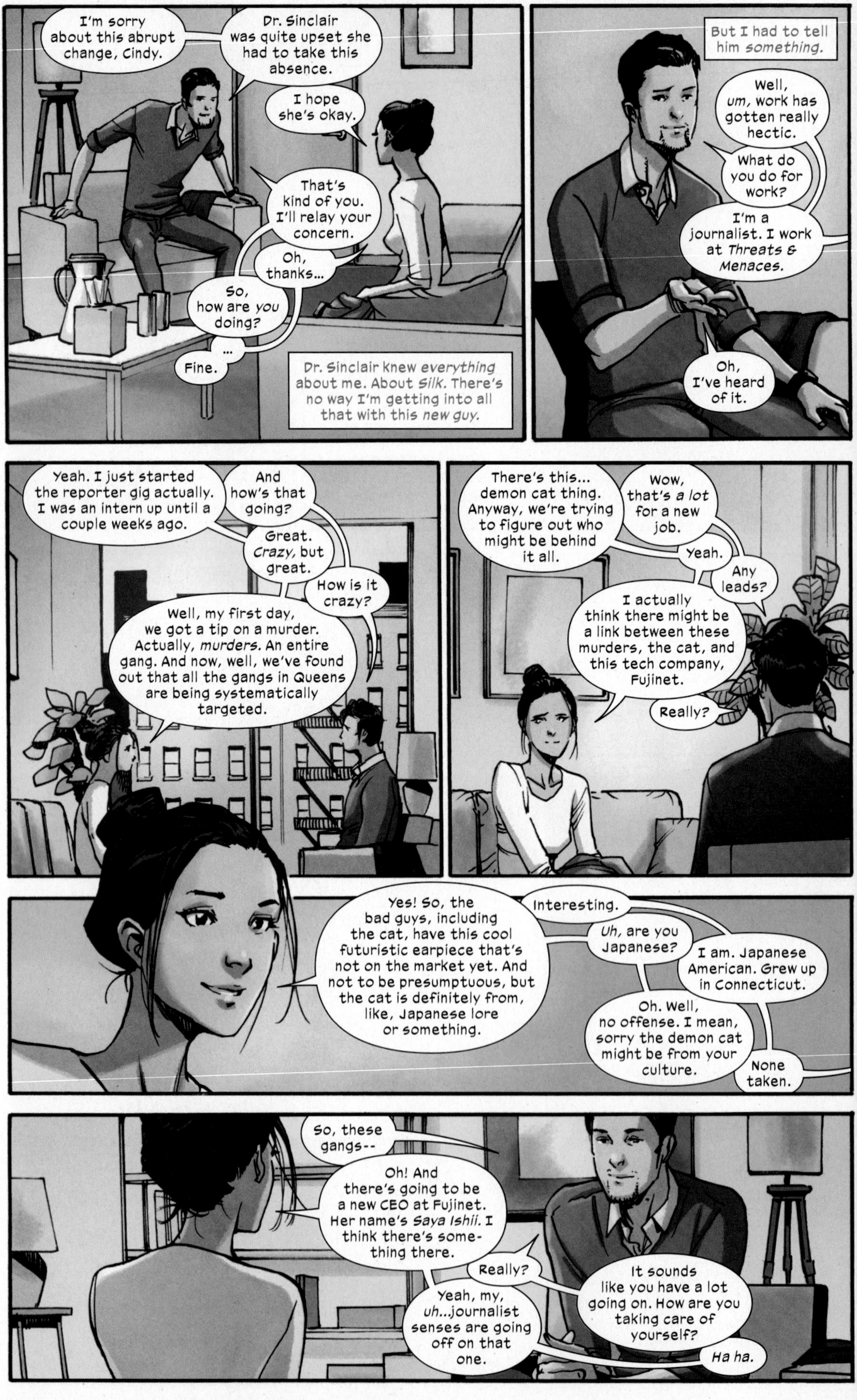

I'm sorry about this abrupt change, Cindy.
Dr. Sinclair was quite upset she had to take this absence.
I hope she's okay.
That's kind of you. I'll relay your concern.
Oh, thanks...
So, how are *you* doing?
...
Fine.
Dr. Sinclair knew *everything* about me. About *Silk*. There's no way I'm getting into all that with this *new guy*.
But I had to tell him *something*.
Well, *um*, work has gotten really hectic.
What do you do for work?
I'm a journalist. I work at *Threats & Menaces*.
Oh, I've heard of it.
Yeah. I just started the reporter gig actually. I was an intern up until a couple weeks ago.
And how's that going?
Great. *Crazy*, but great.
How is it crazy?
Well, my first day, we got a tip on a murder. Actually, *murders*. An entire gang. And now, well, we've found out that all the gangs in Queens are being systematically targeted.
There's this... demon cat thing. Anyway, we're trying to figure out who might be behind it all.
Wow, that's *a lot* for a new job.
Yeah.
Any leads?
I actually think there might be a link between these murders, the cat, and this tech company, Fujinet.
Really?
Yes! So, the bad guys, including the cat, have this cool futuristic earpiece that's not on the market yet. And not to be presumptuous, but the cat is definitely from, like, Japanese lore or something.
Interesting.
Uh, are you Japanese?
I am. Japanese American. Grew up in Connecticut.
Oh. Well, no offense. I mean, sorry the demon cat might be from your culture.
None taken.
So, these gangs--
Oh! And there's going to be a new CEO at Fujinet. Her name's *Saya Ishii*. I think there's something there.
Really?
Yeah, my, *uh*...journalist senses are going off on that one.
It sounds like you have a lot going on. How are you taking care of yourself?
Ha ha.

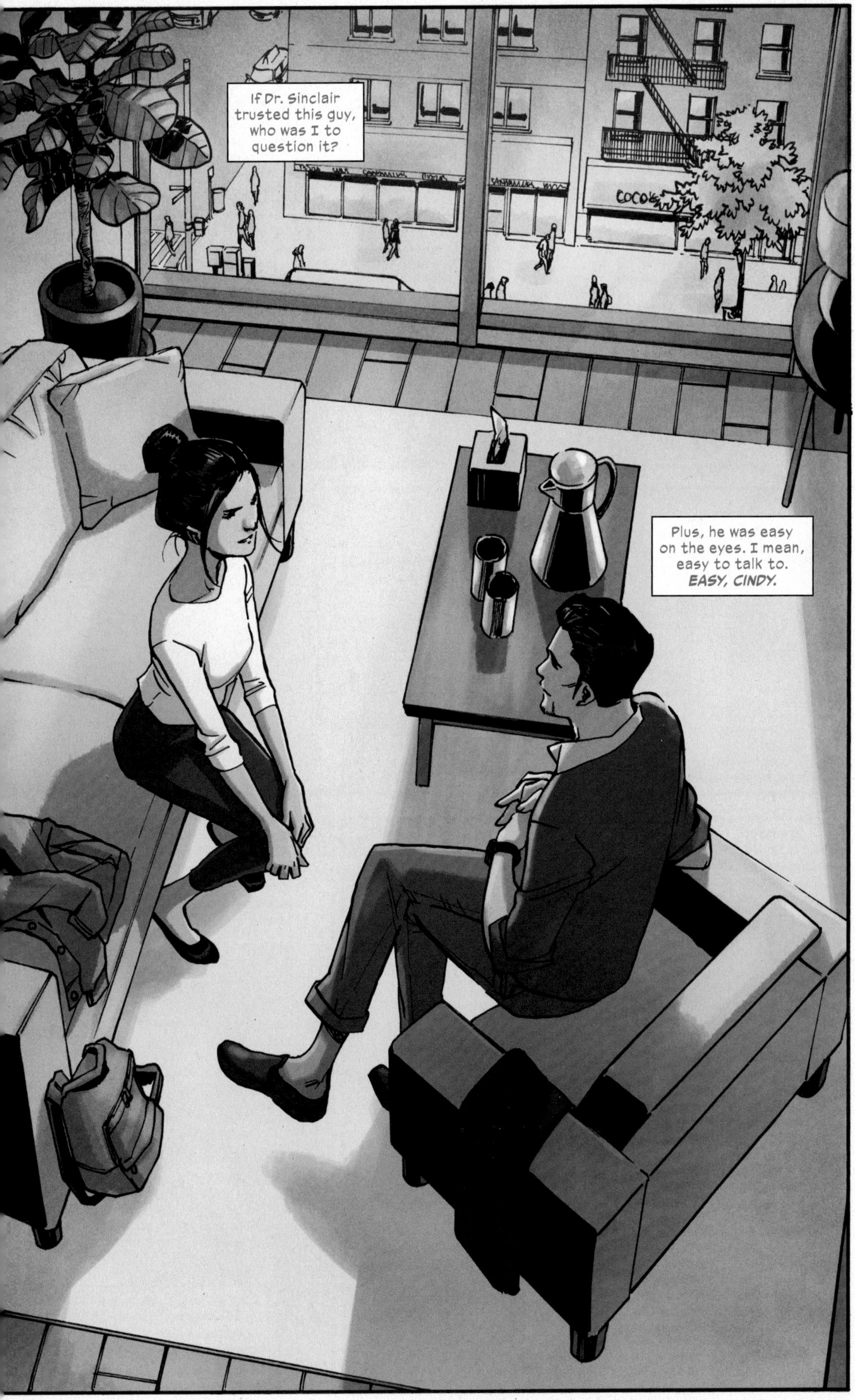
If Dr. Sinclair trusted this guy, who was I to question it?
Plus, he was easy on the eyes. I mean, easy to talk to. EASY, CINDY.

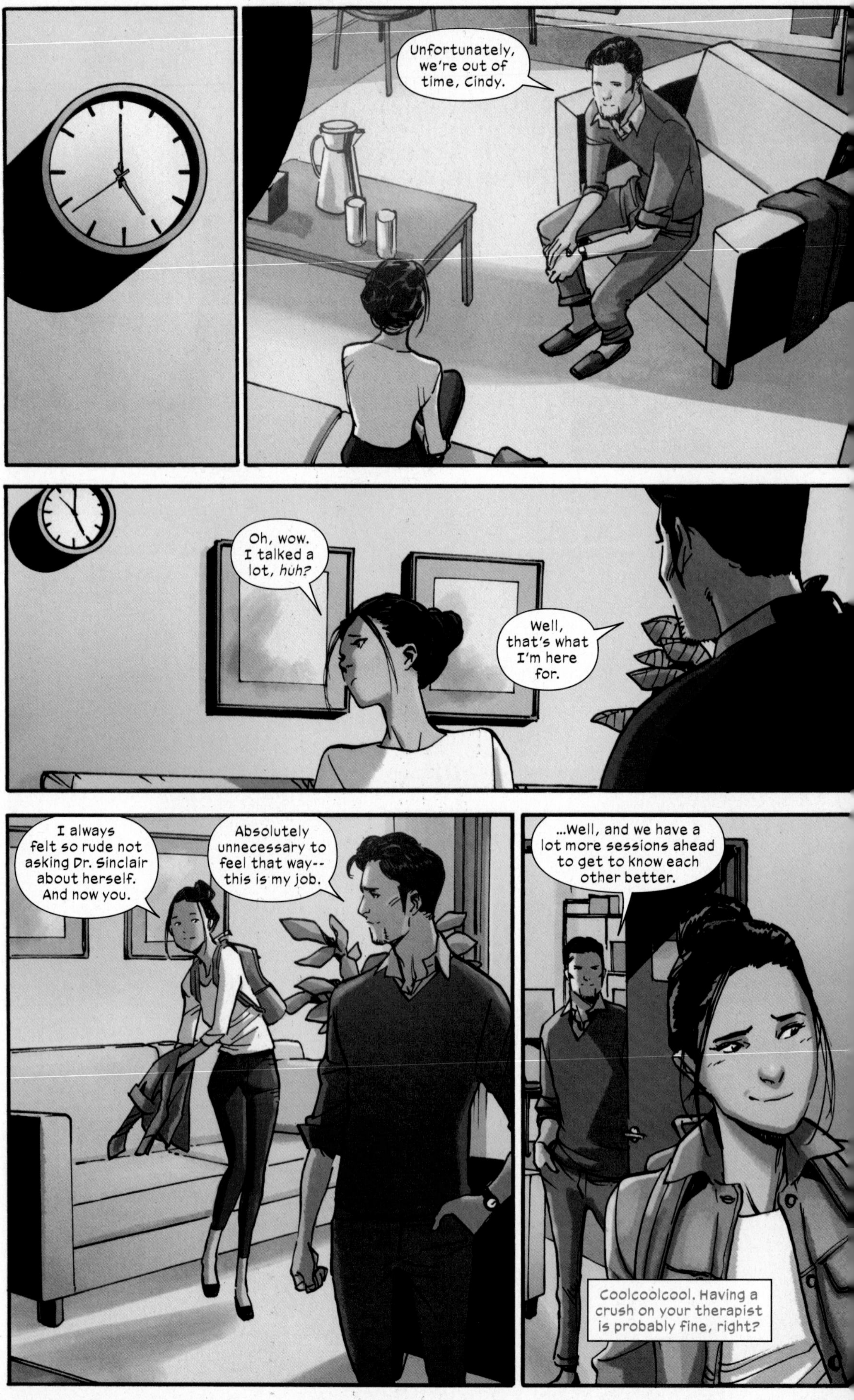
Unfortunately, we're out of time, Cindy.
Oh, wow. I talked a lot, *huh?*
Well, that's what I'm here for.
I always felt so rude not asking Dr. Sinclair about herself. And now you.
Absolutely unnecessary to feel that way-- this is my job.
...Well, and we have a lot more sessions ahead to get to know each other better.
Coolcoolcool. Having a crush on your therapist is probably fine, right?

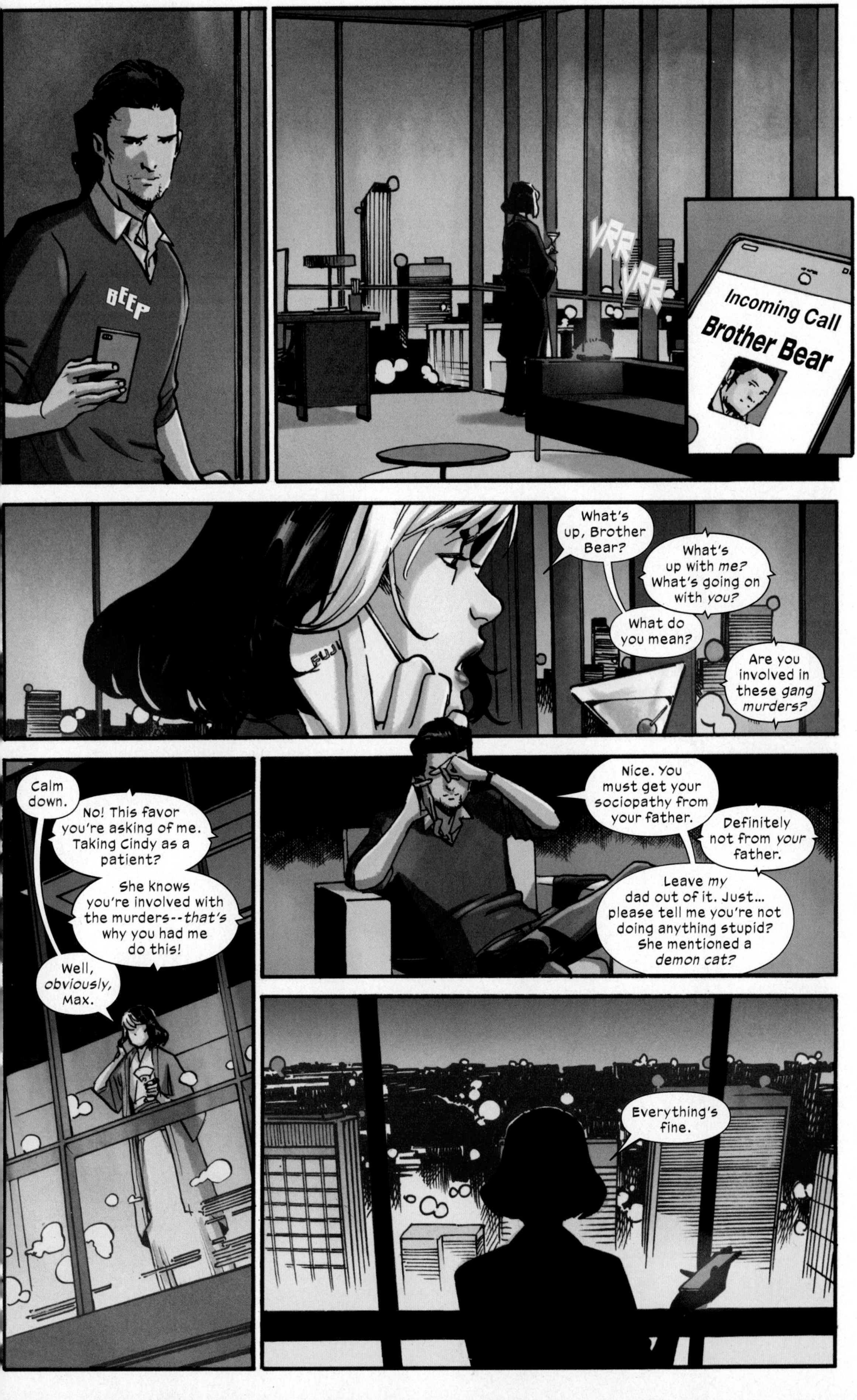
BEEP
VRR VRR
Incoming Call
Brother Bear
What's up, Brother Bear?
What's up with *me?* What's going on with *you?*
What do you mean?
Are you involved in these *gang murders?*
Calm down.
No! This favor you're asking of me. Taking Cindy as a patient?
She knows you're involved with the murders--*that's* why you had me do this!
Well, *obviously,* Max.
Nice. You must get your sociopathy from your father.
Definitely not from *your* father.
Leave *my* dad out of it. Just... please tell me you're not doing anything stupid? She mentioned a *demon cat?*
Everything's fine.

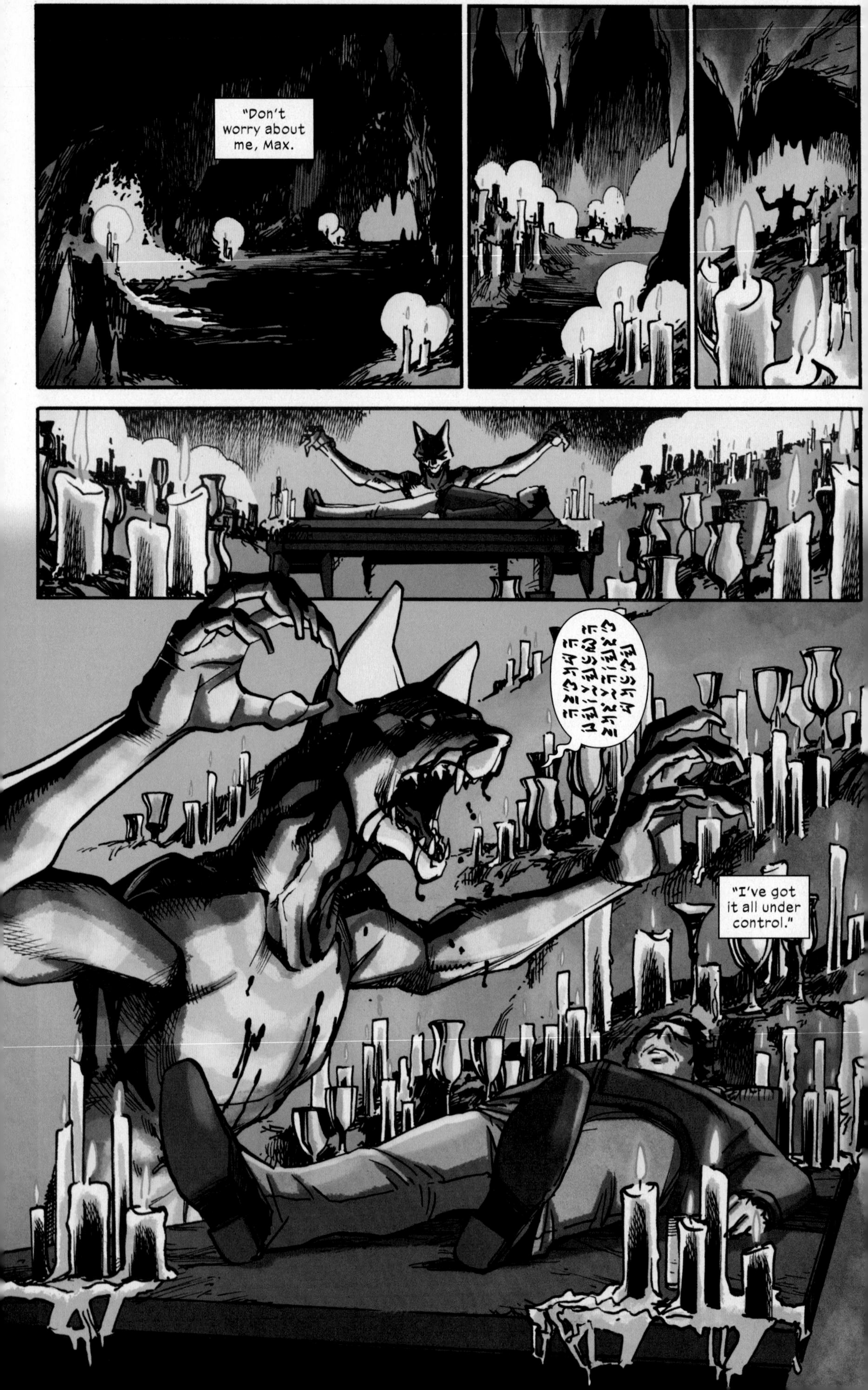
"Don't worry about me, Max.
"I've got it all under control."

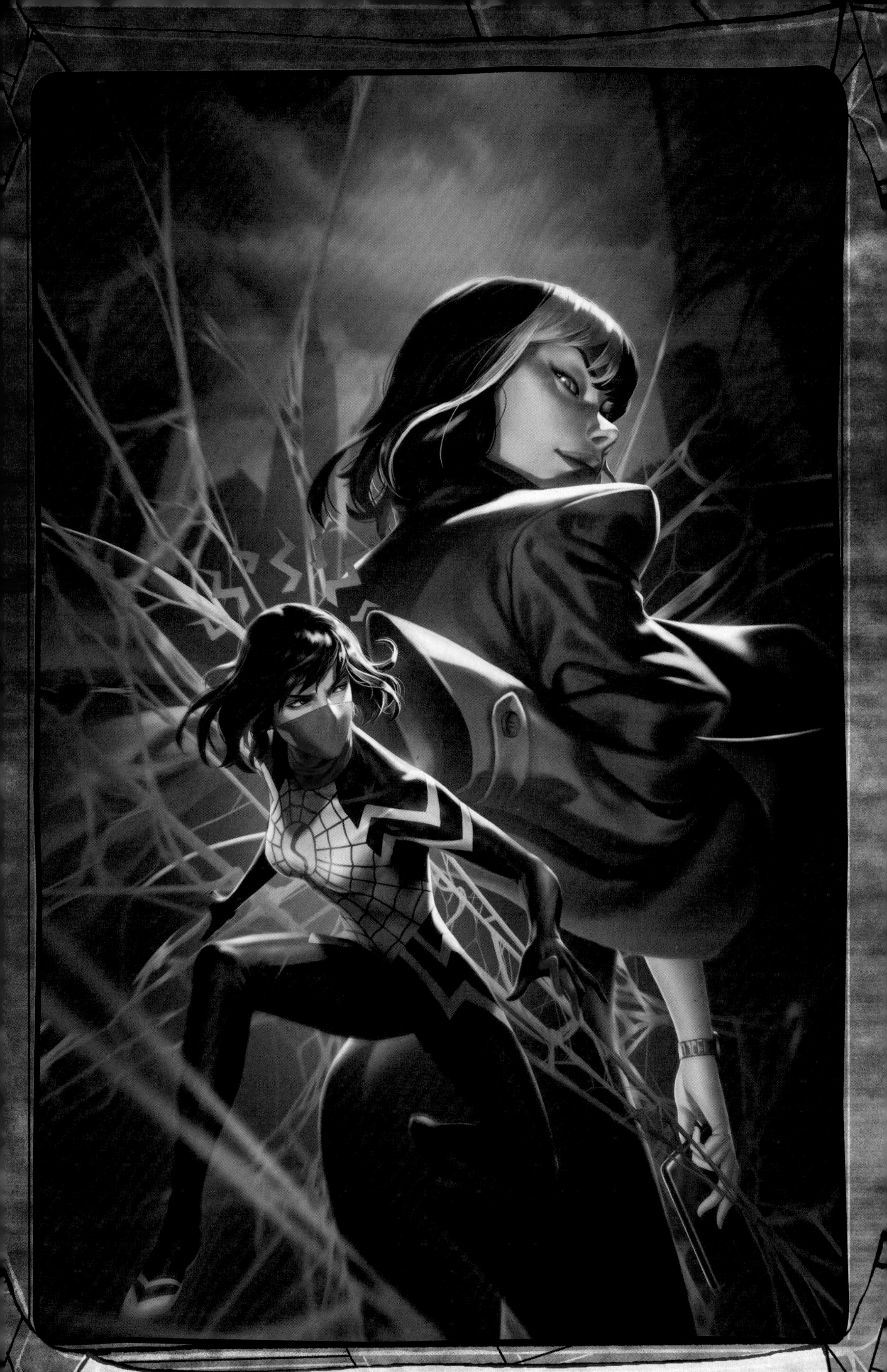

SILK #3

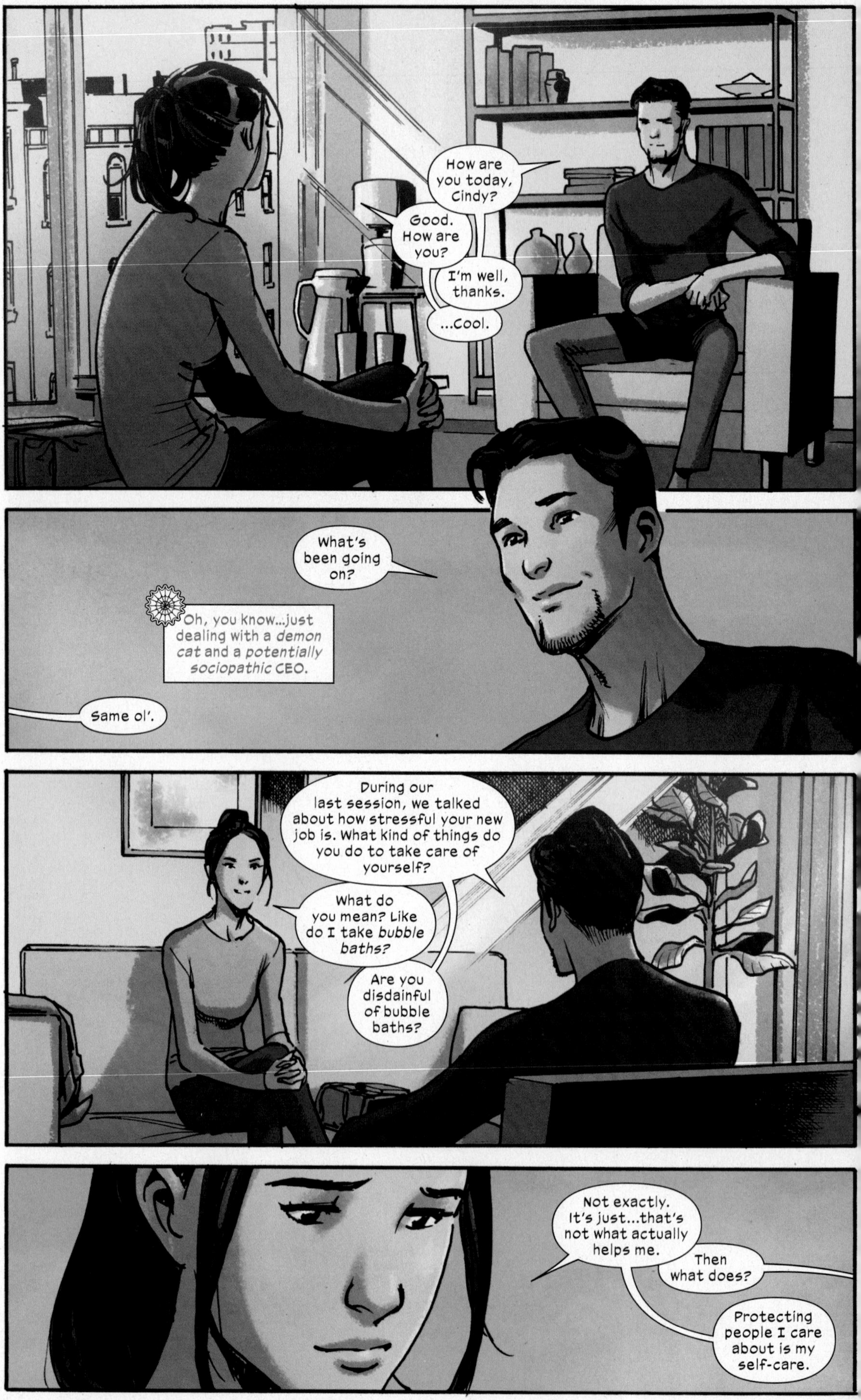
How are you today, Cindy?
Good. How are you?
I'm well, thanks.
...Cool.
What's been going on?
Oh, you know...just dealing with a *demon cat* and a *potentially sociopathic* CEO.
Same ol'.
During our last session, we talked about how stressful your new job is. What kind of things do you do to take care of yourself?
What do you mean? Like do I take *bubble baths?*
Are you disdainful of bubble baths?
Not exactly. It's just...that's not what actually helps me.
Then what does?
Protecting people I care about is my self-care.

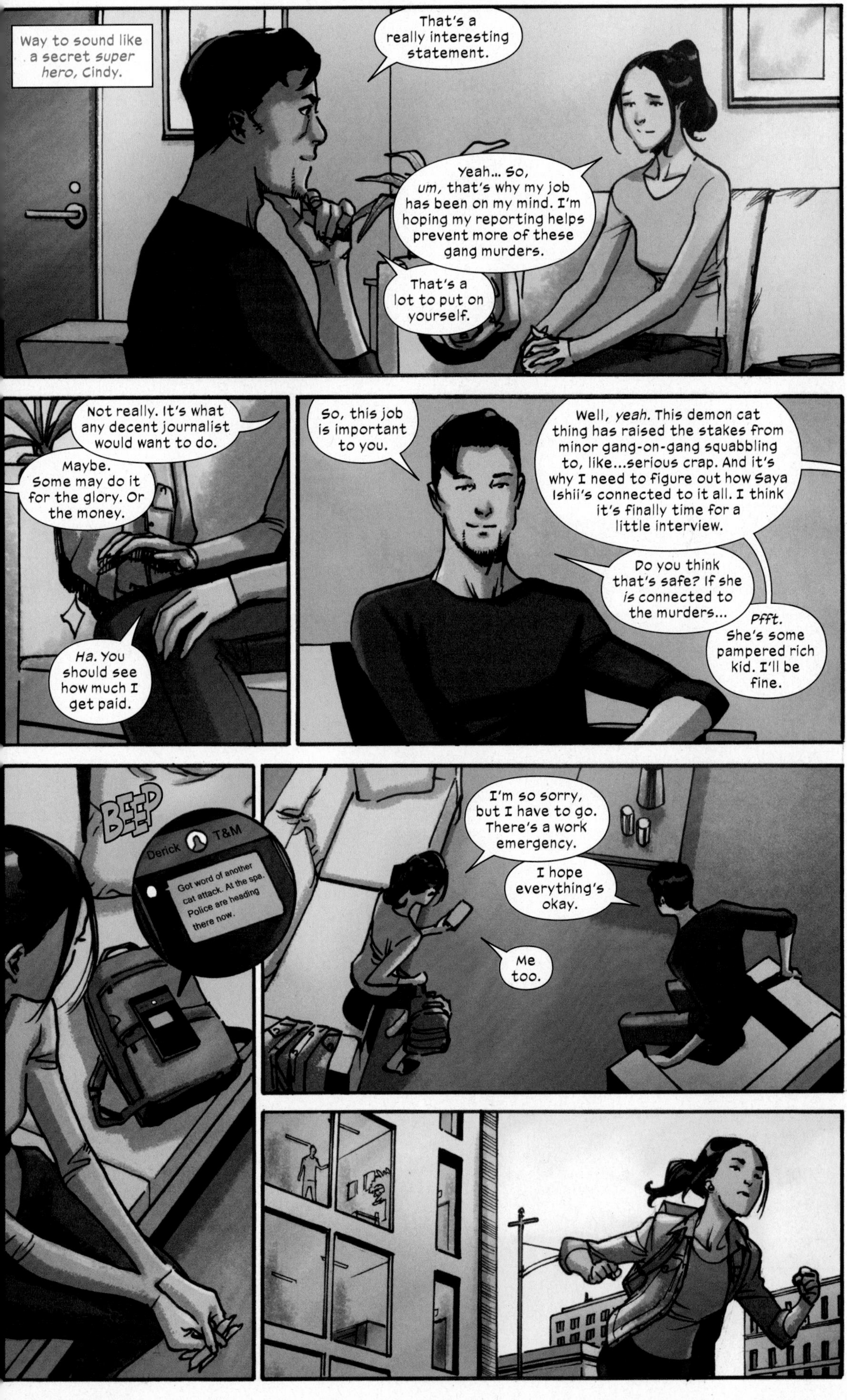
Way to sound like a secret *super hero,* Cindy.
That's a really interesting statement.
Yeah... So, *um,* that's why my job has been on my mind. I'm hoping my reporting helps prevent more of these gang murders.
That's a lot to put on yourself.
Not really. It's what any decent journalist would want to do.
Maybe. Some may do it for the glory. Or the money.
Ha. You should see how much I get paid.
So, this job is important to you.
Well, *yeah.* This demon cat thing has raised the stakes from minor gang-on-gang squabbling to, like...serious crap. And it's why I need to figure out how Saya Ishii's connected to it all. I think it's finally time for a little interview.
Do you think that's safe? If she *is* connected to the murders...
Pfft. She's some pampered rich kid. I'll be fine.
BEEP
Derick T&M
Got word of another cat attack. At the spa. Police are heading there now.
I'm so sorry, but I have to go. There's a work emergency.
I hope everything's okay.
Me too.

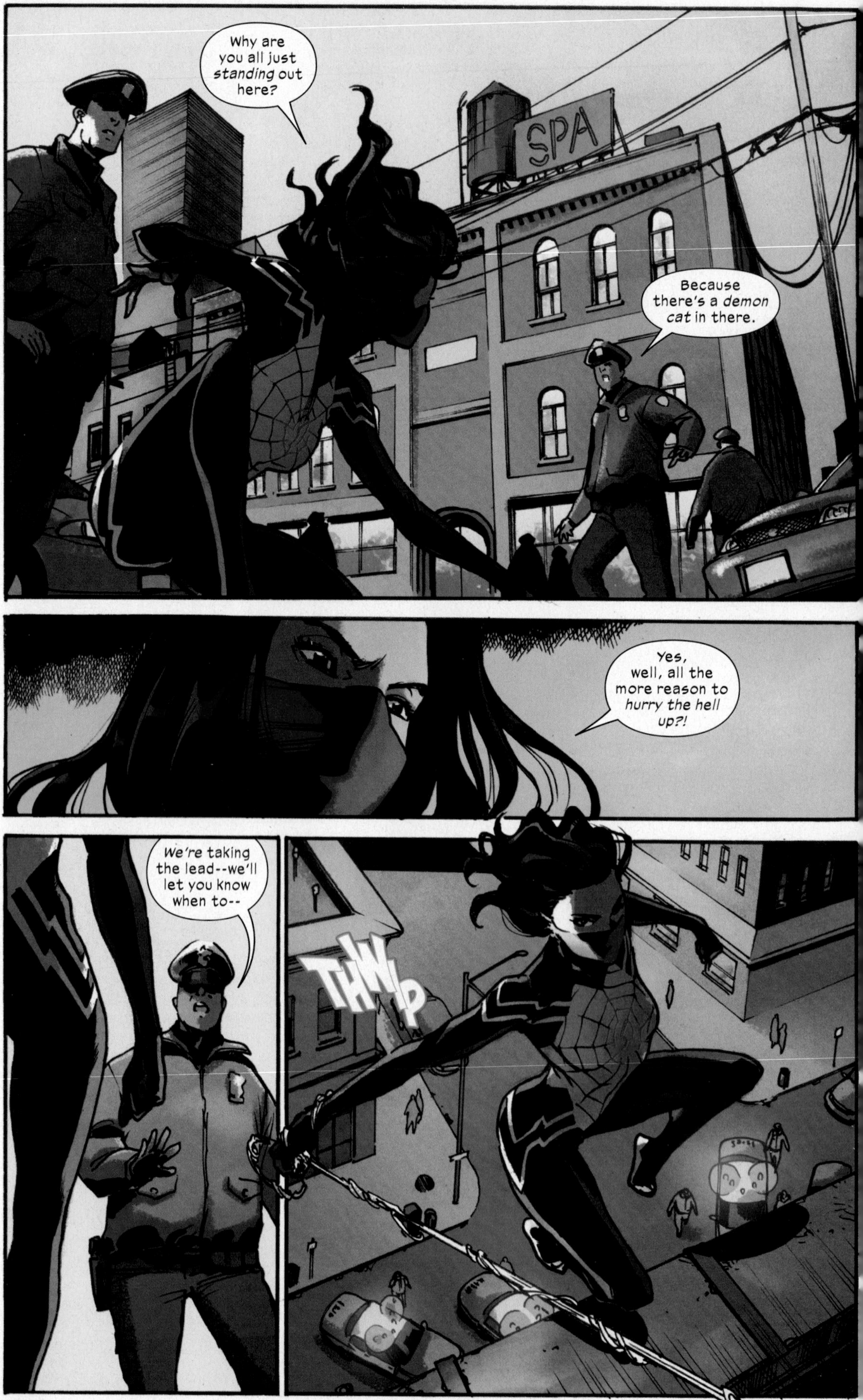
Why are you all just *standing* out here?
SPA
Because there's a *demon cat* in there.
Yes, well, all the more reason to *hurry the hell up?!*
We're taking the lead--we'll let you know when to--
THWIP

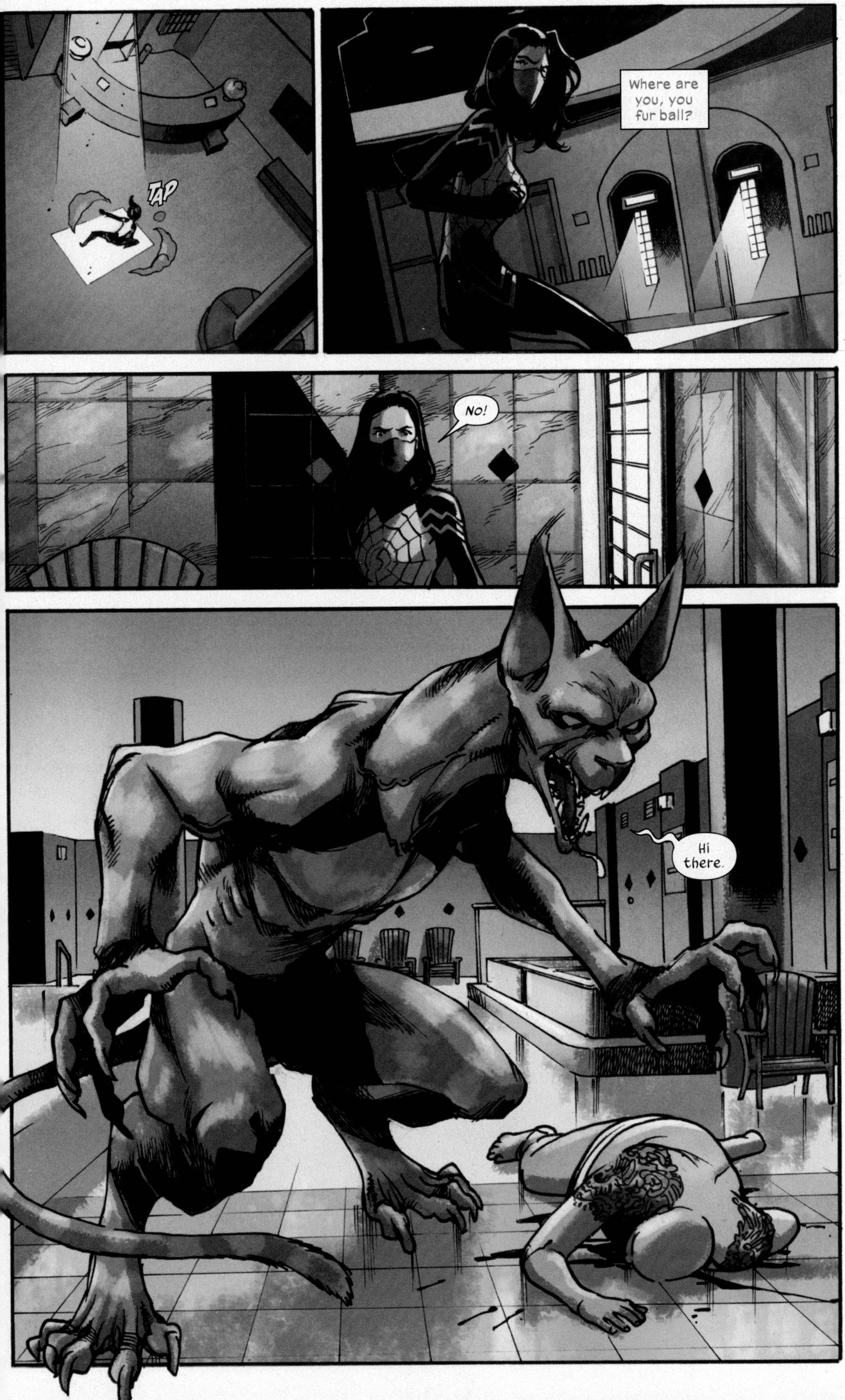

TAP
Where are you, you fur ball?
No!
Hi there.

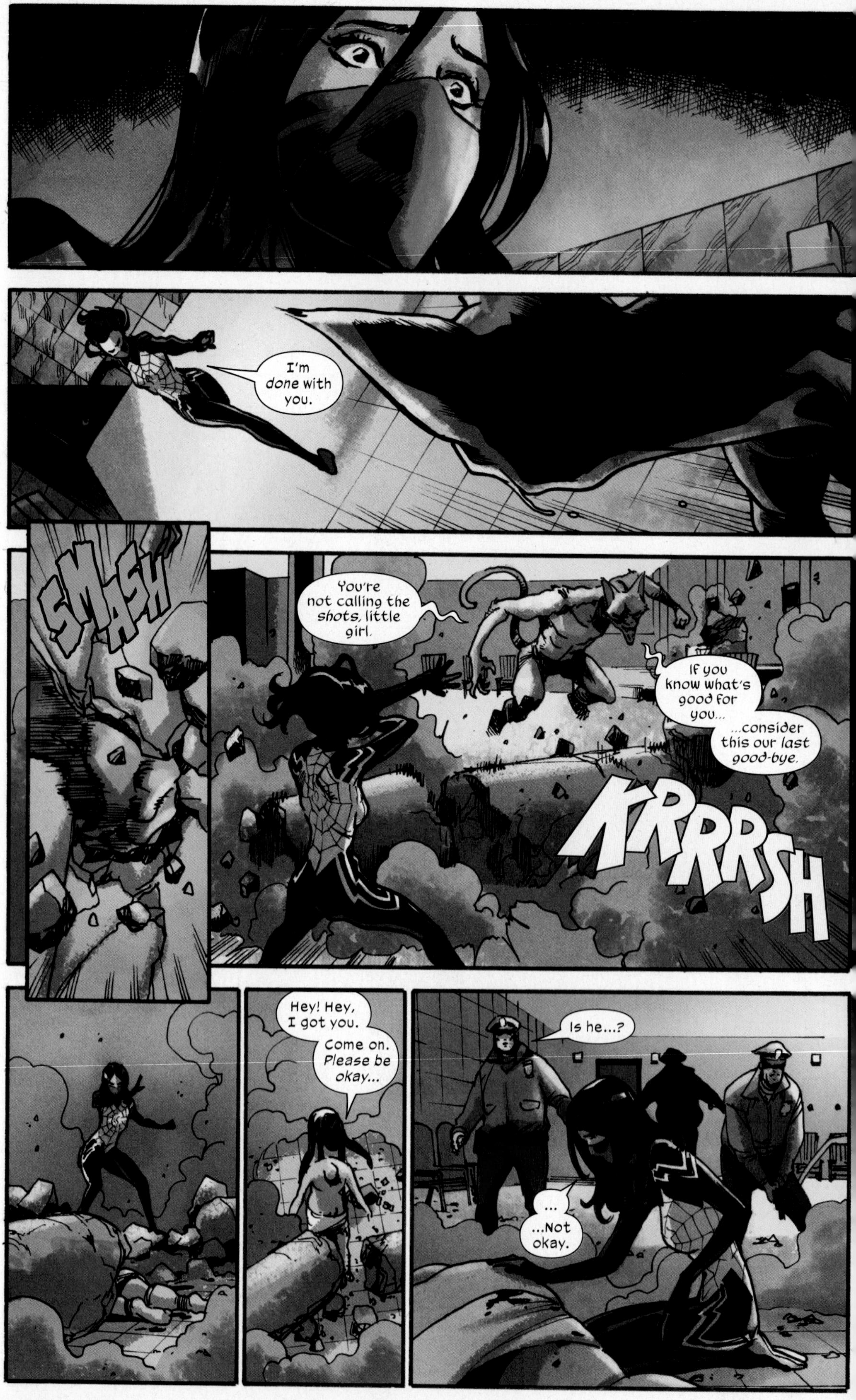
I'm done with you.
You're not calling the shots, little girl.
If you know what's good for you...
...consider this our last good-bye.
SMASH
KRRRSH
Hey! Hey, I got you.
Come on. Please be okay...
Is he...?
...
...Not okay.

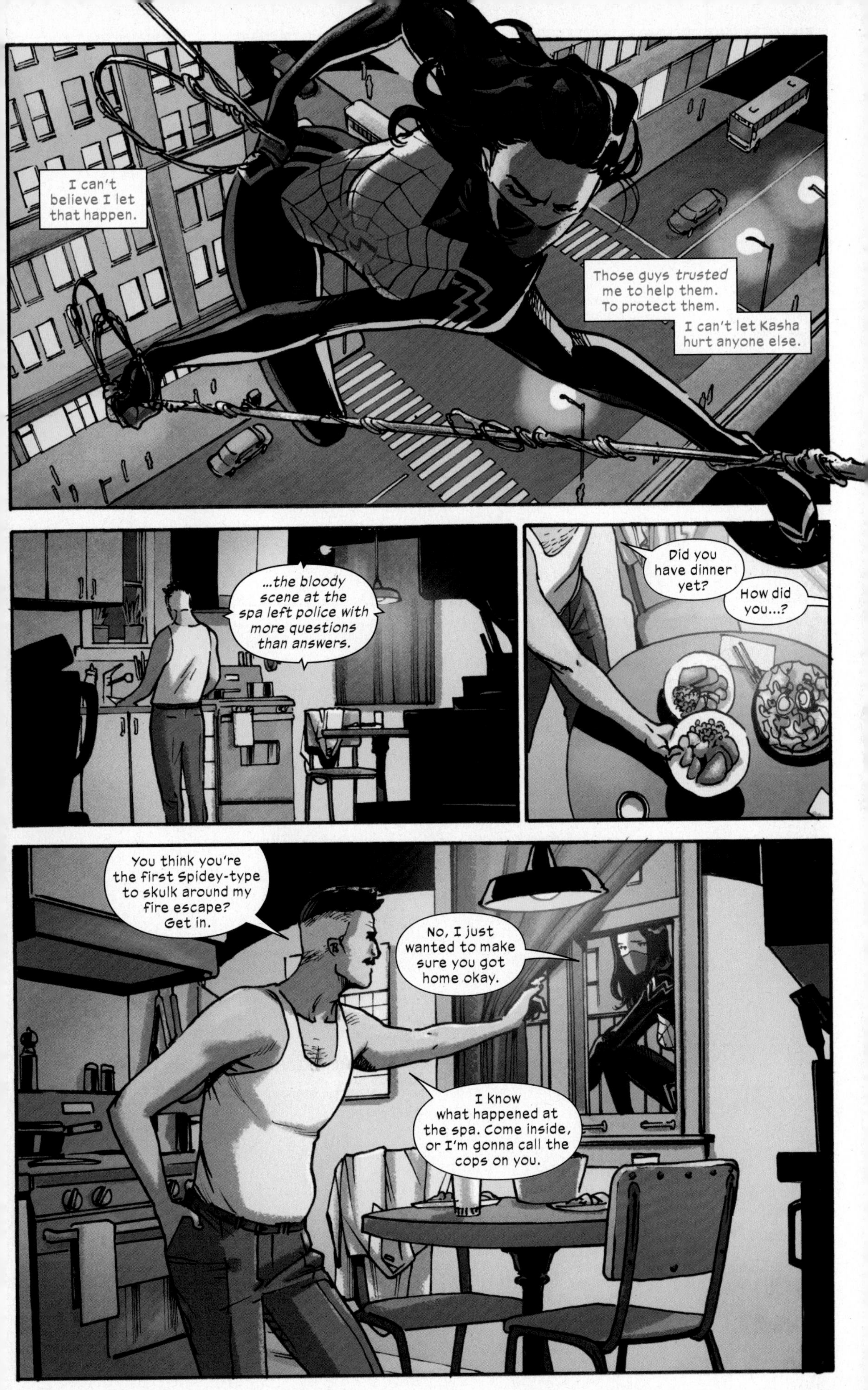
I can't believe I let that happen.
Those guys *trusted* me to help them. To protect them.
I can't let Kasha hurt anyone else.
...the bloody scene at the spa left police with more questions than answers.
Did you have dinner yet?
How did you...?
You think you're the first Spidey-type to skulk around my fire escape? Get in.
No, I just wanted to make sure you got home okay.
I know what happened at the spa. Come inside, or I'm gonna call the cops on you.

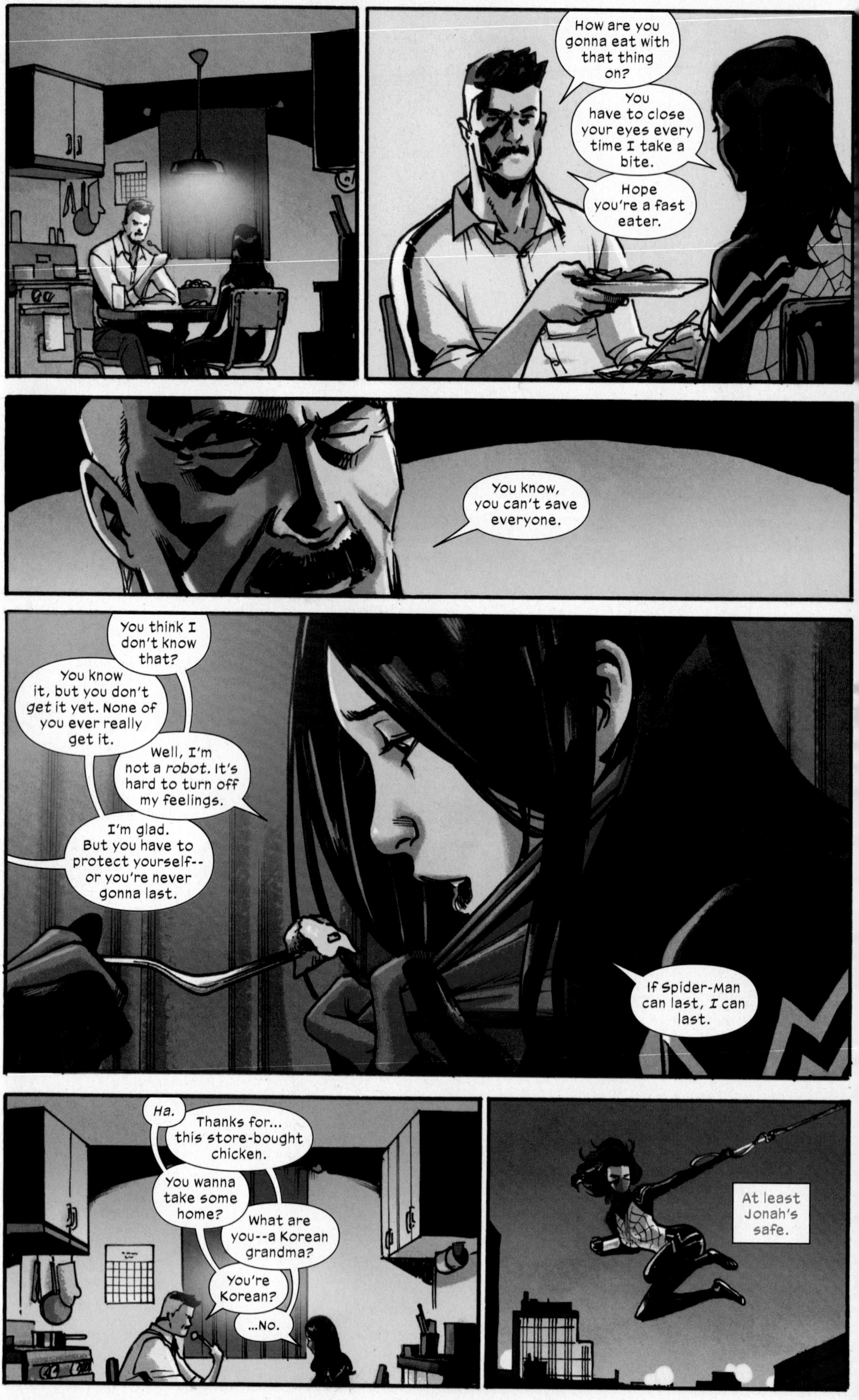
How are you gonna eat with that thing on?
You have to close your eyes every time I take a bite.
Hope you're a fast eater.
You know, you can't save everyone.
You think I don't know that?
You know it, but you don't *get* it yet. None of you ever really get it.
Well, I'm not a *robot*. It's hard to turn off my feelings.
I'm glad. But you have to protect yourself--or you're never gonna last.
If Spider-Man can last, *I* can last.
Ha.
Thanks for... this store-bought chicken.
You wanna take some home?
What are you--a Korean grandma?
You're Korean?
...No.
At least Jonah's safe.

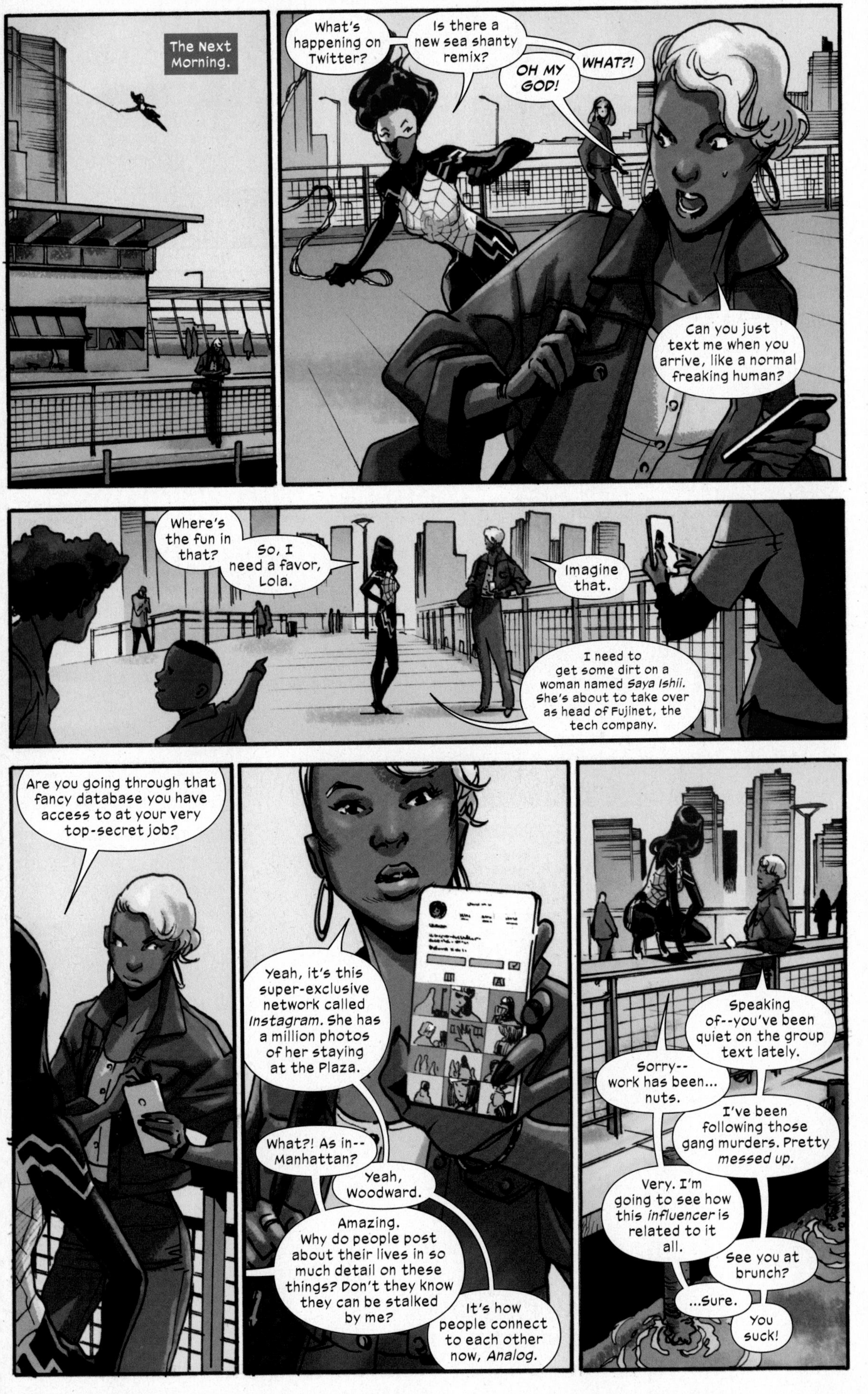
The Next Morning.
What's happening on Twitter?
Is there a new sea shanty remix?
OH MY GOD!
WHAT?!
Can you just text me when you arrive, like a normal freaking human?
Where's the fun in that?
So, I need a favor, Lola.
Imagine that.
I need to get some dirt on a woman named *Saya Ishii.* She's about to take over as head of Fujinet, the tech company.
Are you going through that fancy database you have access to at your very top-secret job?
Yeah, it's this super-exclusive network called *Instagram*. She has a million photos of her staying at the Plaza.
What?! As in--Manhattan?
Yeah, Woodward.
Amazing. Why do people post about their lives in so much detail on these things? Don't they know they can be stalked by me?
It's how people connect to each other now, *Analog.*
Speaking of--you've been quiet on the group text lately.
Sorry--work has been... nuts.
I've been following those gang murders. Pretty *messed up.*
Very. I'm going to see how this *influencer* is related to it all.
See you at brunch?
...Sure.
You suck!

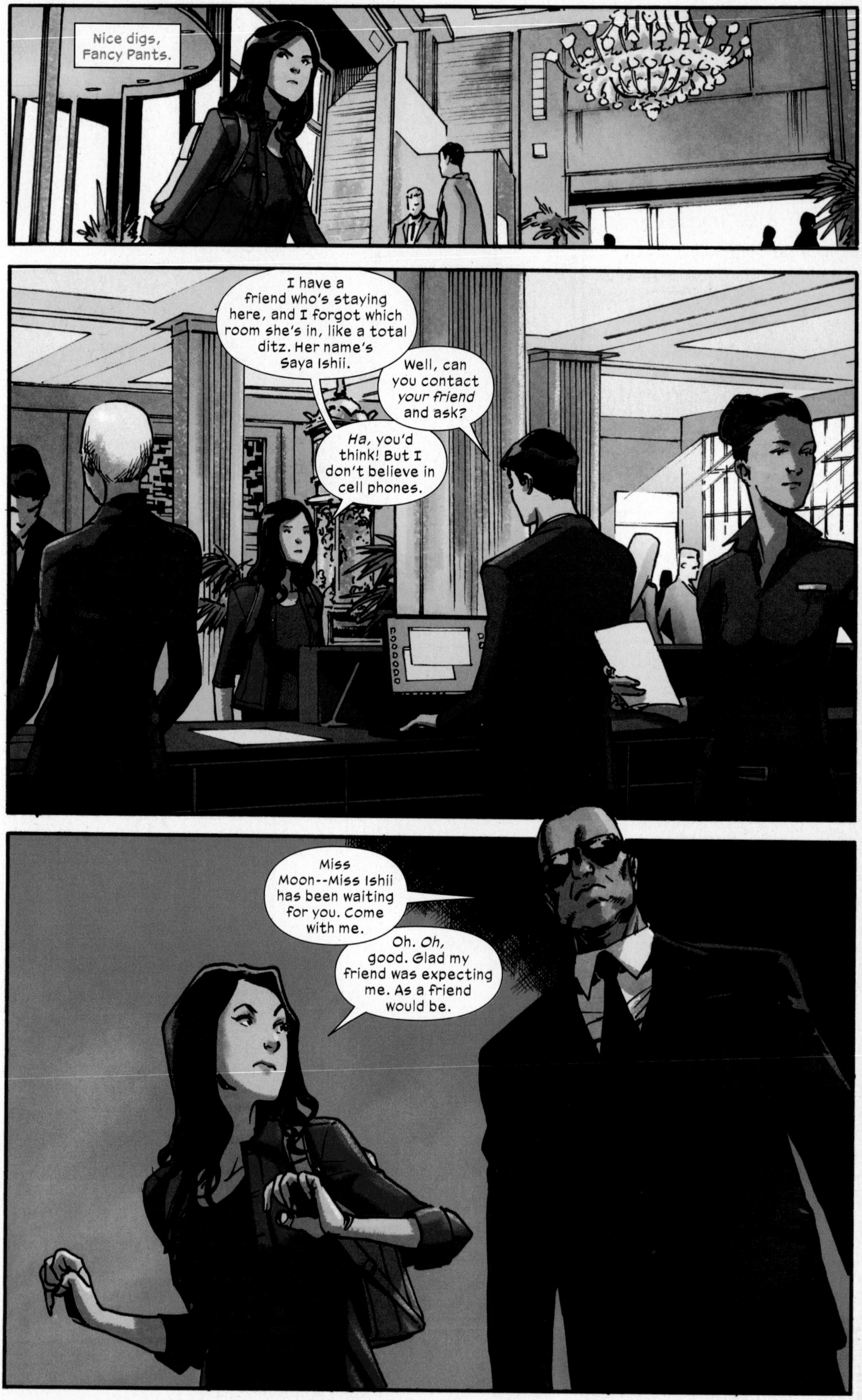
Nice digs, Fancy Pants.
I have a friend who's staying here, and I forgot which room she's in, like a total ditz. Her name's Saya Ishii.
Well, can you contact *your friend* and ask?
Ha, you'd think! But I don't believe in cell phones.
Miss Moon--Miss Ishii has been waiting for you. Come with me.
Oh. *Oh,* good. Glad my friend was expecting me. As a friend would be.

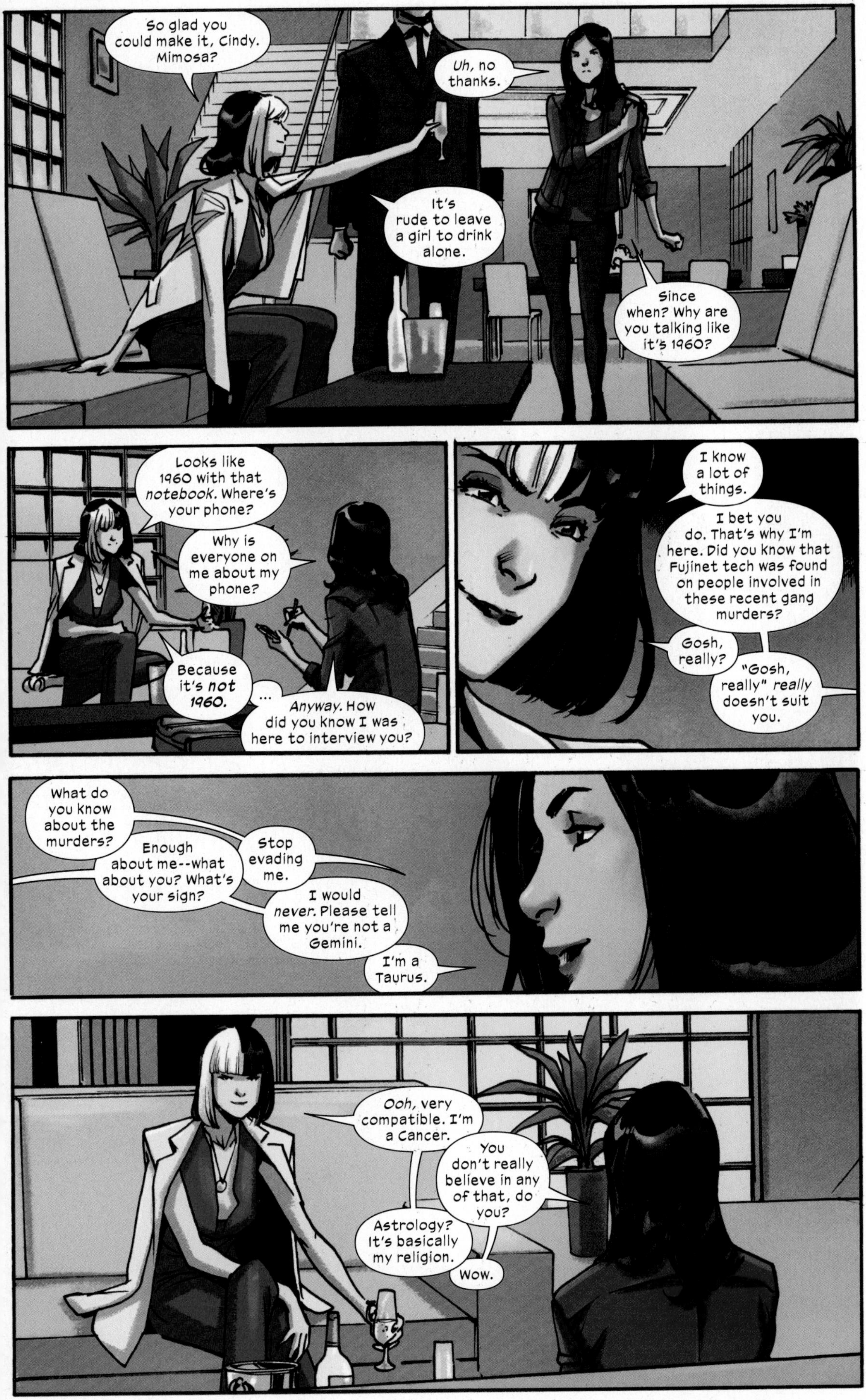

So glad you could make it, Cindy. Mimosa?
Uh, no thanks.
It's rude to leave a girl to drink alone.
Since when? Why are you talking like it's 1960?
Looks like 1960 with that notebook. Where's your phone?
Why is everyone on me about my phone?
Because it's not 1960.
...
Anyway. How did you know I was here to interview you?
I know a lot of things.
I bet you do. That's why I'm here. Did you know that Fujinet tech was found on people involved in these recent gang murders?
Gosh, really?
"Gosh, really" really doesn't suit you.
What do you know about the murders?
Enough about me--what about you? What's your sign?
Stop evading me.
I would never. Please tell me you're not a Gemini.
I'm a Taurus.
Ooh, very compatible. I'm a Cancer.
You don't really believe in any of that, do you?
Astrology? It's basically my religion.
Wow.

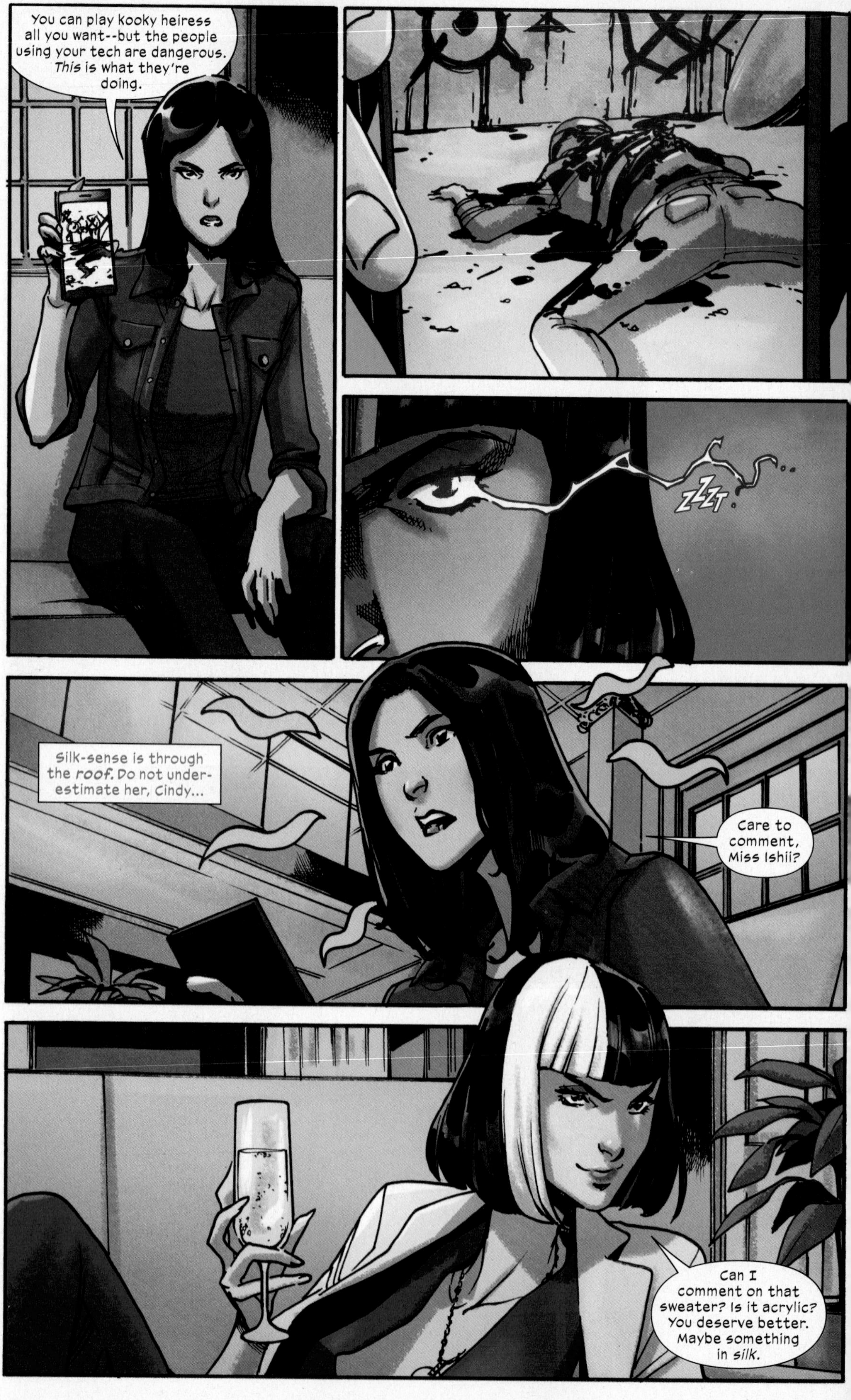

You can play kooky heiress all you want--but the people using your tech are dangerous. *This* is what they're doing.
ZZZT
Silk-sense is through the *roof.* Do not under-estimate her, Cindy...
Care to comment, Miss Ishii?
Can I comment on that sweater? Is it acrylic? You deserve better. Maybe something in *silk.*

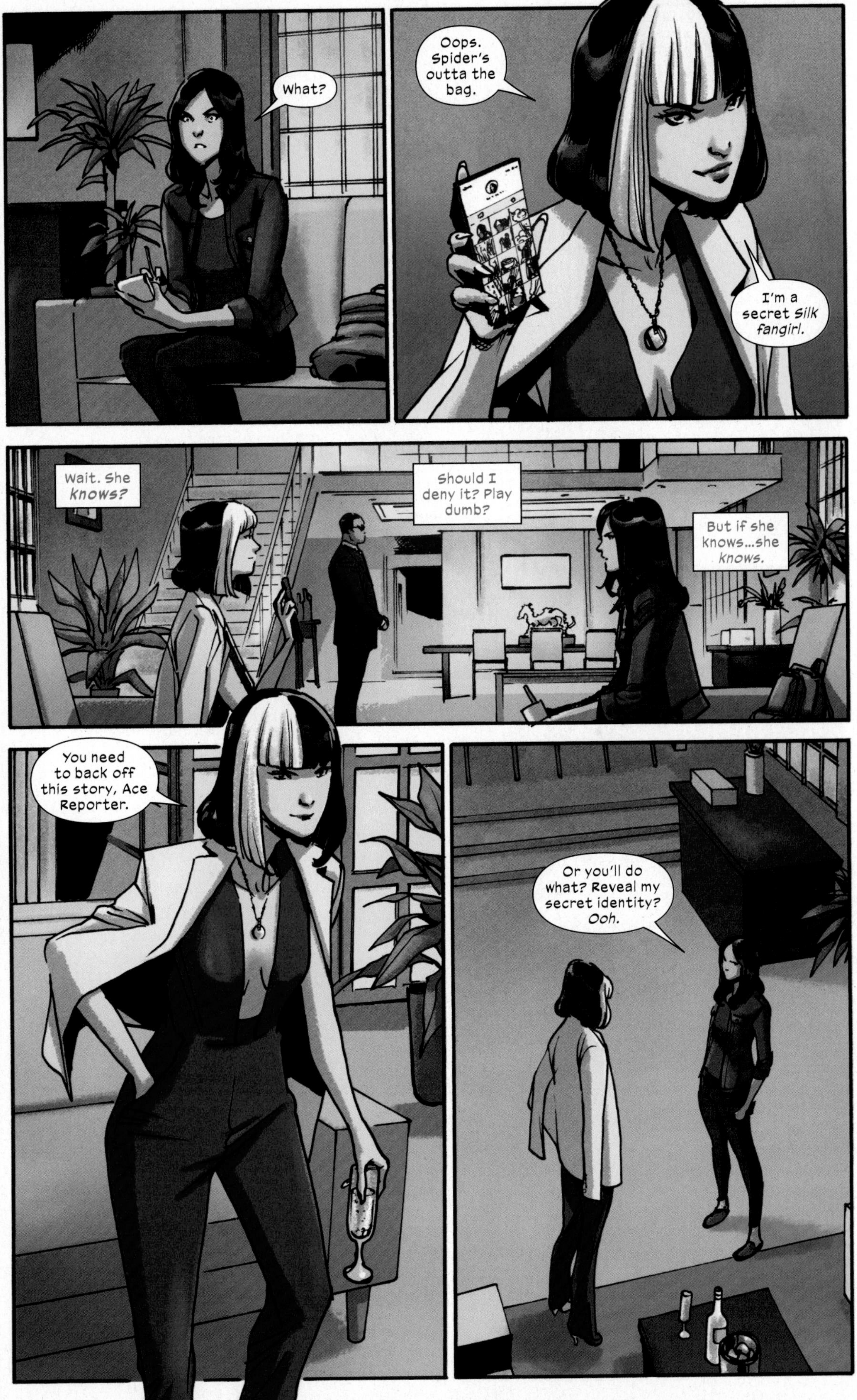
What?
Oops. Spider's outta the bag.
I'm a secret *Silk* *fangirl.*
Wait. She *knows?*
Should I deny it? Play dumb?
But if she knows...she *knows.*
You need to back off this story, Ace Reporter.
Or you'll do what? Reveal my secret identity? *Ooh.*

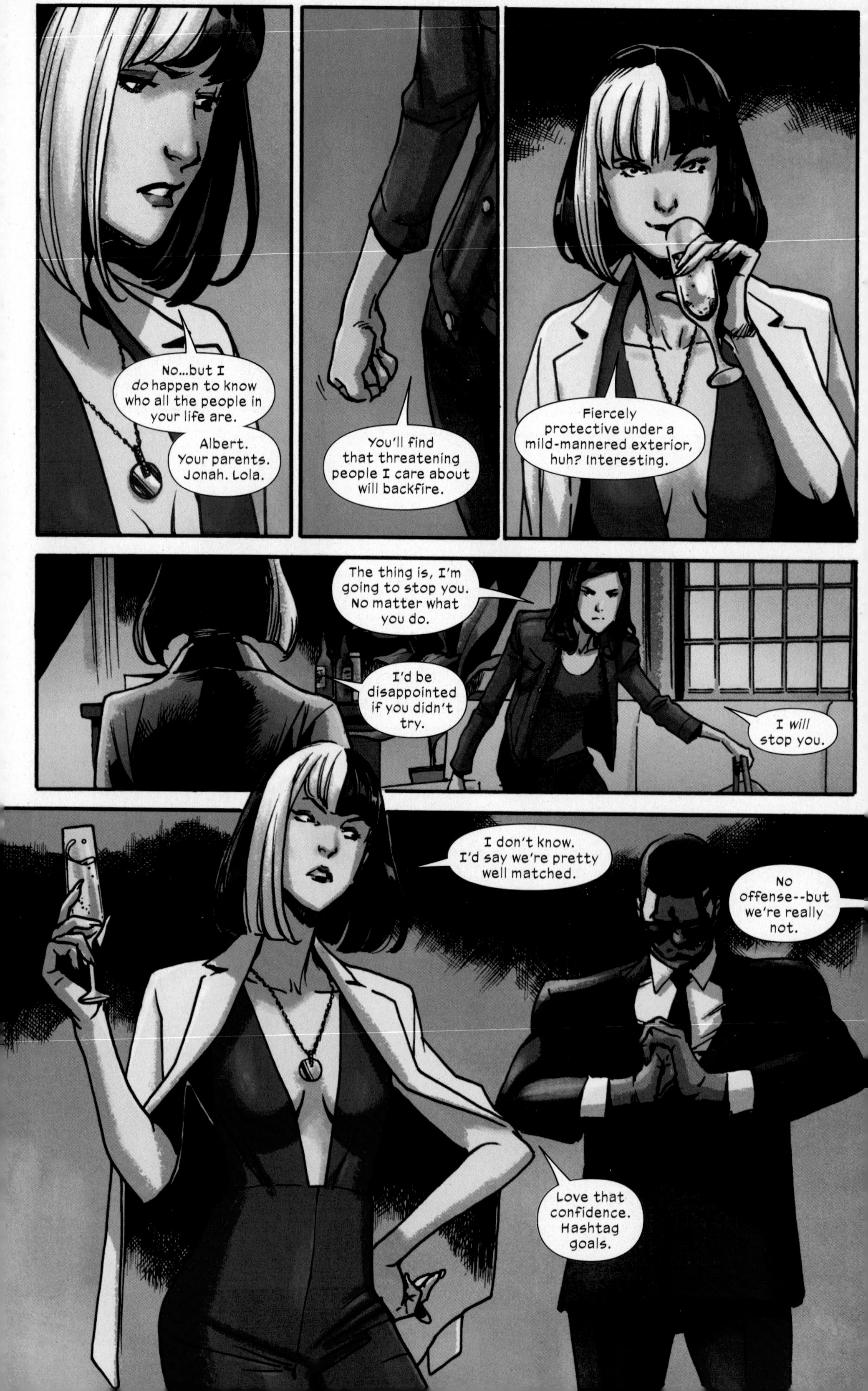
No...but I *do* happen to know who all the people in your life are.
Albert. Your parents. Jonah. Lola.
You'll find that threatening people I care about will backfire.
Fiercely protective under a mild-mannered exterior, huh? Interesting.
The thing is, I'm going to stop you. No matter what you do.
I'd be disappointed if you didn't try.
I *will* stop you.
I don't know. I'd say we're pretty well matched.
No offense--but we're really not.
Love that confidence. Hashtag goals.

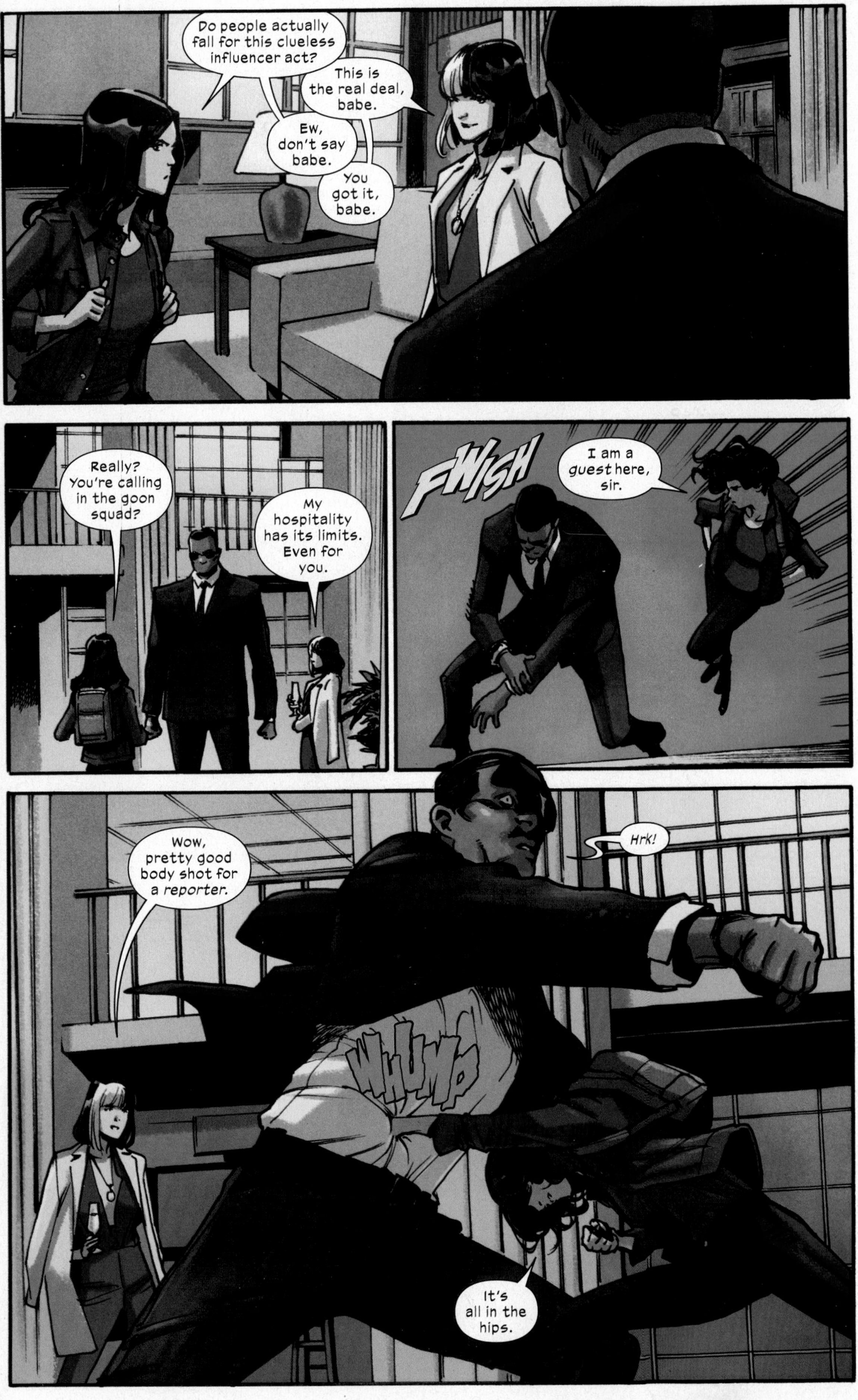
Do people actually fall for this clueless influencer act?
This is the real deal, babe.
Ew, don't say babe.
You got it, babe.
Really? You're calling in the goon squad?
My hospitality has its limits. Even for you.
FWISH
I am a *guest* here, sir.
Wow, pretty good body shot for a *reporter*.
Hrk!
WHUMP
It's all in the hips.

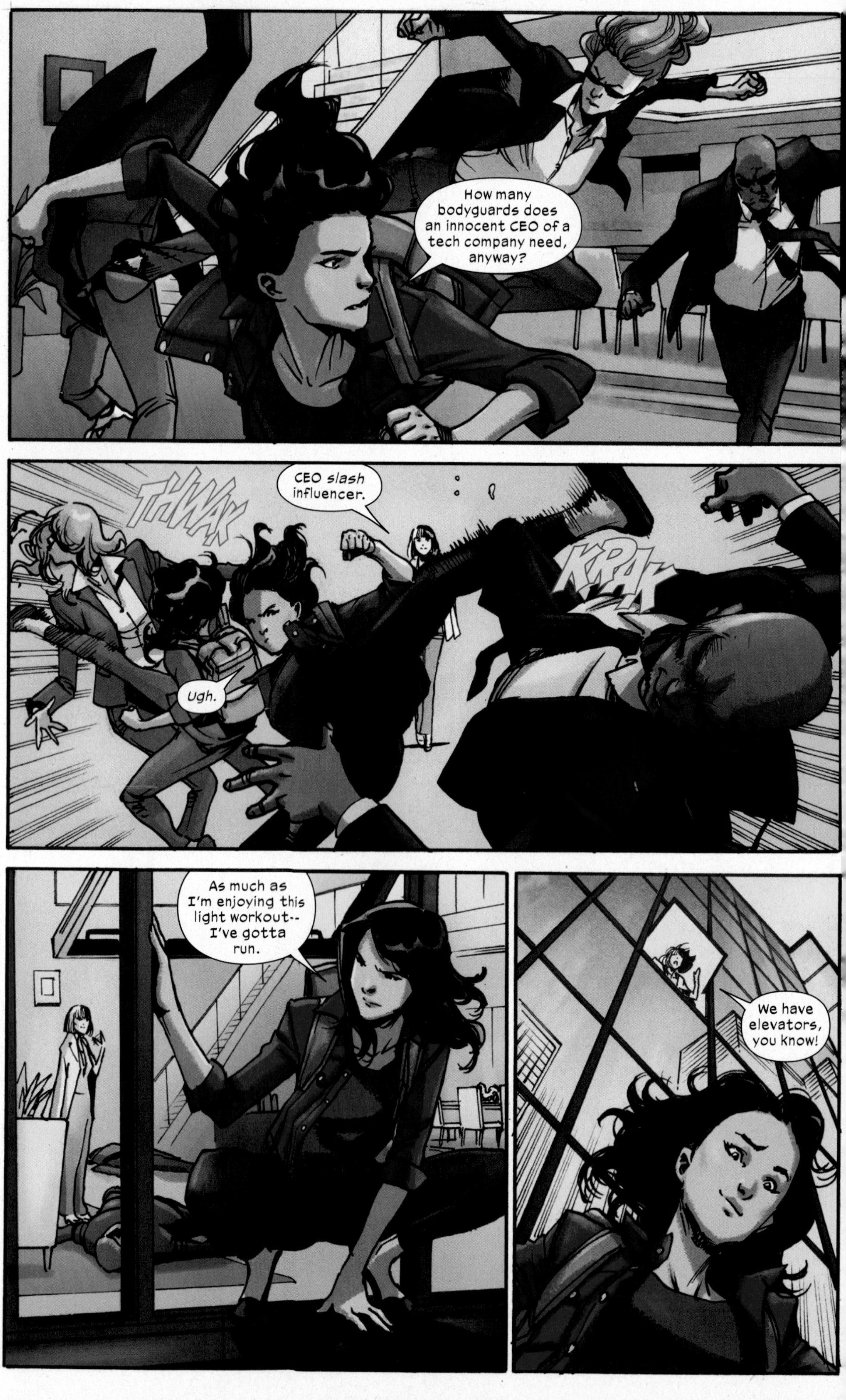
How many bodyguards does an innocent CEO of a tech company need, anyway?
THWAK
CEO slash influencer.
KRAK
Ugh.
As much as I'm enjoying this light workout-- I've gotta run.
We have elevators, you know!

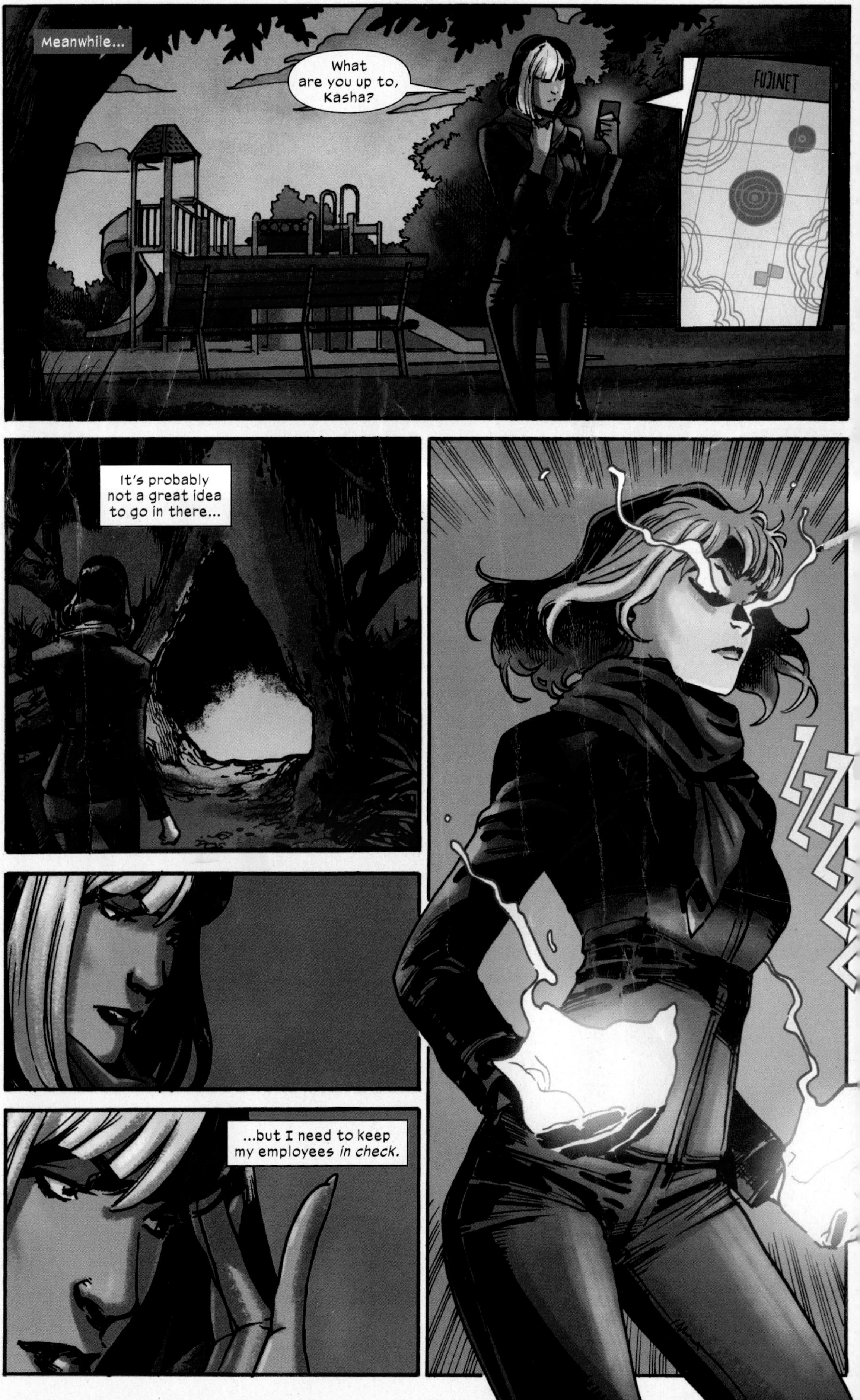
Meanwhile...
What are you up to, Kasha?
FUJINET
It's probably not a great idea to go in there...
...but I need to keep my employees *in check*.
ZZZZZ

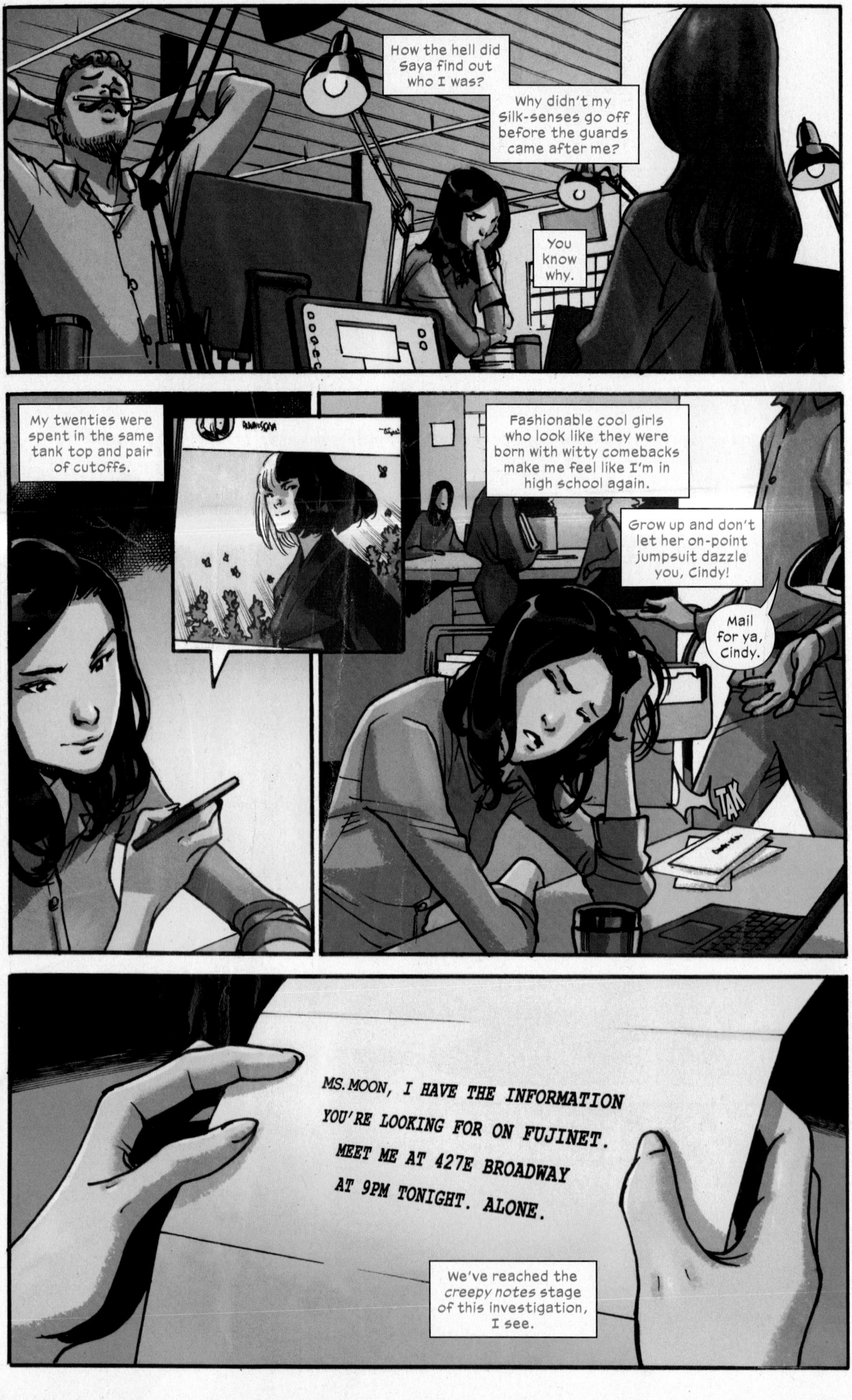
How the hell did Saya find out who I was?
Why didn't my Silk-senses go off before the guards came after me?
You know why.
My twenties were spent in the same tank top and pair of cutoffs.
Fashionable cool girls who look like they were born with witty comebacks make me feel like I'm in high school again.
Grow up and don't let her on-point jumpsuit dazzle you, Cindy!
Mail for ya, Cindy.
TAK
MS. MOON, I HAVE THE INFORMATION YOU'RE LOOKING FOR ON FUJINET. MEET ME AT 427E BROADWAY AT 9PM TONIGHT. ALONE.
We've reached the *creepy notes* stage of this investigation, I see.

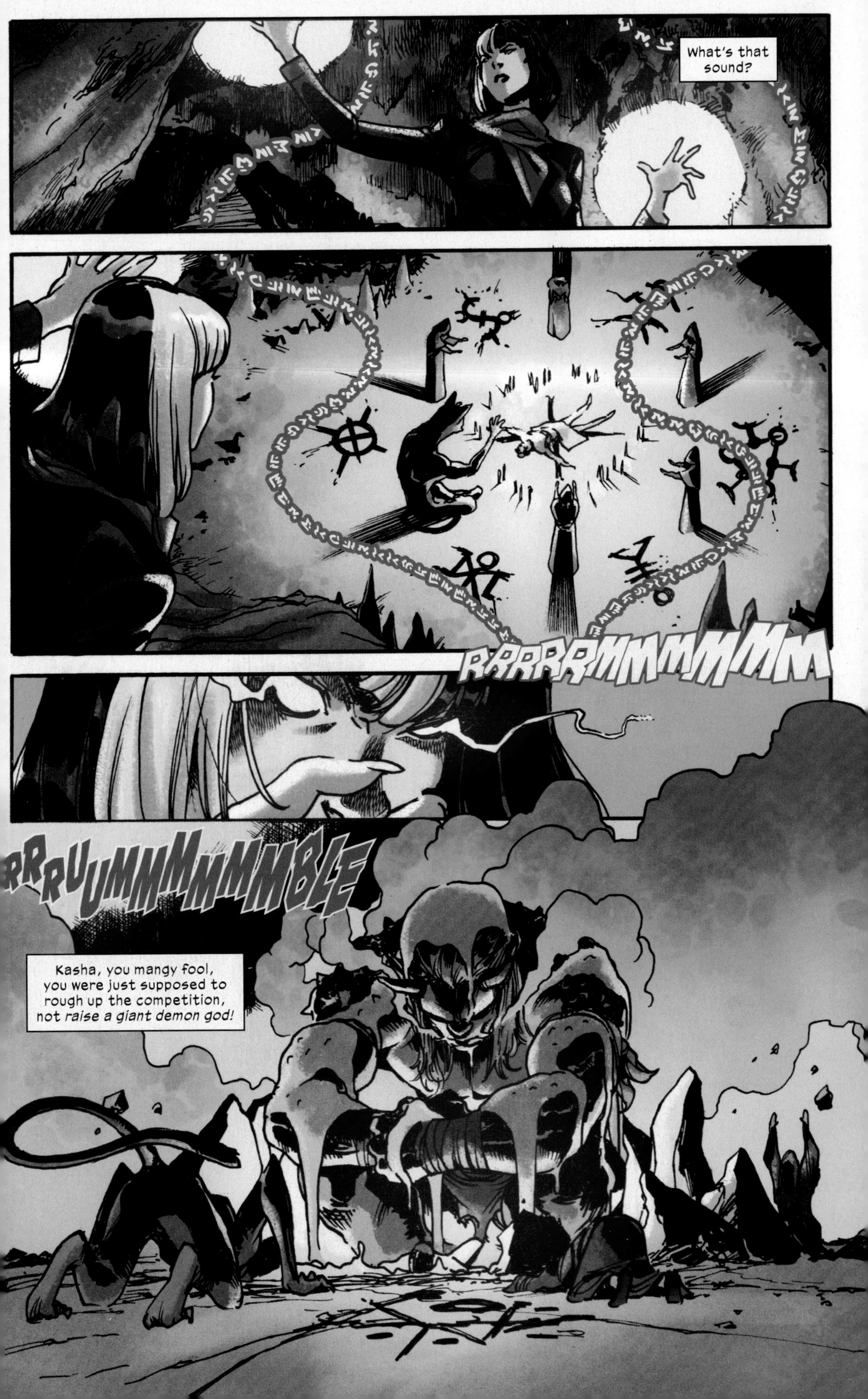
What's that sound?
RRRRRMMMMMMMM
RRRUMMMMMMMMBLE
Kasha, you mangy fool, you were just supposed to rough up the competition, not *raise a giant demon god!*

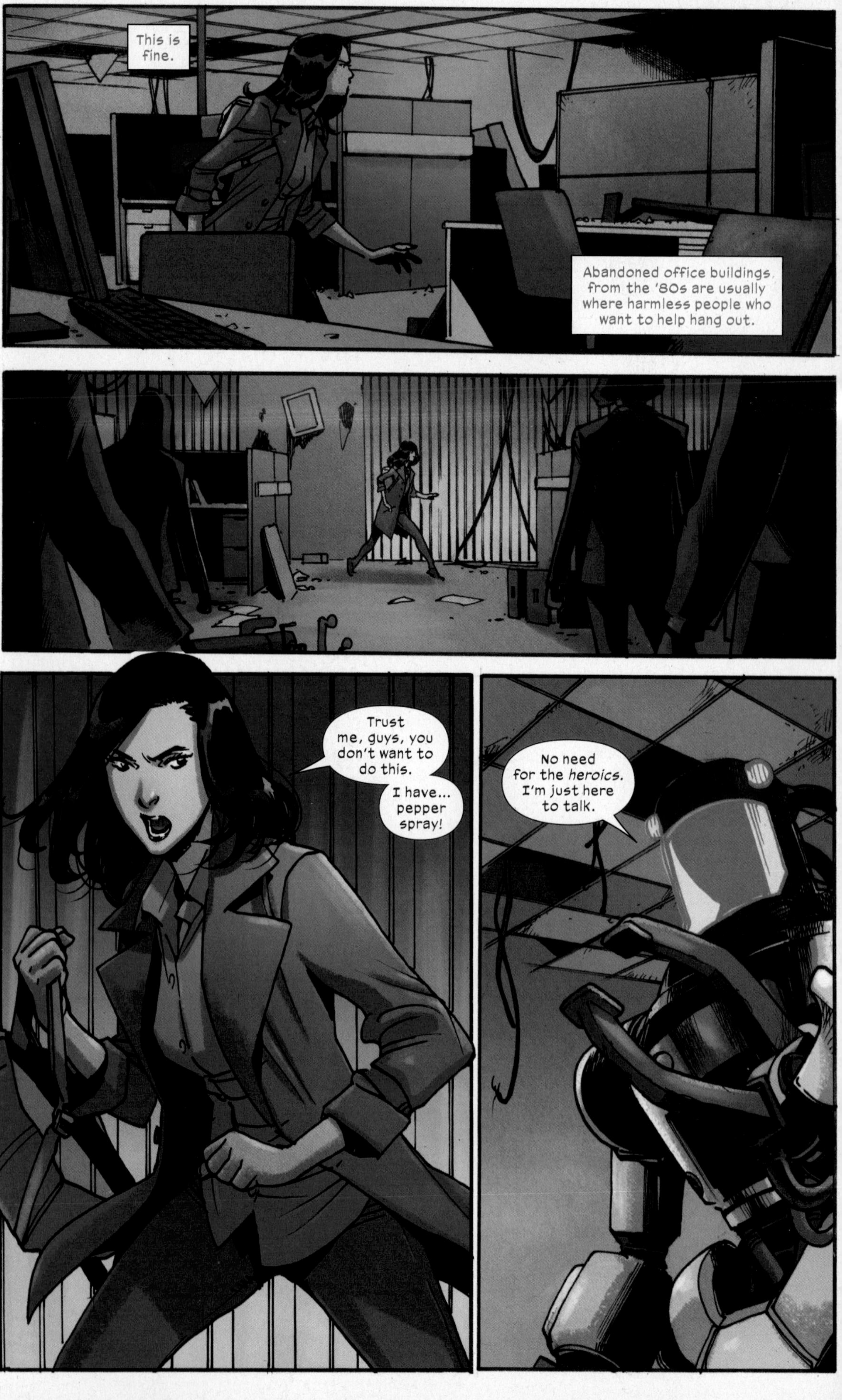
This is fine.
Abandoned office buildings from the '80s are usually where harmless people who want to help hang out.
Trust me, guys, you don't want to do this.
I have... pepper spray!
No need for the *heroics*. I'm just here to talk.

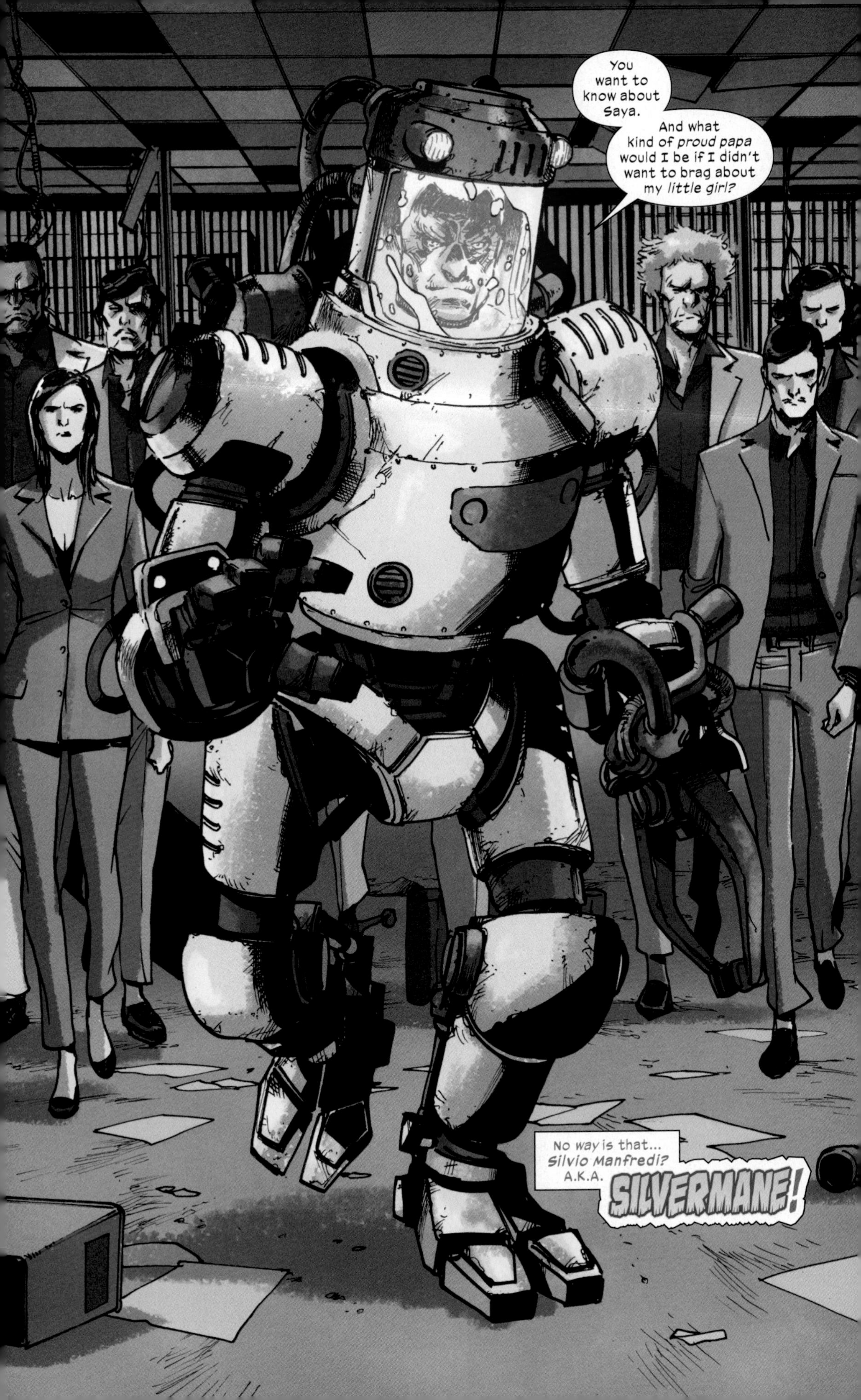
You want to know about Saya.
And what kind of *proud papa* would I be if I didn't want to brag about my *little girl?*
No way is that... *Silvio Manfredi?* A.K.A.
SILVERMANE!

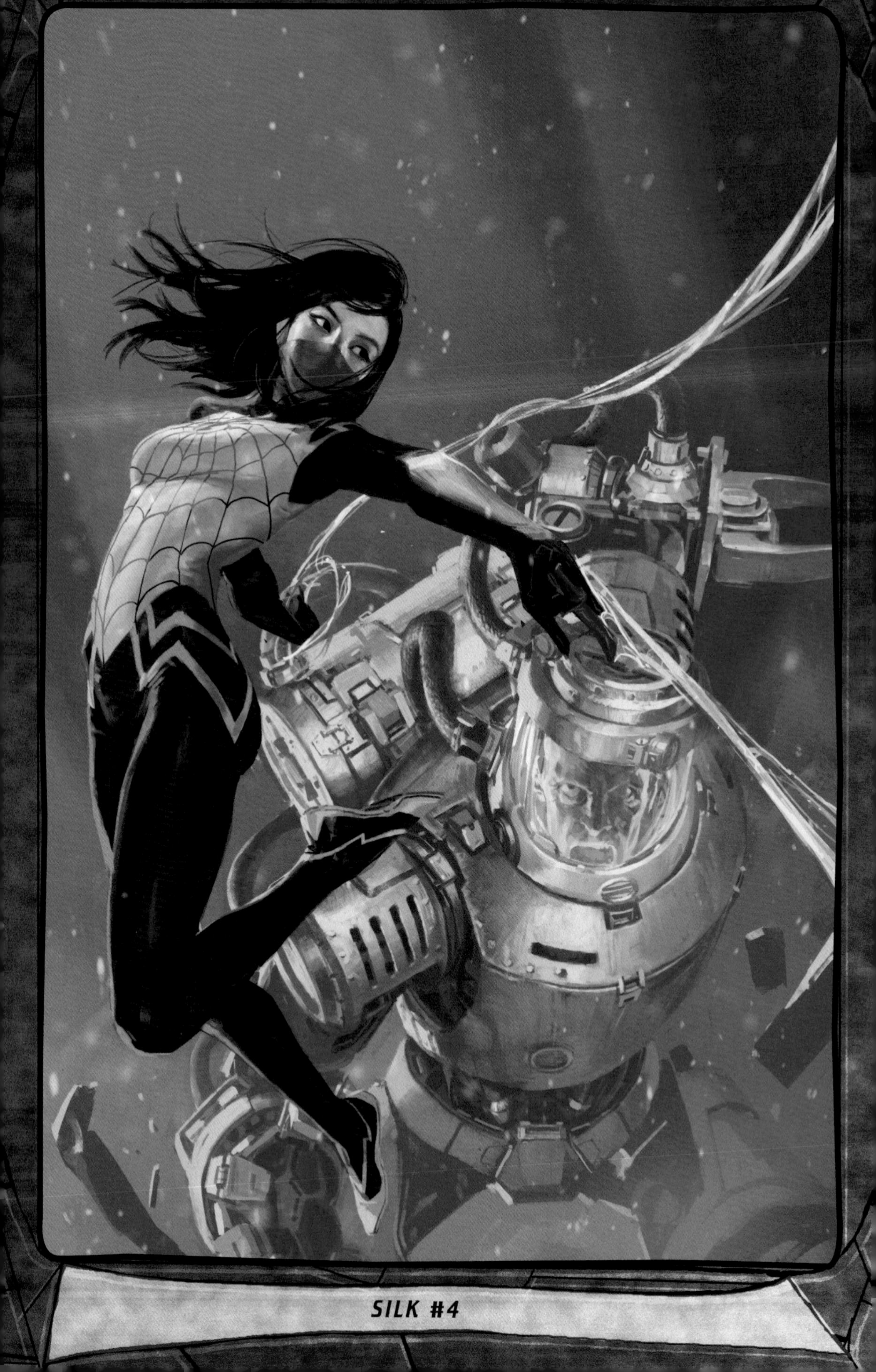

SILK #4

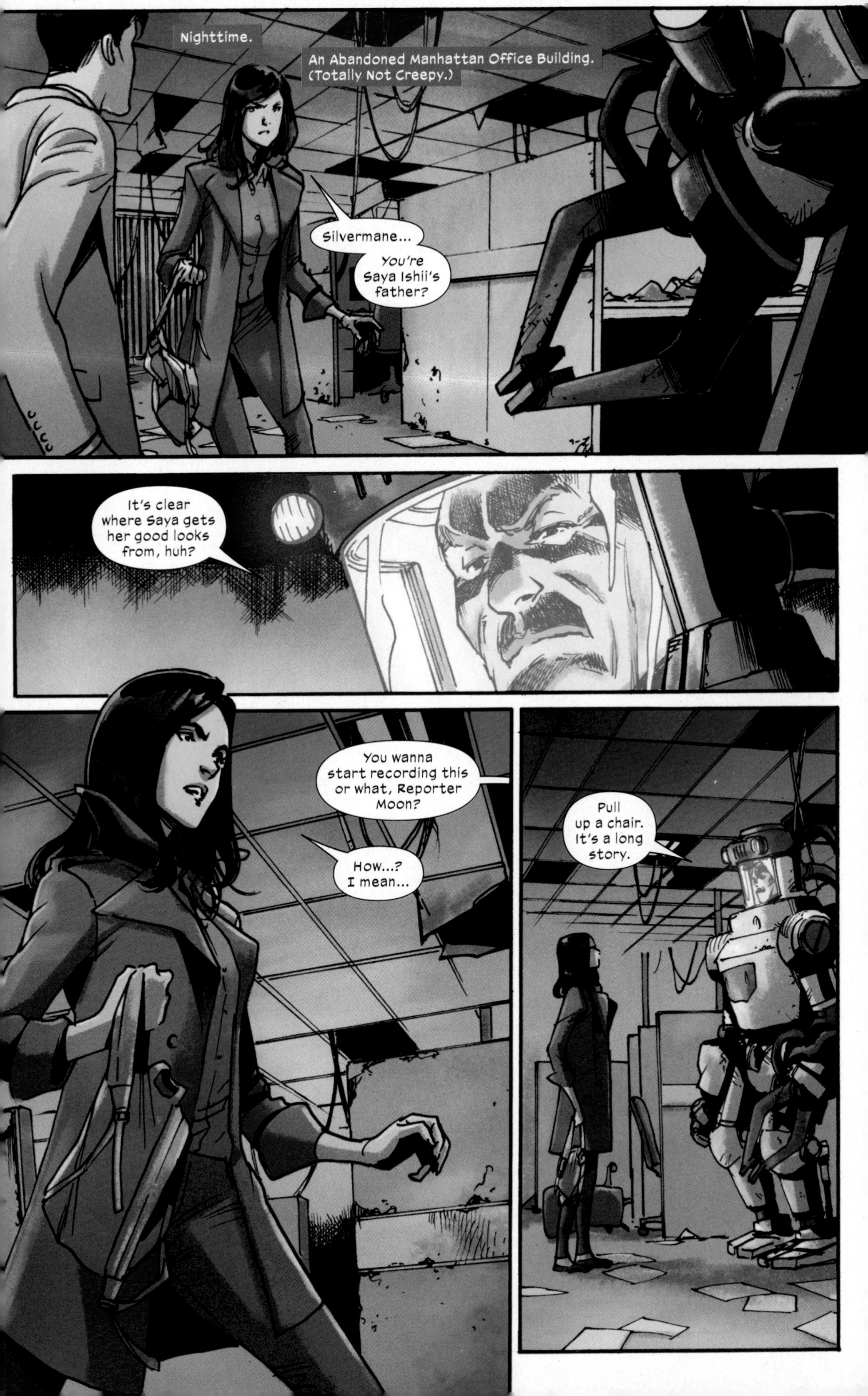
Nighttime.
An Abandoned Manhattan Office Building. (Totally Not Creepy.)
Silvermane...
You're Saya Ishii's father?
It's clear where Saya gets her good looks from, huh?
You wanna start recording this or what, Reporter Moon?
How...? I mean...
Pull up a chair. It's a long story.

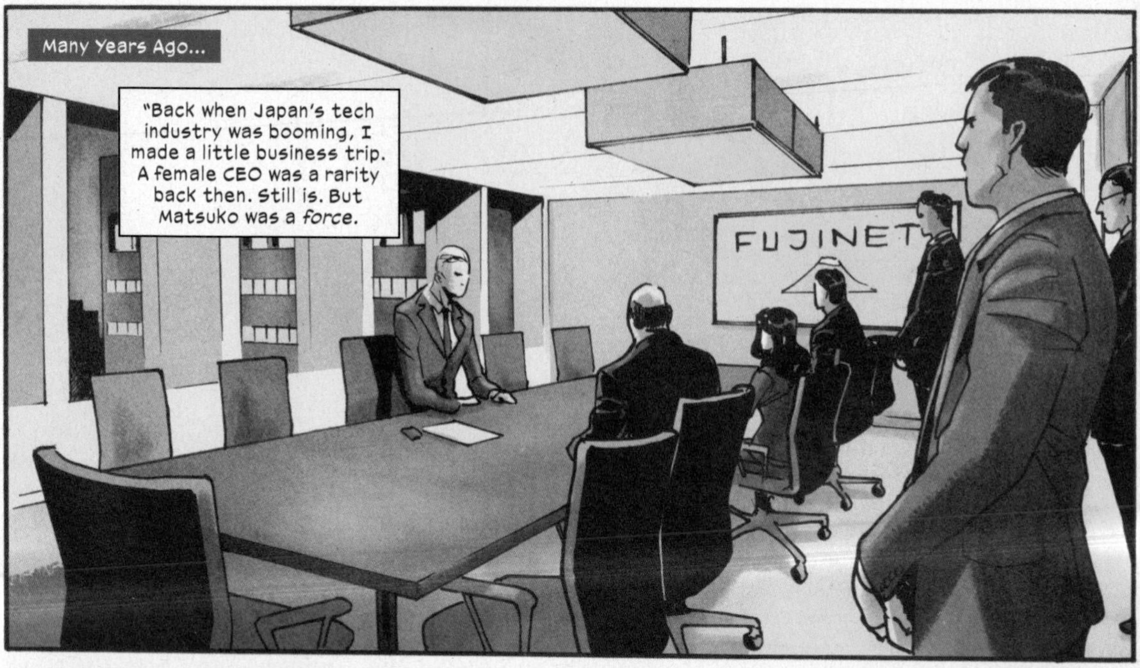
Many Years Ago...
"Back when Japan's tech industry was booming, I made a little business trip. A female CEO was a rarity back then. Still is. But Matsuko was a *force*.
FUJINET

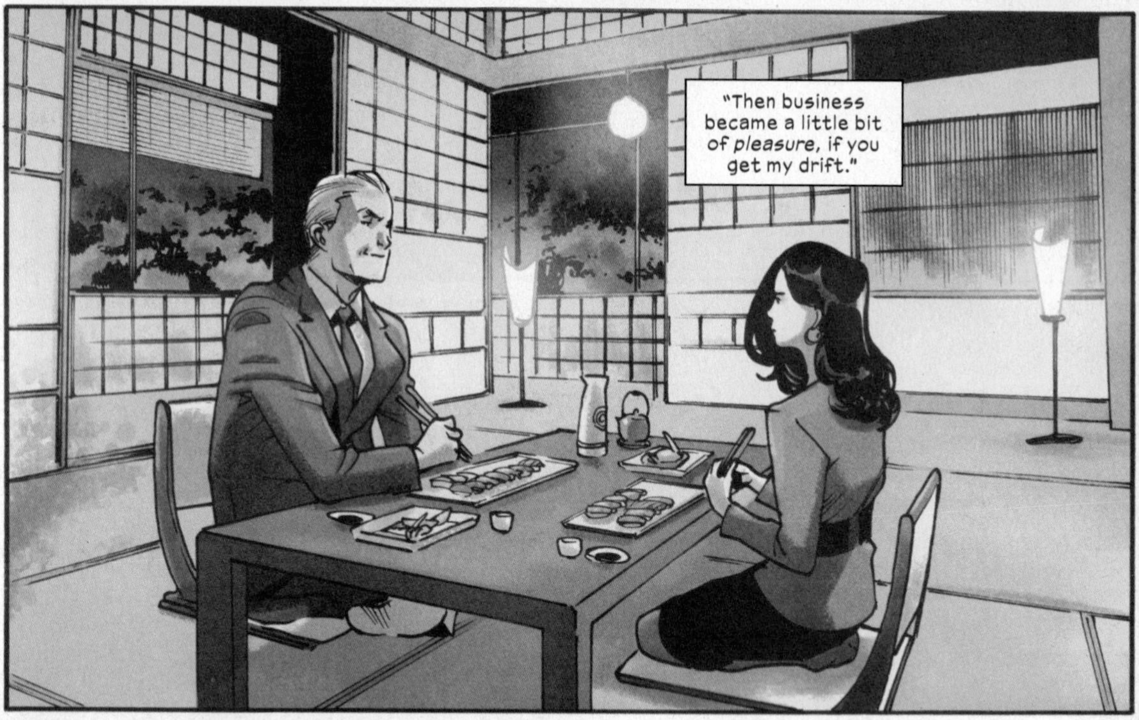
"Then business became a little bit of *pleasure*, if you get my drift."

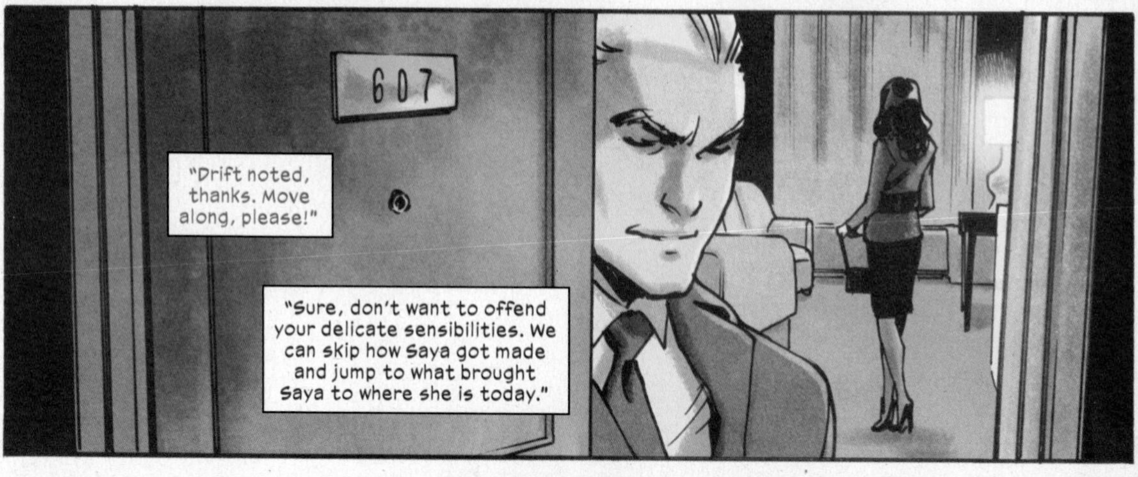
607
"Drift noted, thanks. Move along, please!"
"Sure, don't want to offend your delicate sensibilities. We can skip how Saya got made and jump to what brought Saya to where she is today."

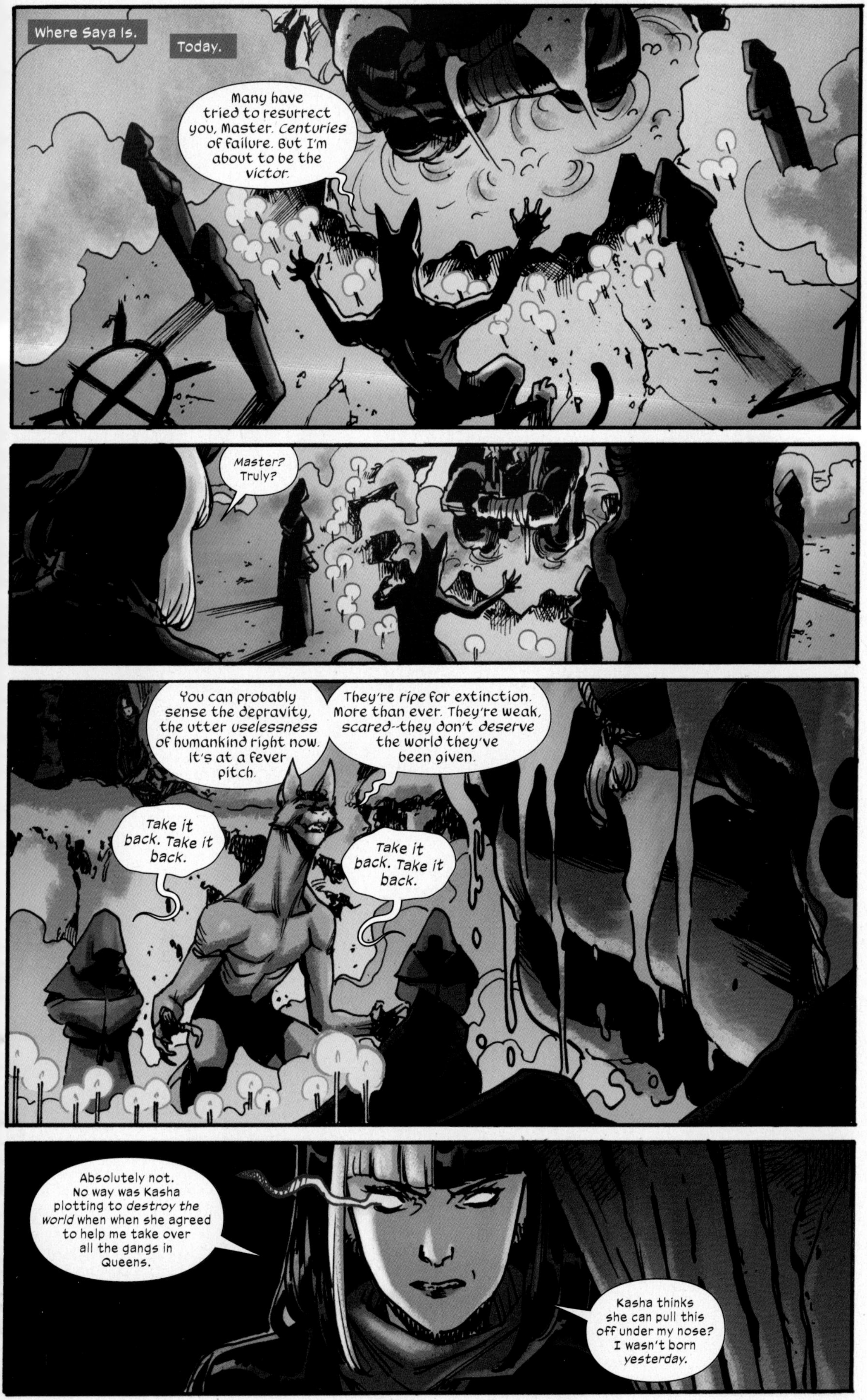

Where Saya Is.
Today.
Many have tried to resurrect you, Master. Centuries of failure. But I'm about to be the victor.
Master? Truly?
You can probably sense the depravity, the utter uselessness of humankind right now. It's at a fever pitch.
They're ripe for extinction. More than ever. They're weak, scared--they don't deserve the world they've been given.
Take it back. Take it back.
Take it back. Take it back.
Absolutely not. No way was Kasha plotting to destroy the world when when she agreed to help me take over all the gangs in Queens.
Kasha thinks she can pull this off under my nose? I wasn't born yesterday.

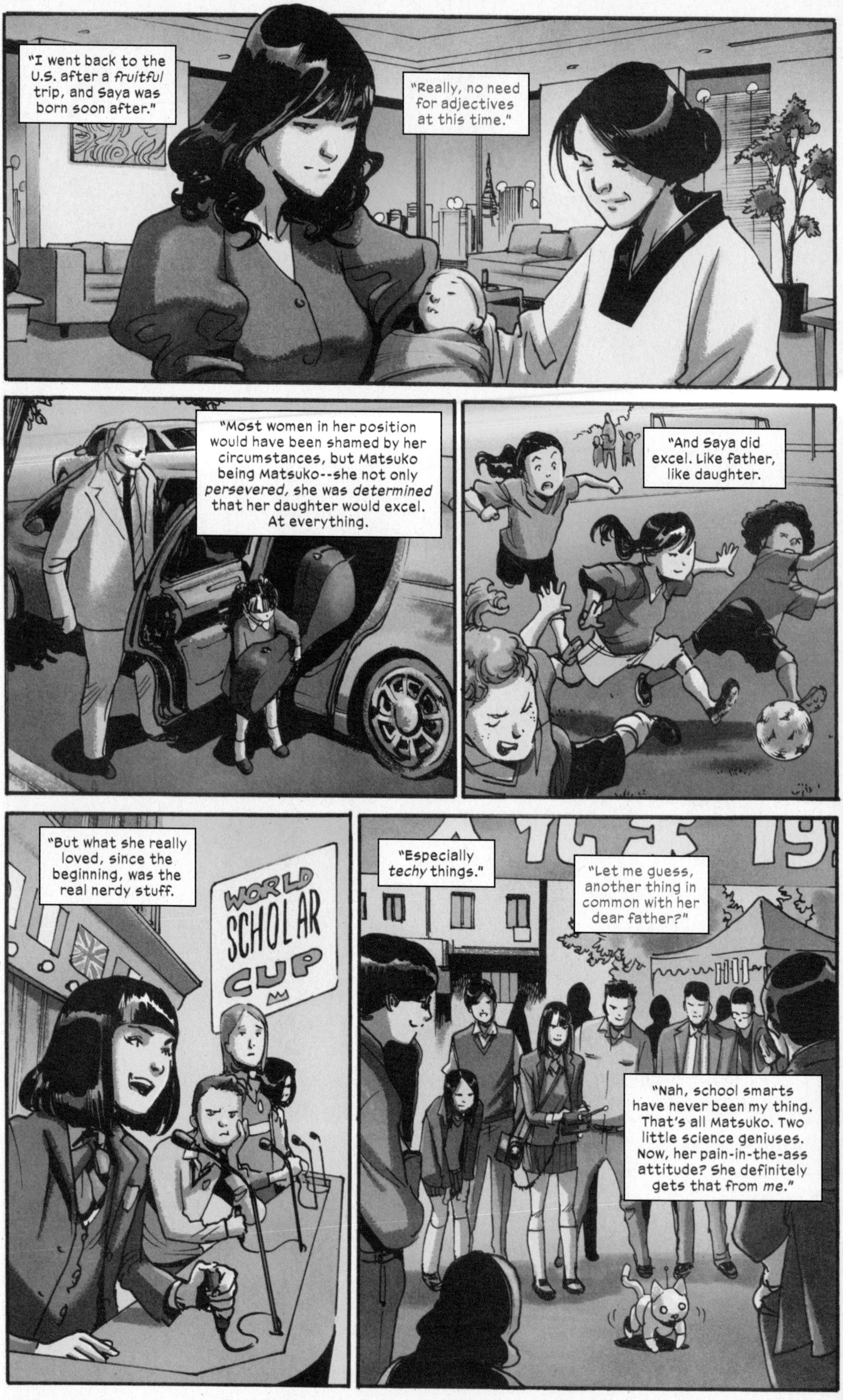
"I went back to the U.S. after a *fruitful* trip, and Saya was born soon after."
"Really, no need for adjectives at this time."
"Most women in her position would have been shamed by her circumstances, but Matsuko being Matsuko--she not only *persevered,* she was *determined* that her daughter would excel. At everything.
"And Saya did excel. Like father, like daughter.
"But what she really loved, since the beginning, was the real nerdy stuff.
WORLD SCHOLAR CUP
"Especially *techy* things."
"Let me guess, another thing in common with her dear father?"
"Nah, school smarts have never been my thing. That's all Matsuko. Two little science geniuses. Now, her pain-in-the-ass attitude? She definitely gets that from *me.*"

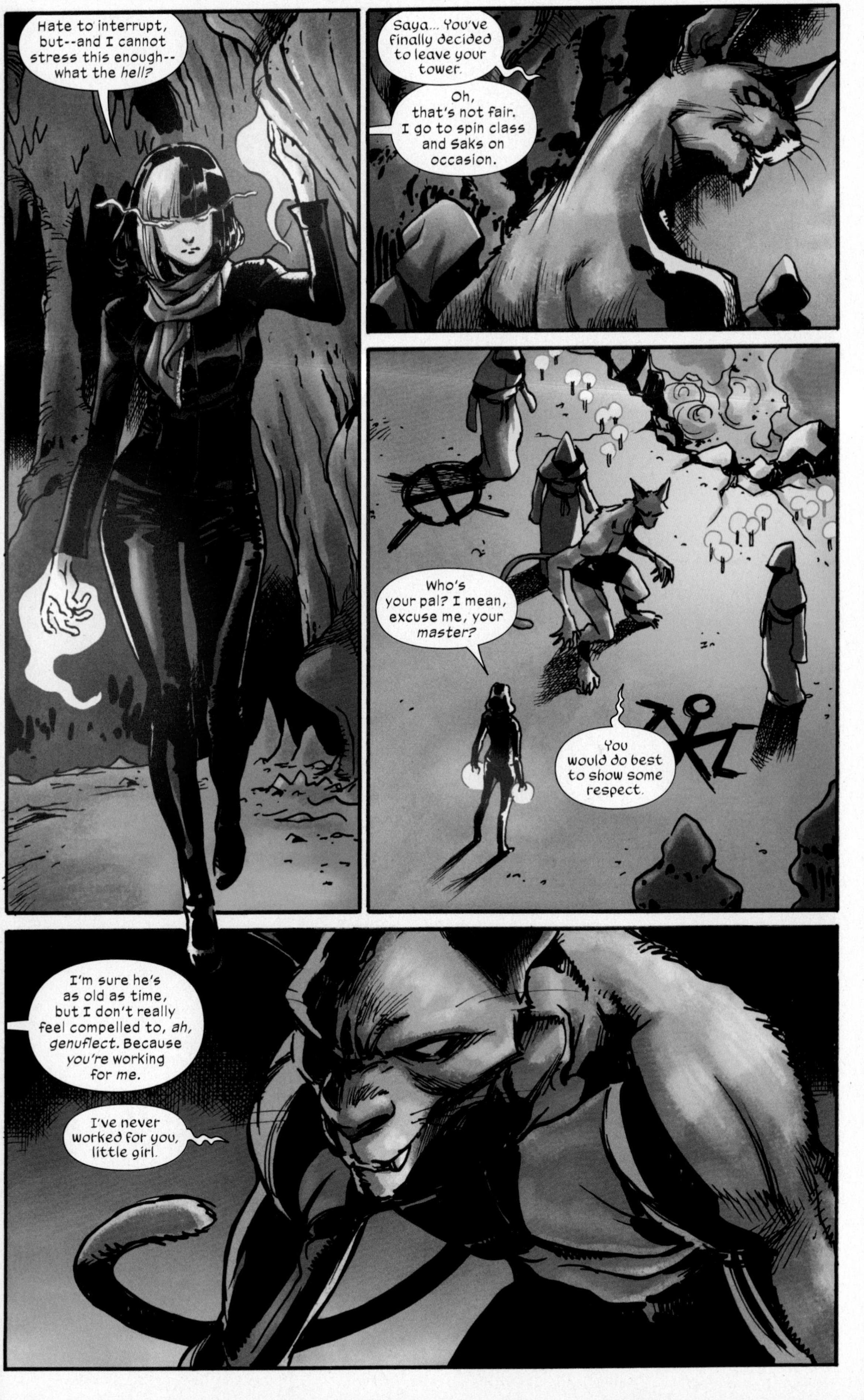
Hate to interrupt, but--and I cannot stress this enough--what the *hell?*
Saya... You've finally decided to leave your tower.
Oh, that's not fair. I go to spin class and Saks on occasion.
Who's your pal? I mean, excuse me, your *master?*
You would do best to show some respect.
I'm sure he's as old as time, but I don't really feel compelled to, *ah, genuflect.* Because *you're* working for *me.*
I've never worked for you, little girl.

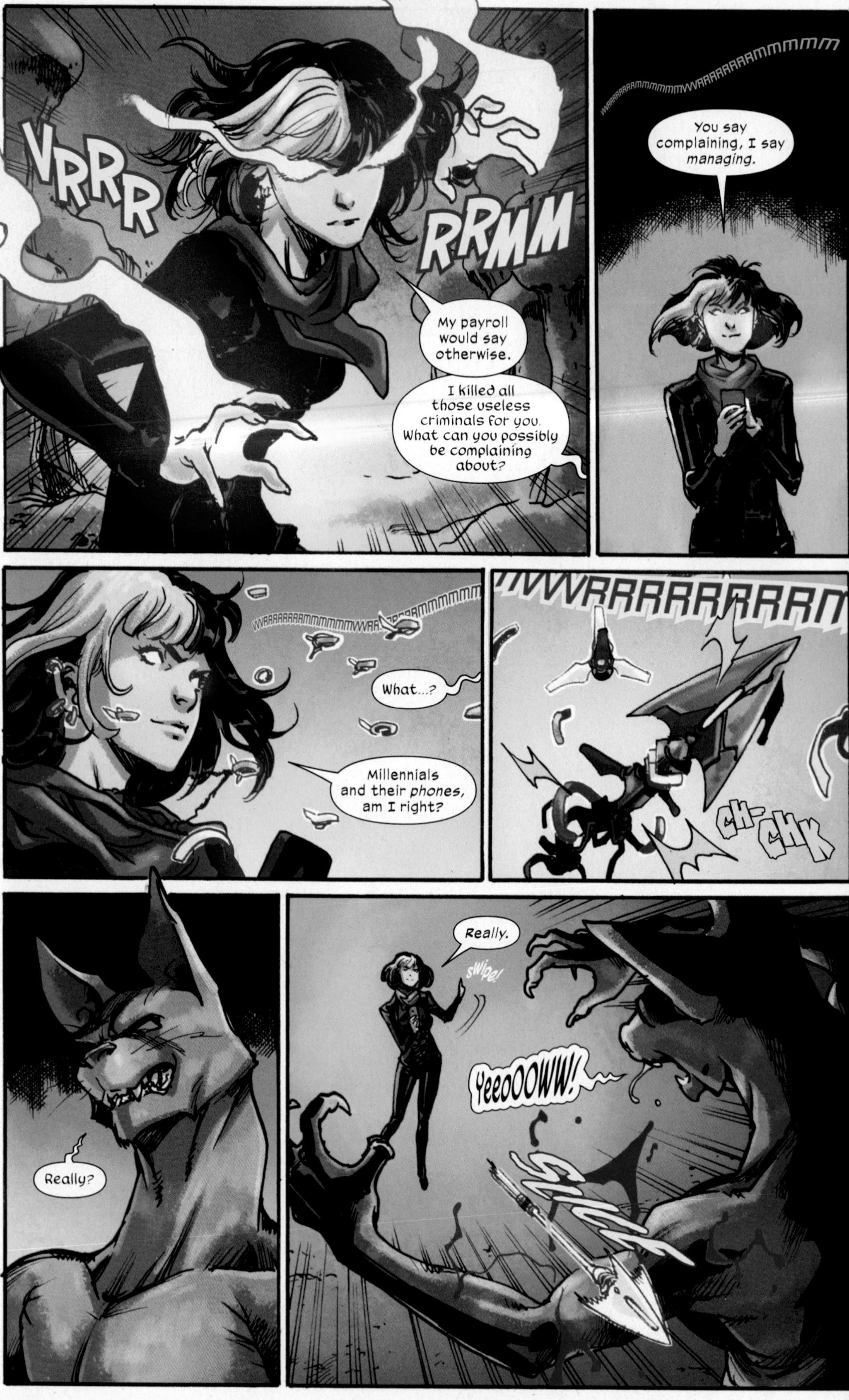
VRRR
RRMM
My payroll would say otherwise.
I killed all those useless criminals for you. What can you possibly be complaining about?
WRRRRRRRMMMMMMMWRRRRRRRMMMMMM
You say complaining, I say *managing.*
What...?
Millennials and their *phones,* am I right?
WRRRRRRRRMMMMMMWRRRRRRMMMMMM
WRRRRRRRRRRM
CH-CHK
Really?
Really.
swipe!
YeeoOOWW!
SHUNK

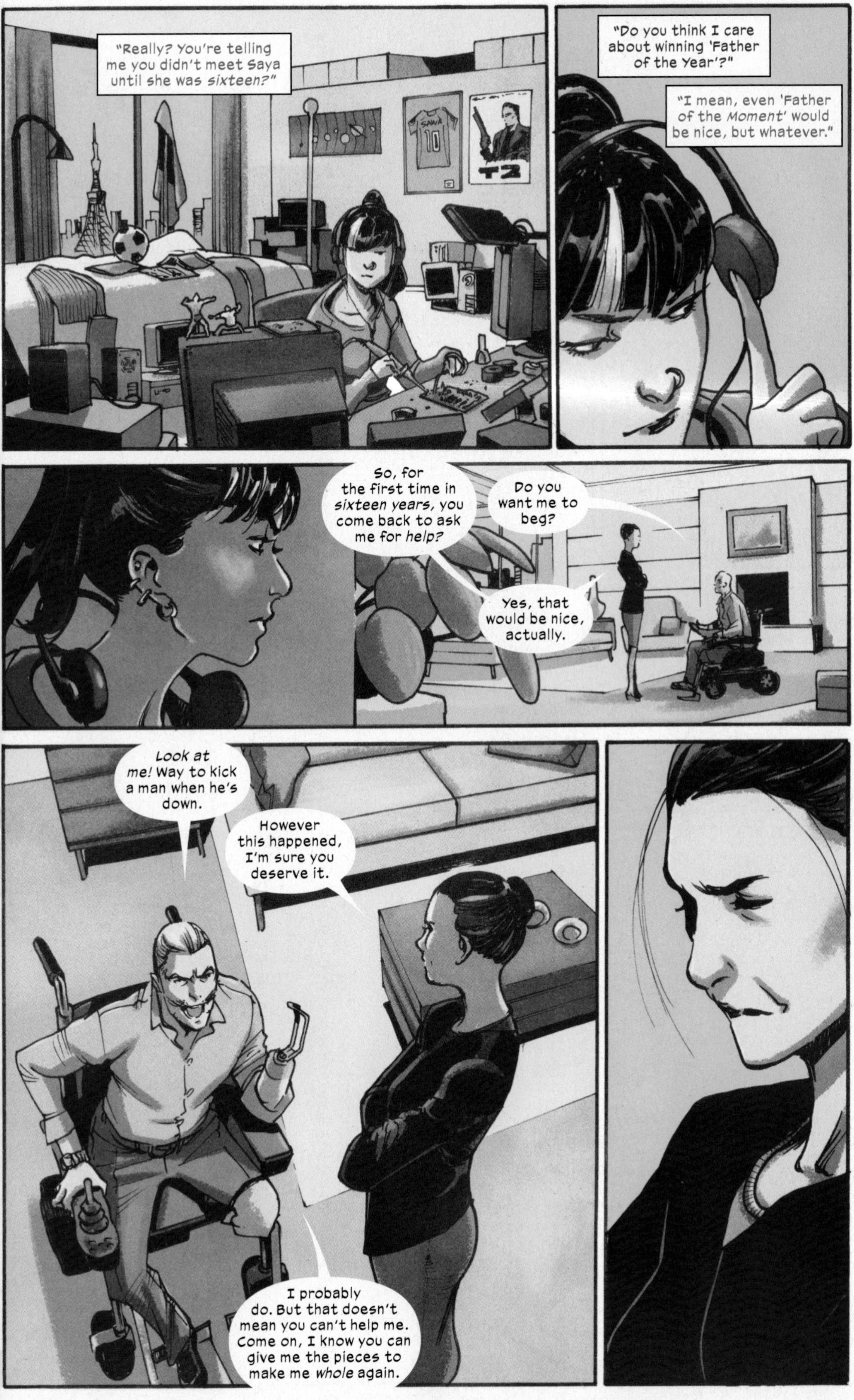
"Really? You're telling me you didn't meet Saya until she was *sixteen?*"
SAWA 10
T2
"Do you think I care about winning 'Father of the Year'?"
"I mean, even 'Father of the *Moment*' would be nice, but whatever."
So, for the first time in *sixteen years,* you come back to ask me for *help?*
Do you want me to beg?
Yes, that would be nice, actually.
Look at me! Way to kick a man when he's down.
However this happened, I'm sure you deserve it.
I probably do. But that doesn't mean you can't help me. Come on, I know you can give me the pieces to make me *whole* again.

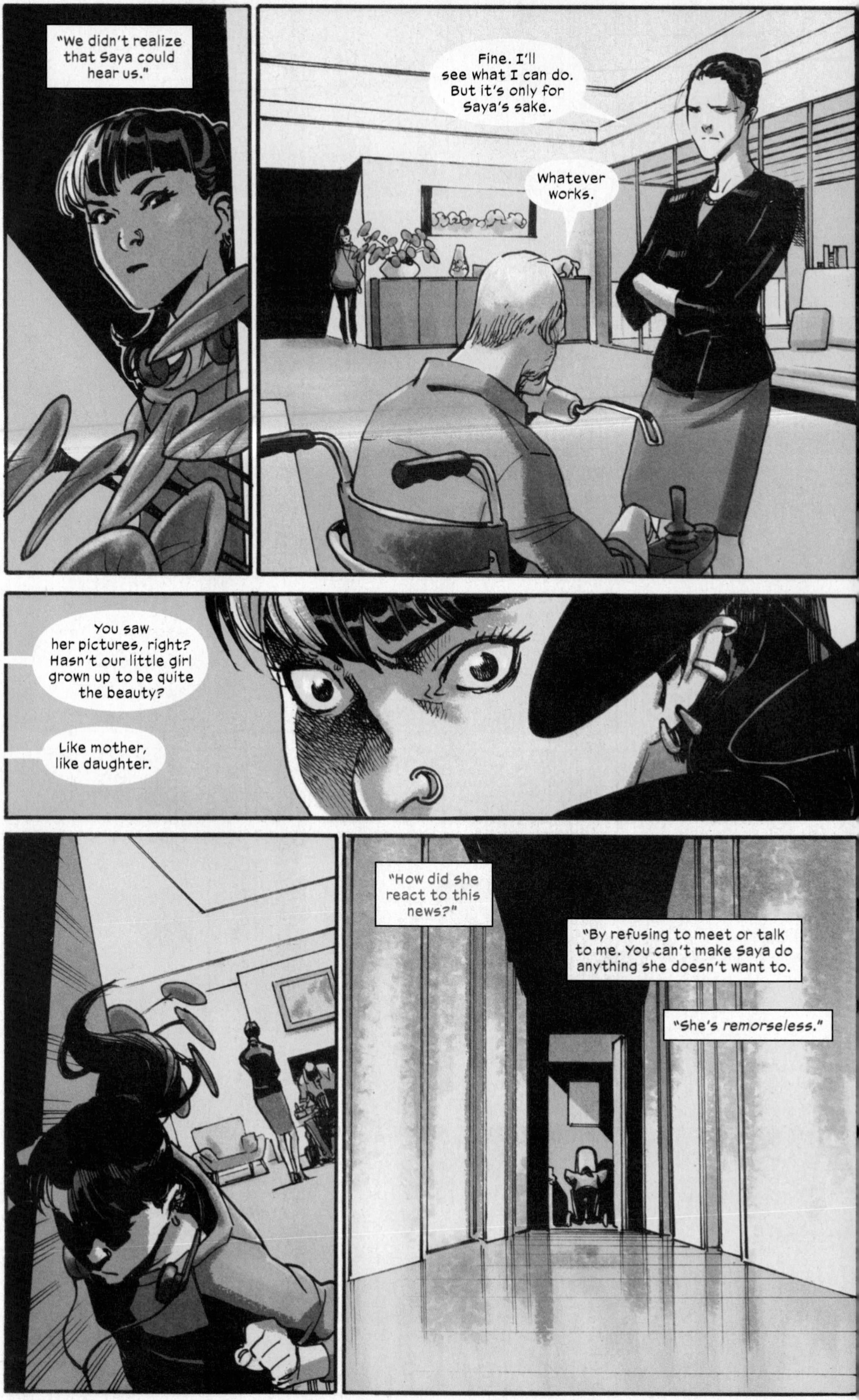
"We didn't realize that Saya could hear us."
Fine. I'll see what I can do. But it's only for Saya's sake.
Whatever works.
You saw her pictures, right? Hasn't our little girl grown up to be quite the beauty?
Like mother, like daughter.
"How did she react to this news?"
"By refusing to meet or talk to me. You can't make Saya do anything she doesn't want to.
"She's *remorseless*."

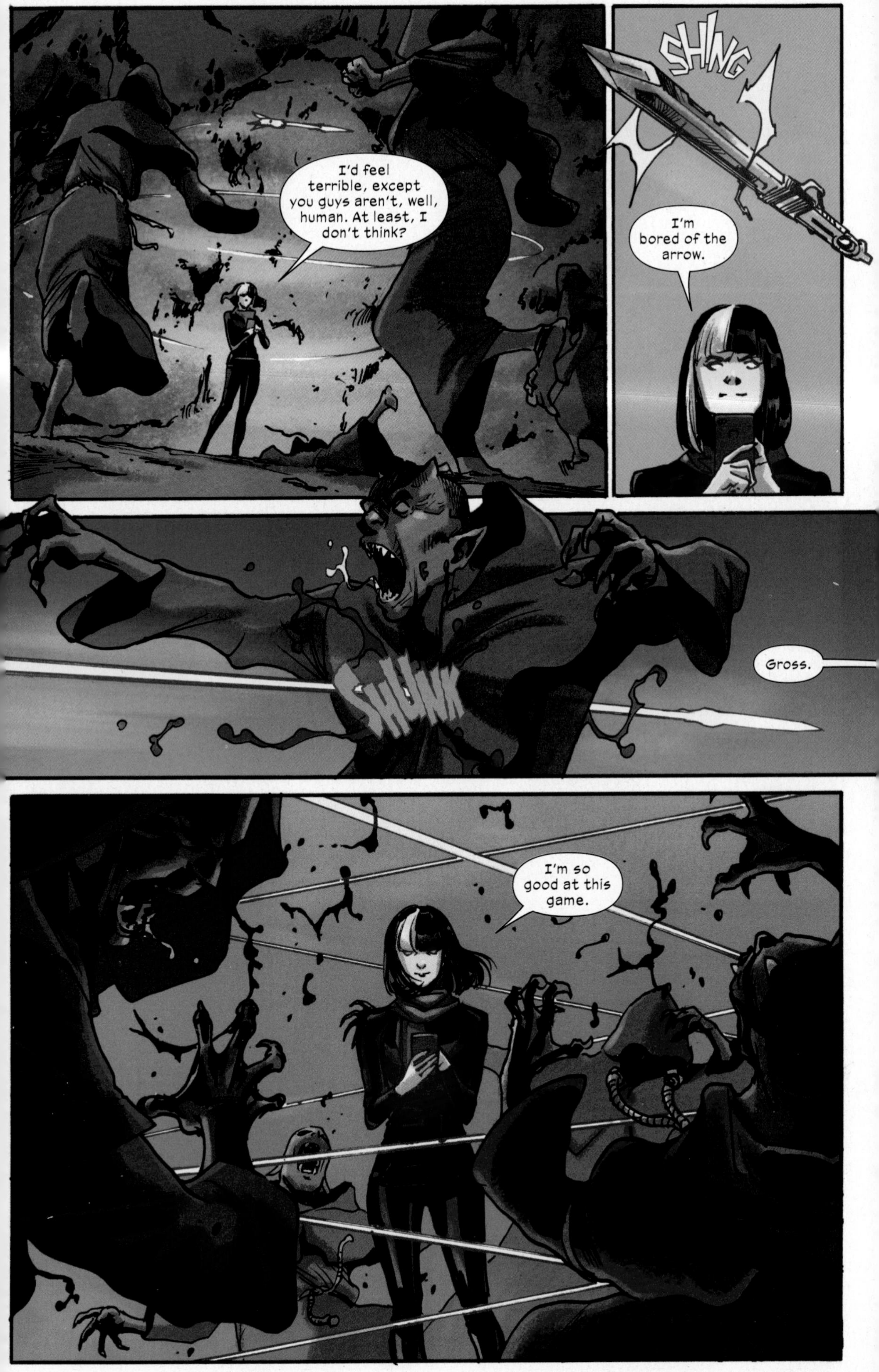
I'd feel terrible, except you guys aren't, well, human. At least, I don't think?
SHING
I'm bored of the arrow.
SHUNK
Gross.
I'm so good at this game.

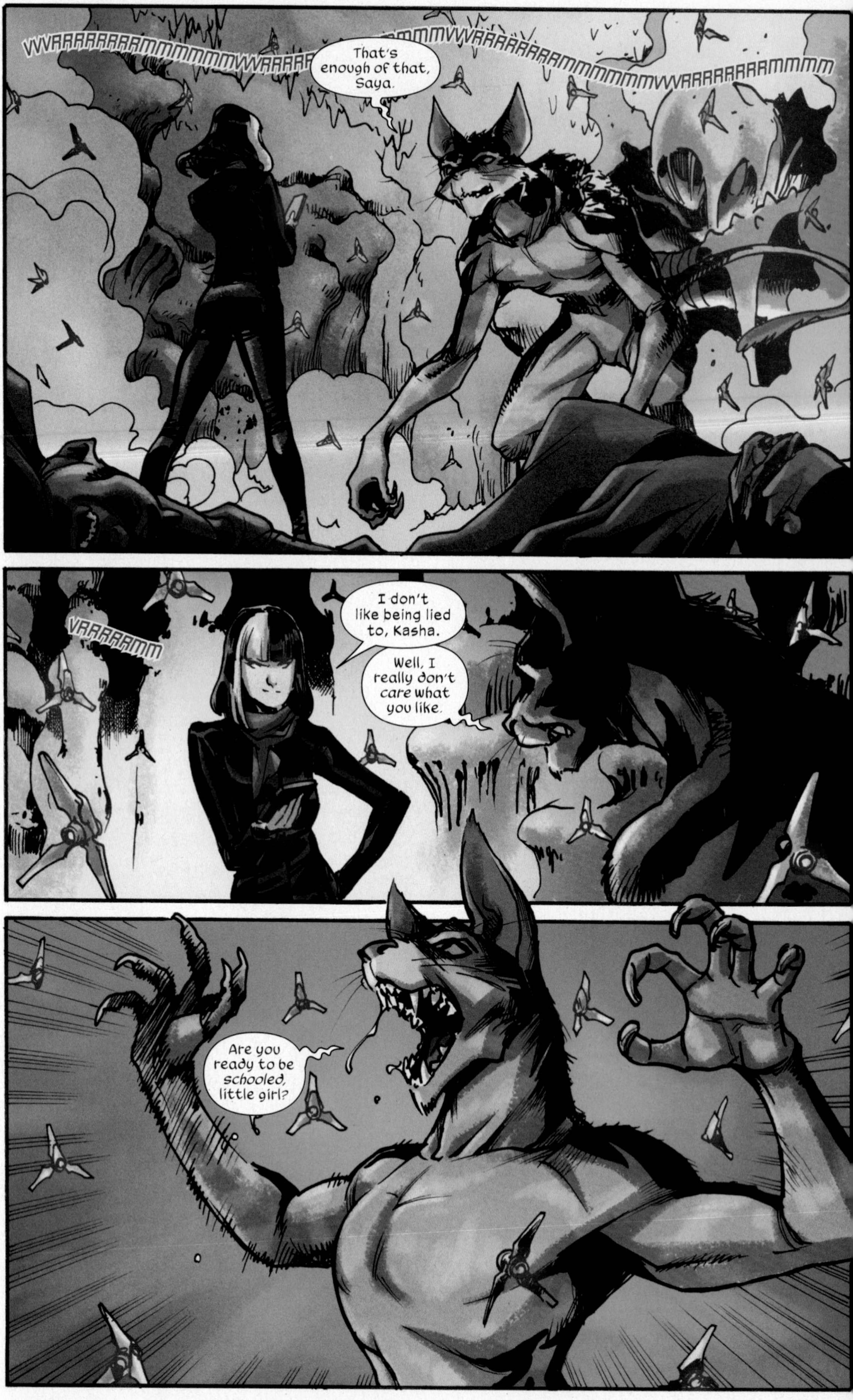
VVVRRRRRRRRRMMMMMMMMVVVRRRRR
That's enough of that, Saya.
MMMMVVVRRRRRRRRRMMMMMMMMVVVRRRRRRRRRMMMMM
VRRRRRMM
I don't like being lied to, Kasha.
Well, I really don't *care* what you like.
Are you ready to be *schooled*, little girl?

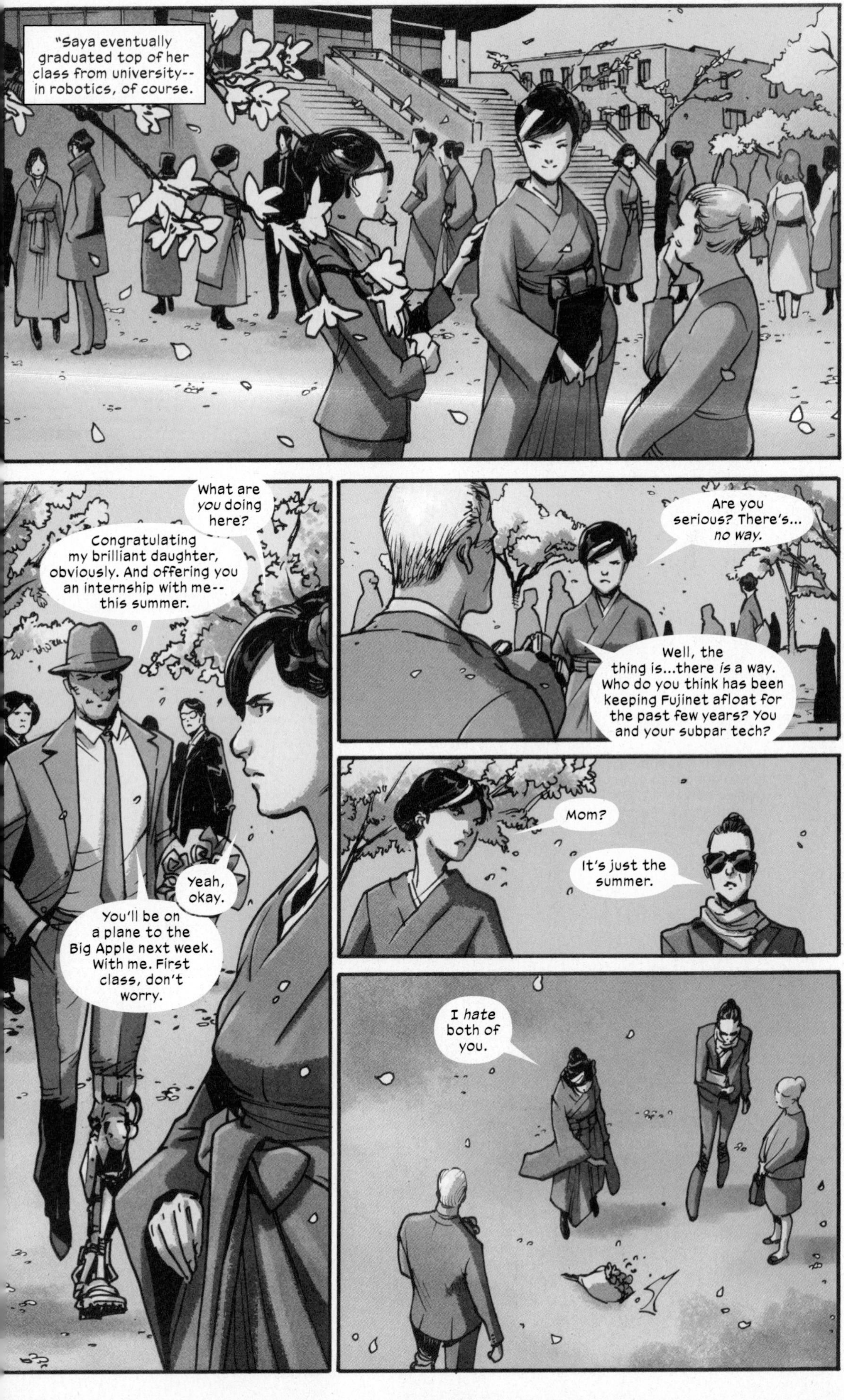
"Saya eventually graduated top of her class from university-- in robotics, of course.
What are *you* doing here?
Congratulating my brilliant daughter, obviously. And offering you an internship with me-- this summer.
Yeah, okay.
You'll be on a plane to the Big Apple next week. With me. First class, don't worry.
Are you serious? There's... *no way.*
Well, the thing is...there *is* a way. Who do you think has been keeping Fujinet afloat for the past few years? You and your subpar tech?
Mom?
It's just the summer.
I *hate* both of you.

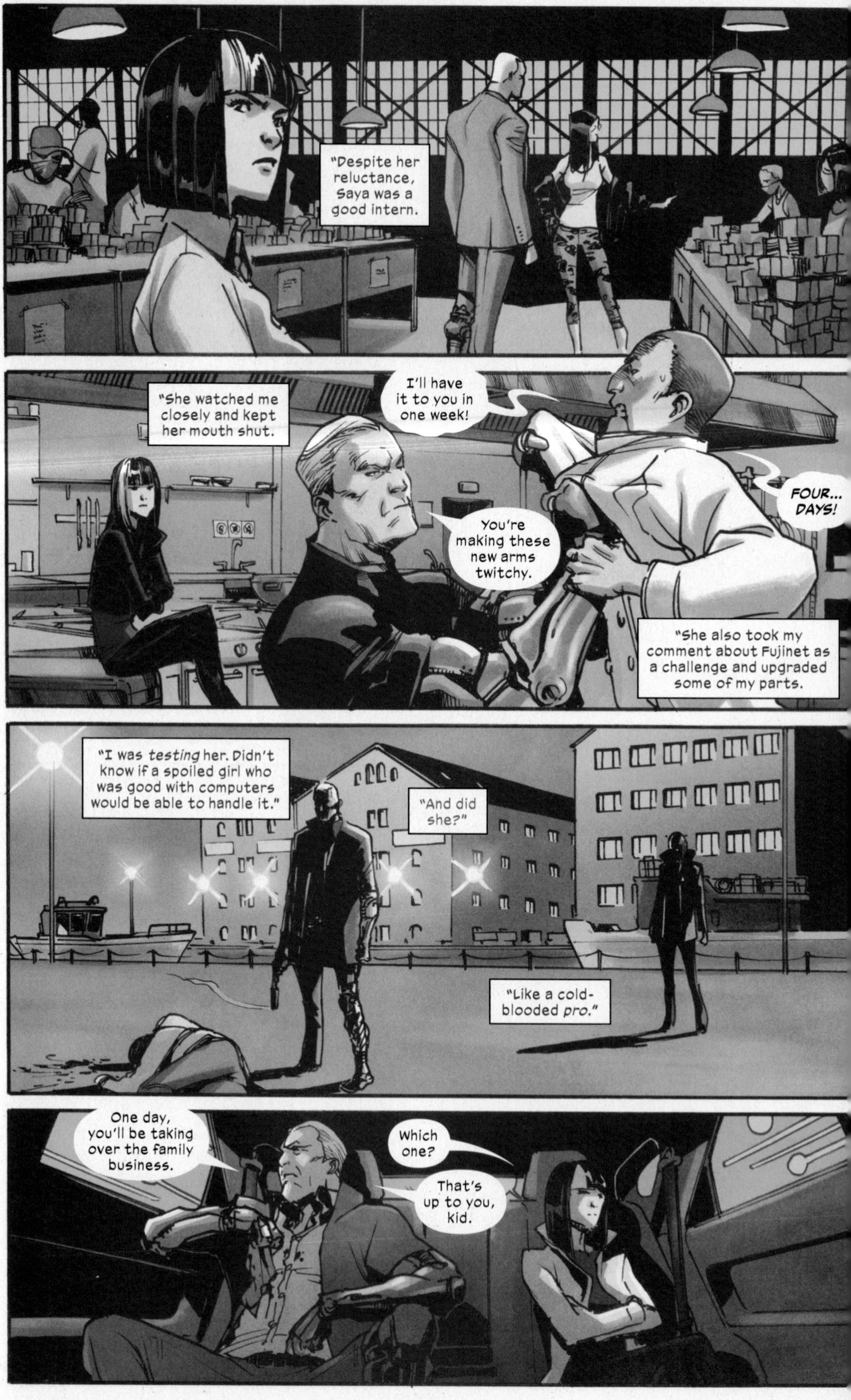
"Despite her reluctance, Saya was a good intern.
"She watched me closely and kept her mouth shut.
I'll have it to you in one week!
FOUR... DAYS!
You're making these new arms twitchy.
"She also took my comment about Fujinet as a challenge and upgraded some of my parts.
"I was *testing* her. Didn't know if a spoiled girl who was good with computers would be able to handle it."
"And did she?"
"Like a cold-blooded *pro*."
One day, you'll be taking over the family business.
Which one?
That's up to you, kid.

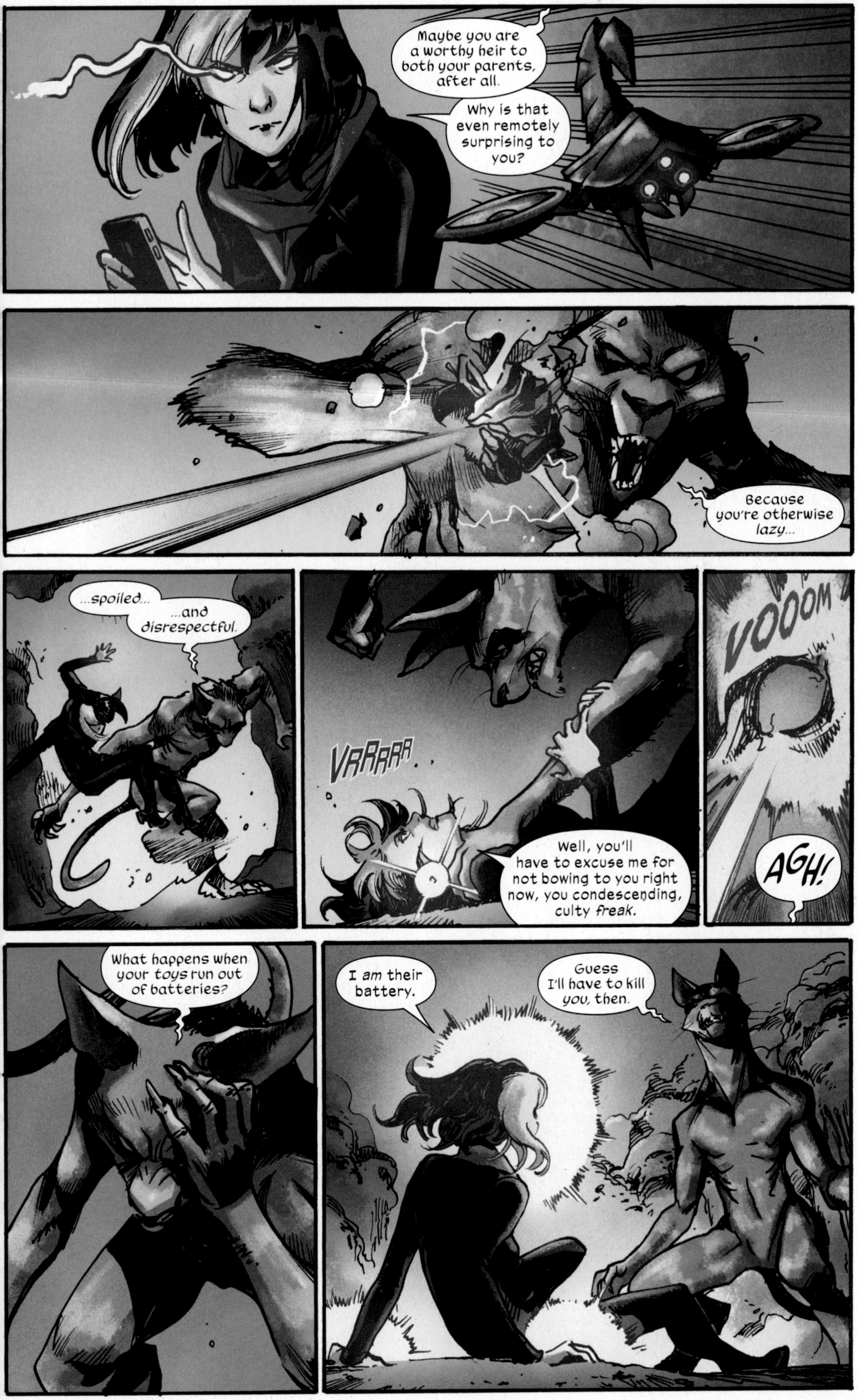

Maybe you are a worthy heir to both your parents, after all.
Why is that even remotely surprising to you?
Because you're otherwise lazy...
...spoiled...
...and disrespectful.
VRRRRR
Well, you'll have to excuse me for not bowing to you right now, you condescending, culty *freak*.
VOOOM
AGH!
What happens when your *toys* run out of batteries?
I *am* their battery.
Guess I'll have to kill *you*, then.

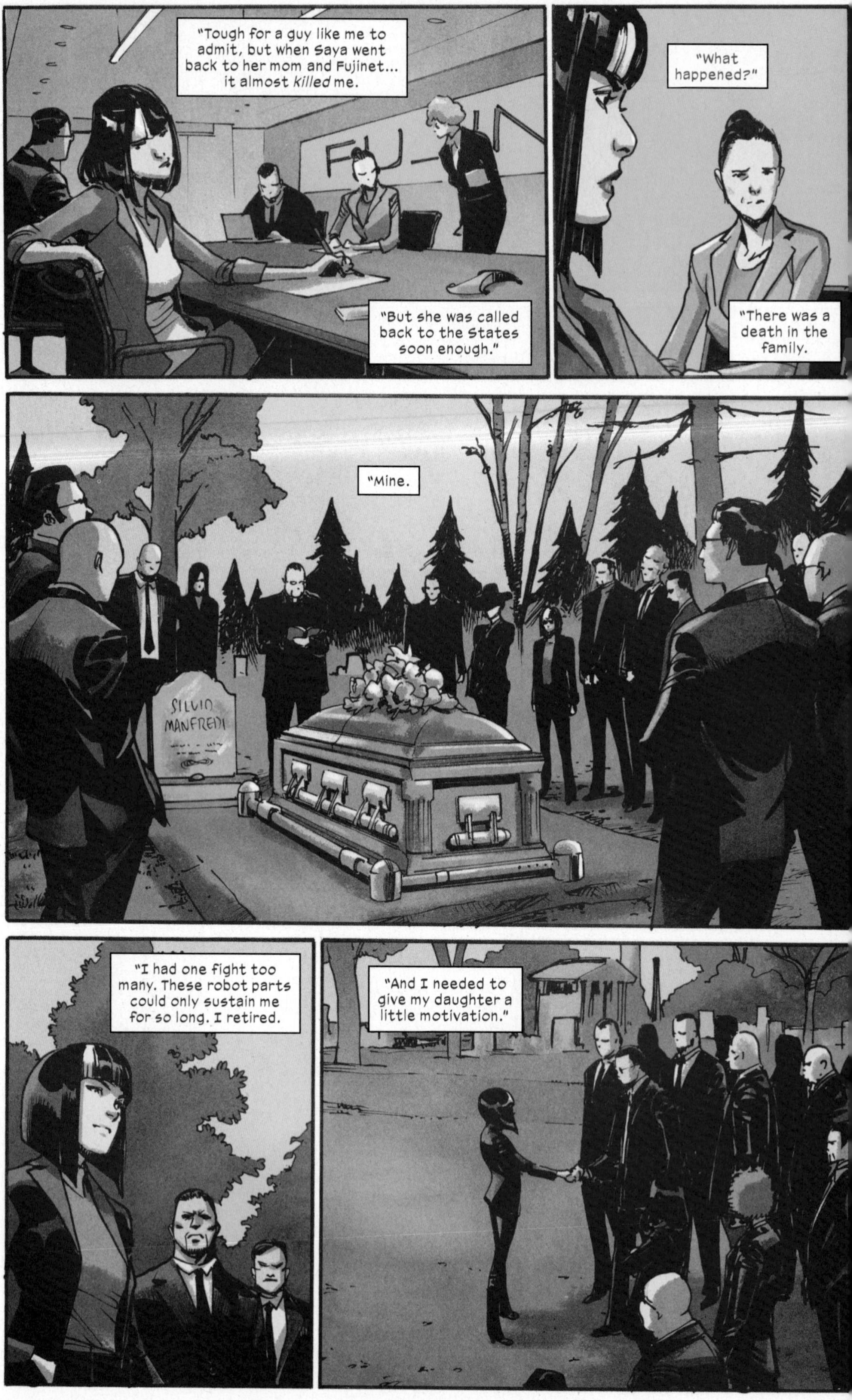
"Tough for a guy like me to admit, but when Saya went back to her mom and Fujinet... it almost *killed* me.
"But she was called back to the States soon enough."
"What happened?"
"There was a death in the family.
"Mine.
SILVIO MANFREDI
"I had one fight too many. These robot parts could only sustain me for so long. I retired.
"And I needed to give my daughter a little motivation."

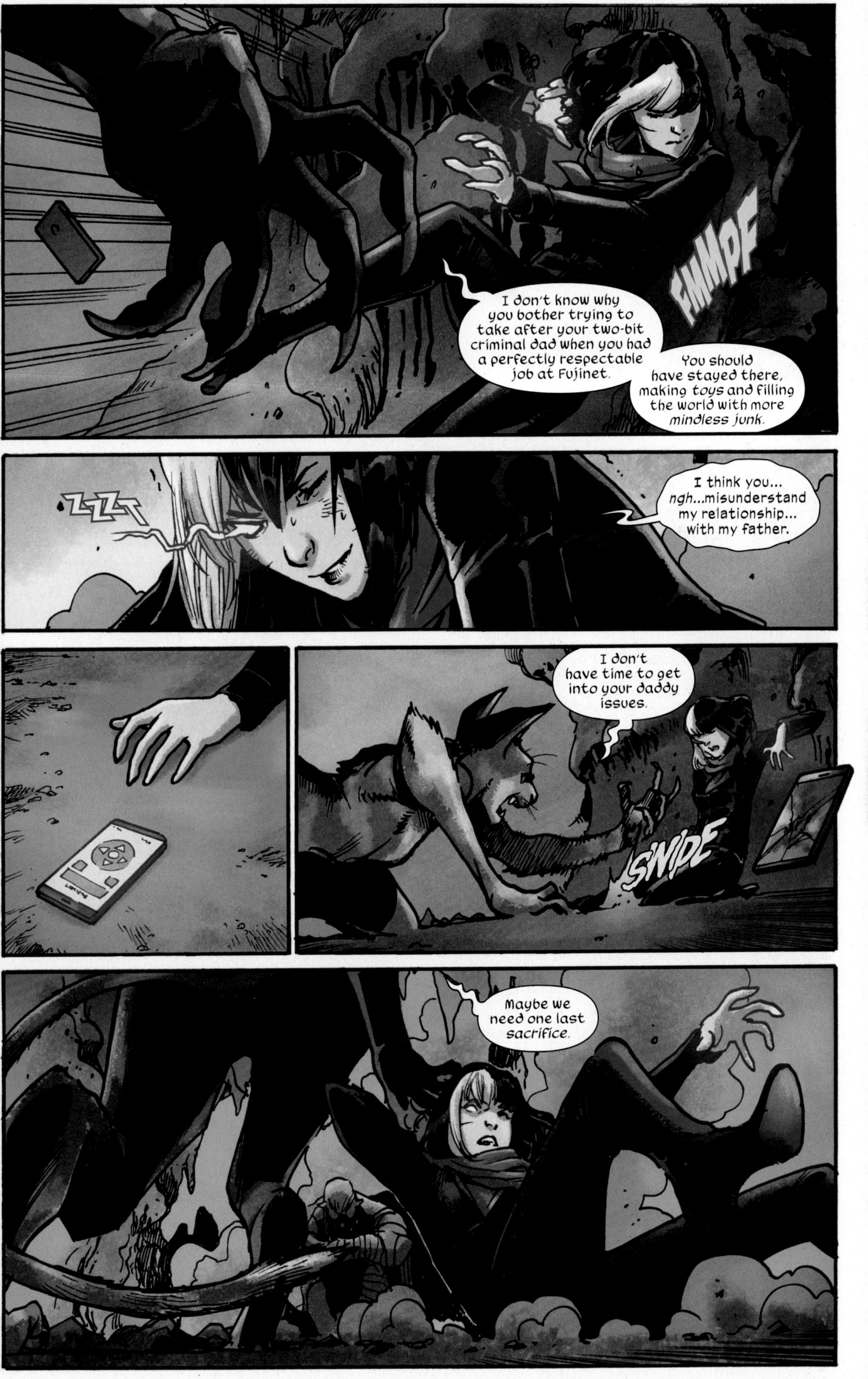
FMMPF
I don't know why you bother trying to take after your two-bit criminal dad when you had a perfectly respectable job at Fujinet.
You should have stayed there, making *toys* and filling the world with more *mindless junk*.
ZZZT
I think you... *ngh*...misunderstand my relationship... with my father.
I don't have time to get into your daddy issues.
SWIPE
Maybe we need one last *sacrifice*.

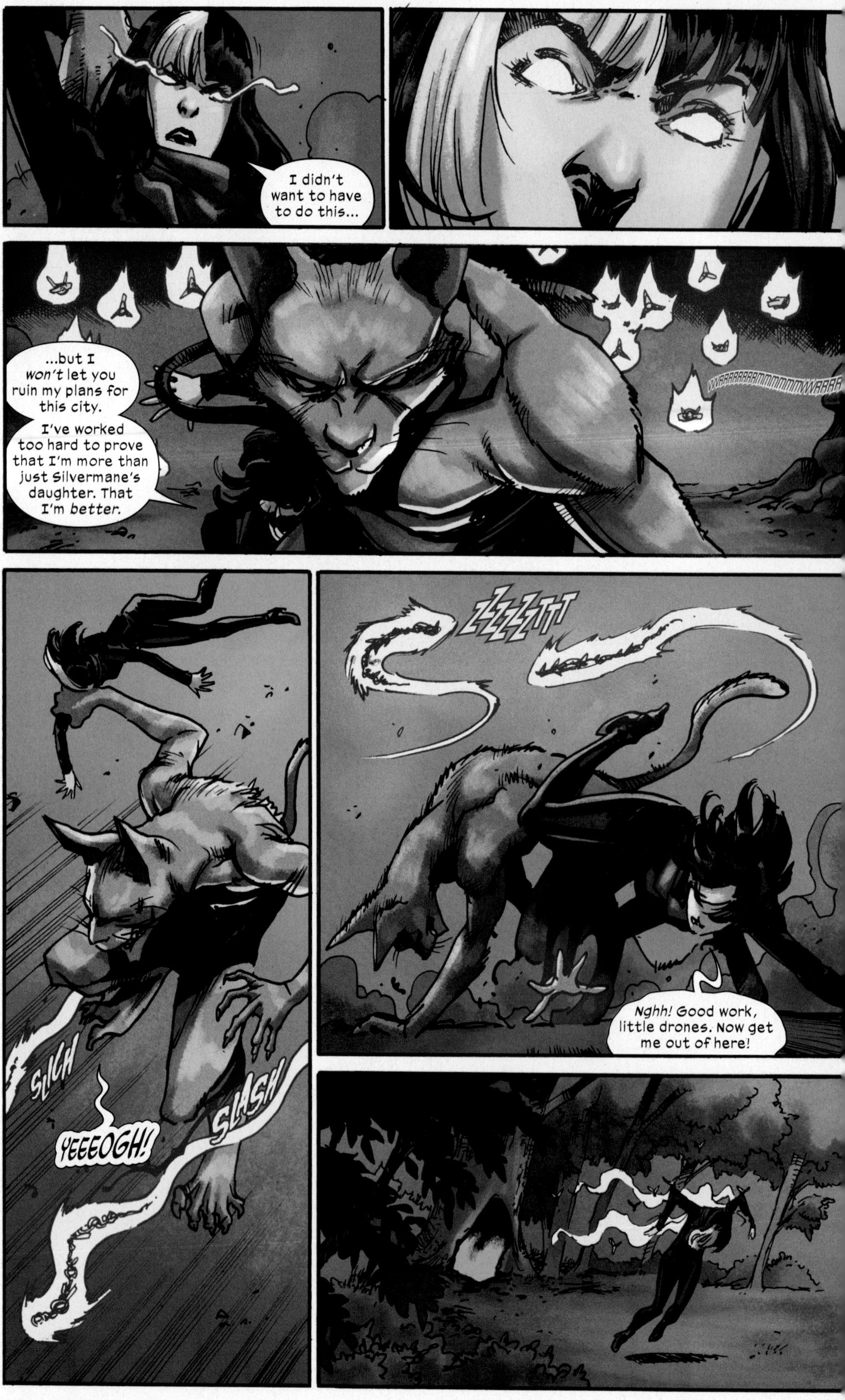
I didn't want to have to do this...
...but I *won't* let you ruin my plans for this city.
I've worked too hard to prove that I'm more than just Silvermane's daughter. That I'm *better*.
WRAAAAAAMMMMMMWAAAA
SLICH
YEEEOGH!
SLASH
ZZZZZTTT
Nghh! Good work, little drones. Now get me out of here!

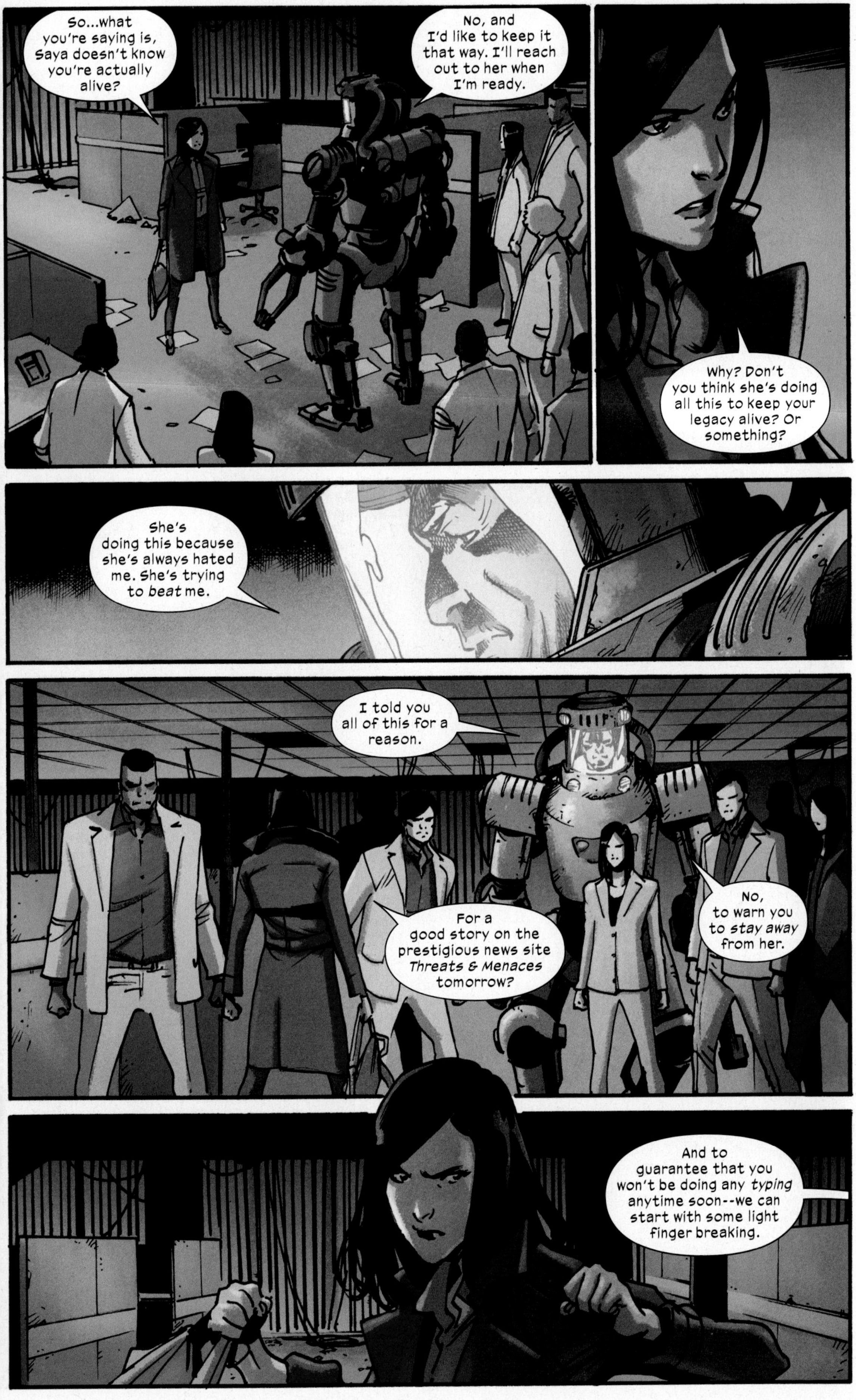
So...what you're saying is, Saya doesn't know you're actually alive?
No, and I'd like to keep it that way. I'll reach out to her when I'm ready.
Why? Don't you think she's doing all this to keep your legacy alive? Or something?
She's doing this because she's always hated me. She's trying to *beat* me.
I told you all of this for a reason.
For a good story on the prestigious news site *Threats & Menaces* tomorrow?
No, to warn you to *stay away* from her.
And to guarantee that you won't be doing any *typing* anytime soon--we can start with some light finger breaking.

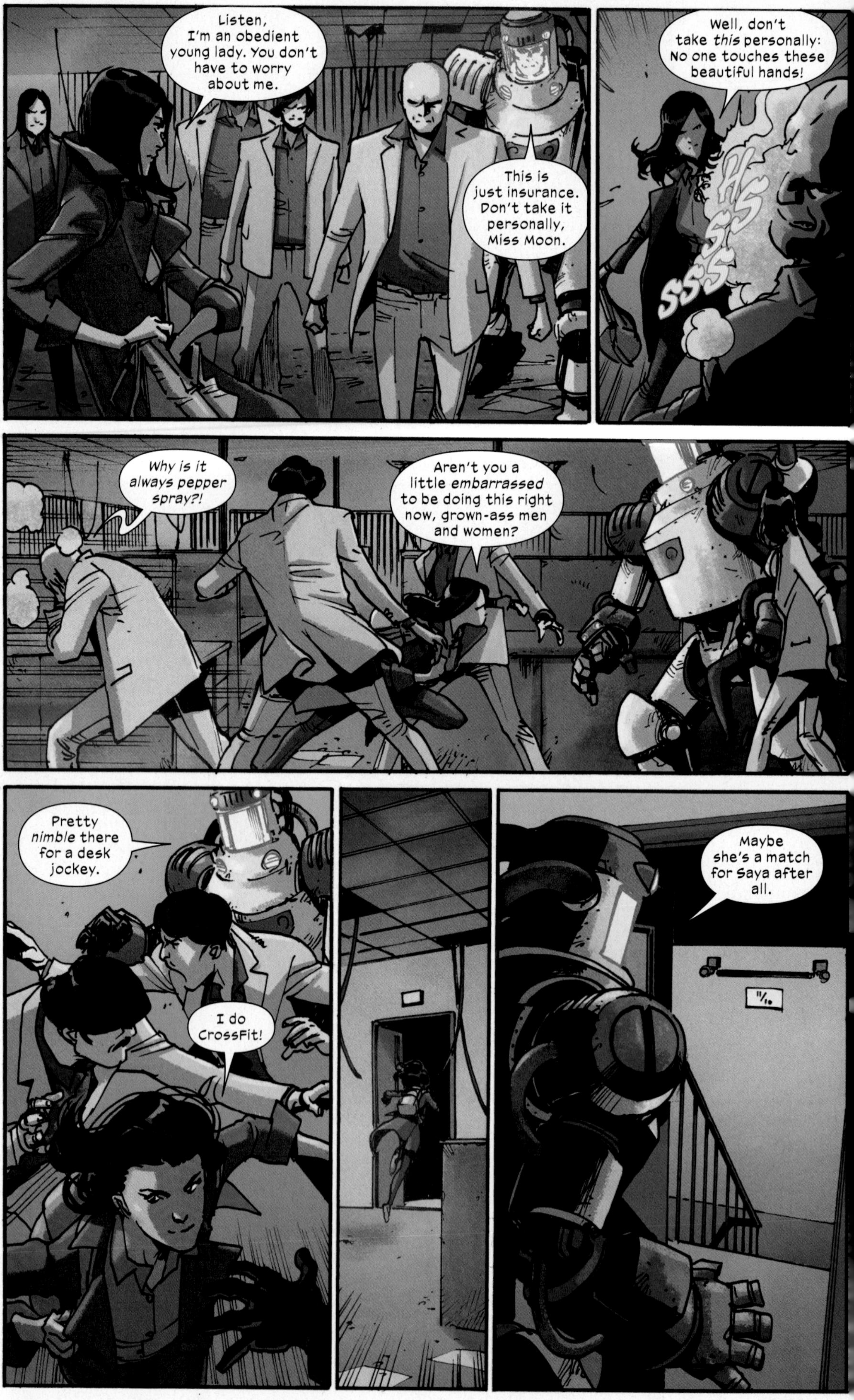
Listen, I'm an obedient young lady. You don't have to worry about me.
This is just insurance. Don't take it personally, Miss Moon.
Well, don't take *this* personally: No one touches these beautiful hands!
HSSSSSS
Why is it always pepper spray?!
Aren't you a little *embarrassed* to be doing this right now, grown-ass men and women?
Pretty *nimble* there for a desk jockey.
I do CrossFit!
Maybe she's a match for Saya after all.

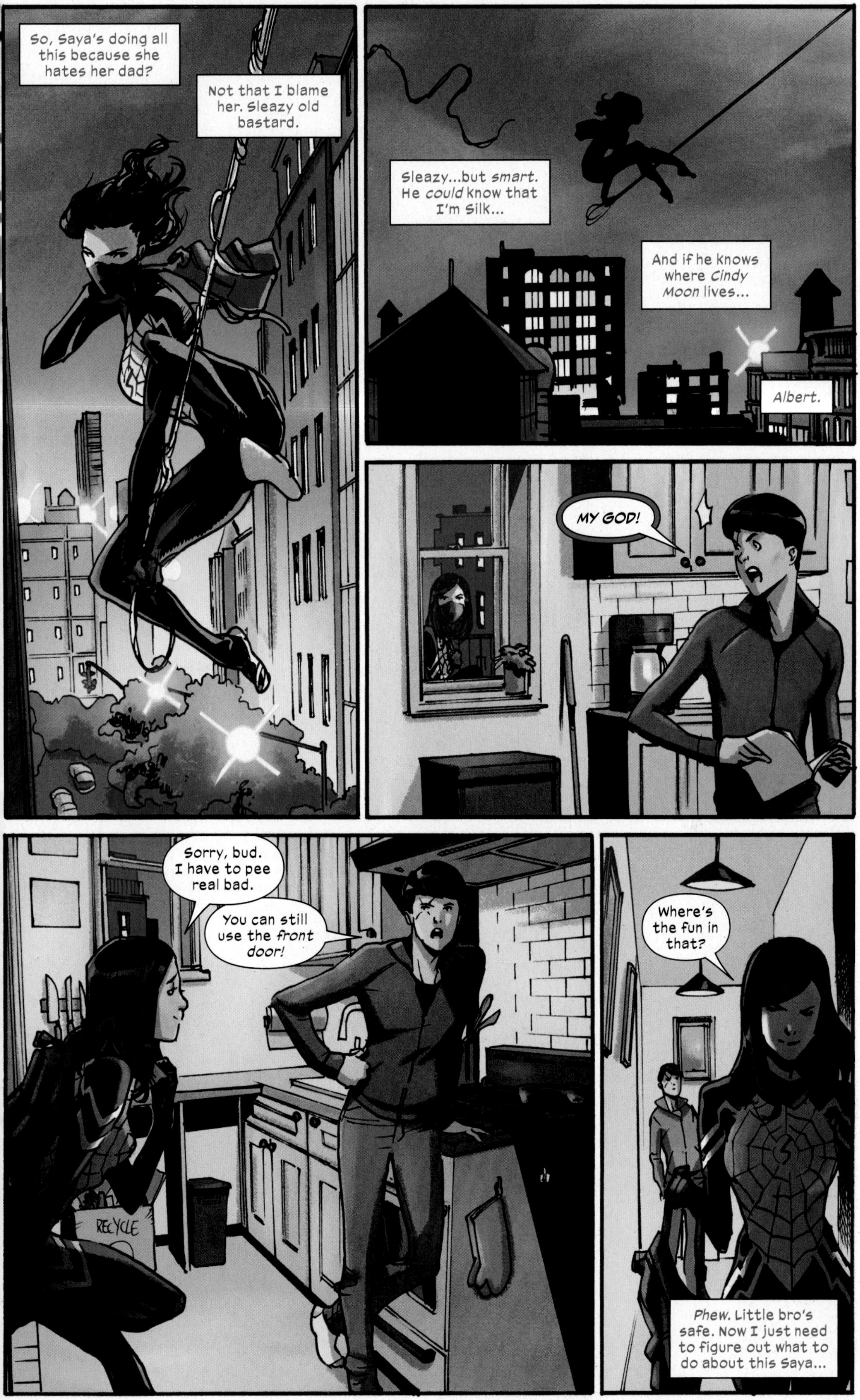
So, Saya's doing all this because she hates her dad?
Not that I blame her. Sleazy old bastard.
Sleazy...but *smart*. He *could* know that I'm Silk...
And if he knows where *Cindy Moon* lives...
Albert.
MY GOD!
Sorry, bud. I have to pee real bad.
You can still use the *front* door!
Where's the fun in that?
Phew. Little bro's safe. Now I just need to figure out what to do about this Saya...
RECYCLE

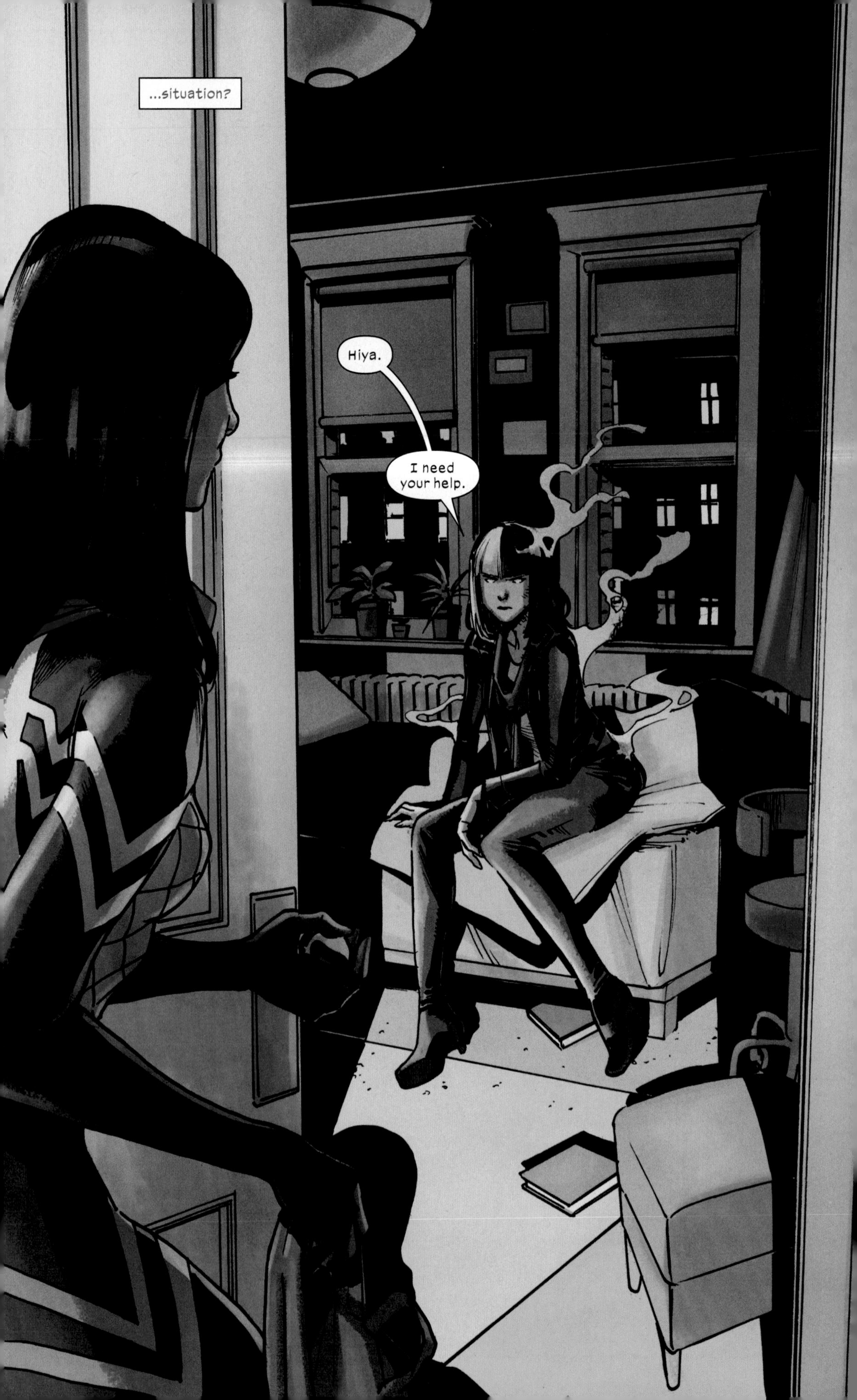
...situation?
Hiya.
I need your help.

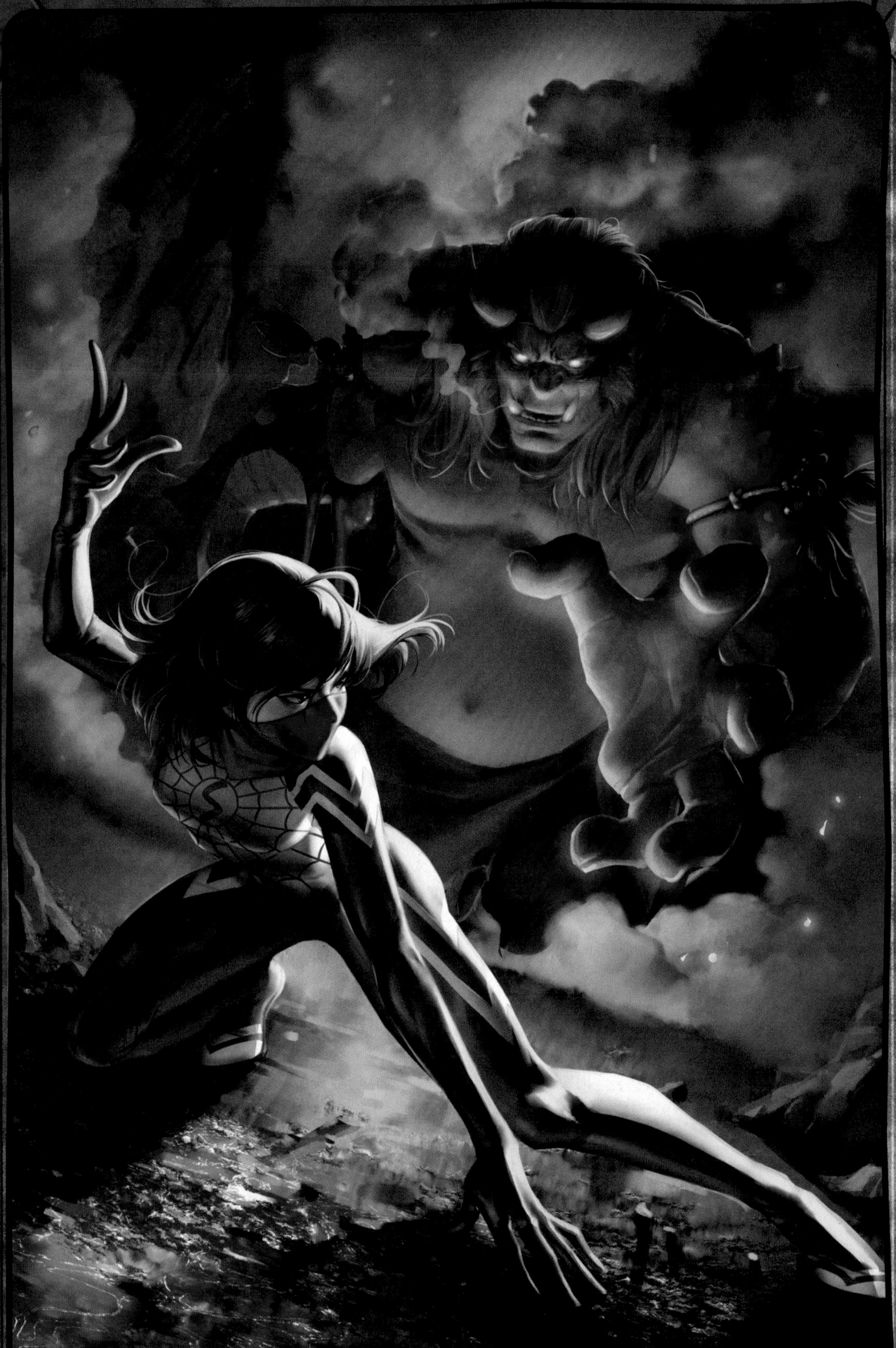

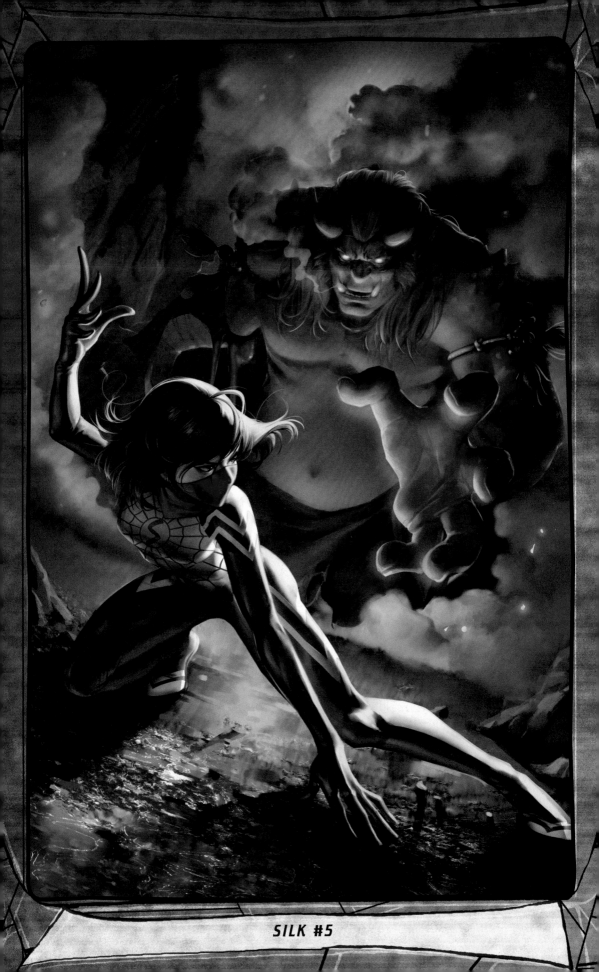

SILK #5

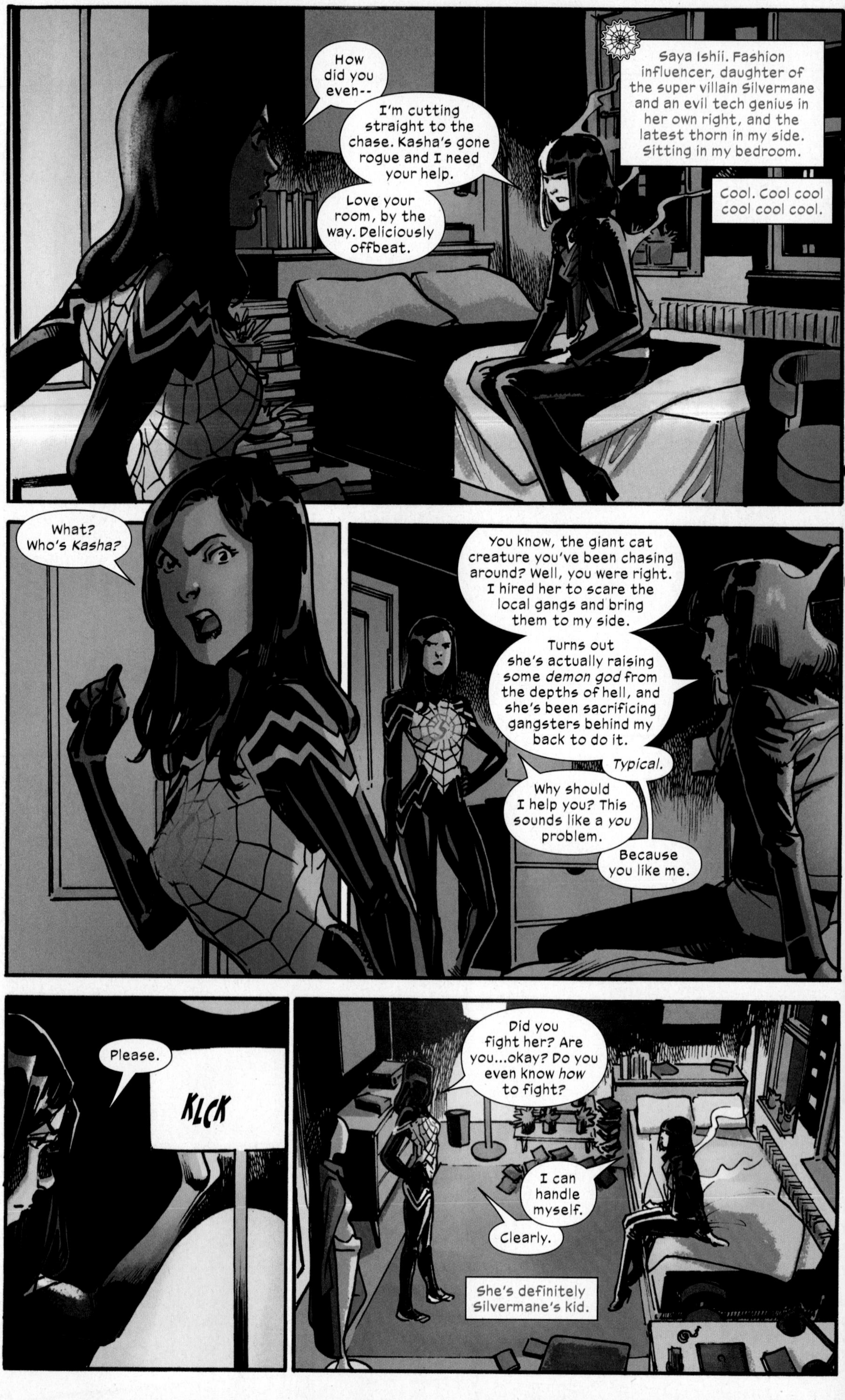
How did you even--
I'm cutting straight to the chase. Kasha's gone rogue and I need your help.
Love your room, by the way. Deliciously offbeat.
Saya Ishii. Fashion influencer, daughter of the super villain Silvermane and an evil tech genius in her own right, and the latest thorn in my side. Sitting in my bedroom.
Cool. Cool cool cool cool cool.
What? Who's *Kasha?*
You know, the giant cat creature you've been chasing around? Well, you were right. I hired her to scare the local gangs and bring them to my side.
Turns out she's actually raising some *demon god* from the depths of hell, and she's been sacrificing gangsters behind my back to do it.
Typical.
Why should I help you? This sounds like a *you* problem.
Because you like me.
Please.
KLCK
Did you fight her? Are you...okay? Do you even know *how* to fight?
I can handle myself.
Clearly.
She's definitely Silvermane's kid.

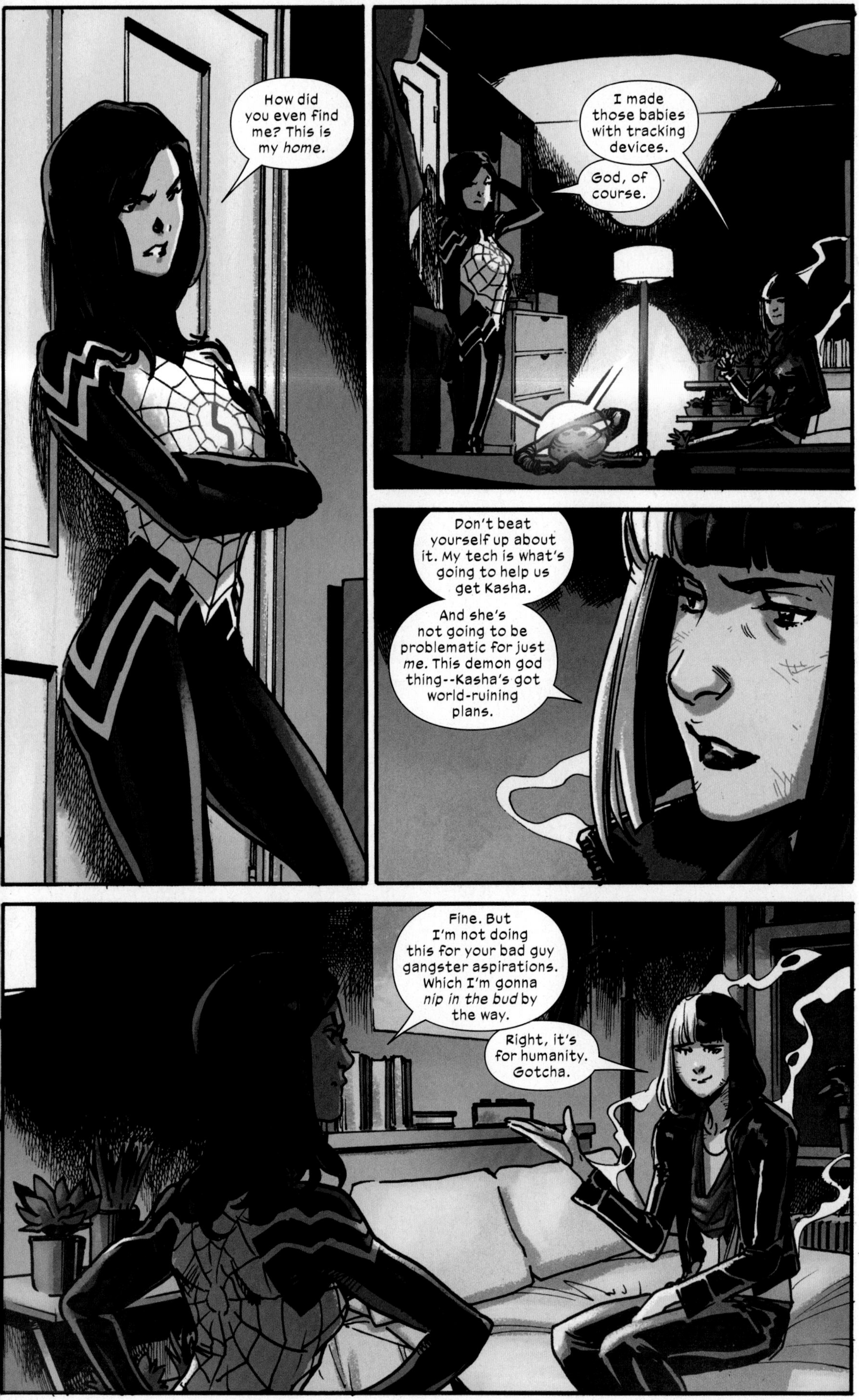
How did you even find me? This is my *home.*
I made those babies with tracking devices.
God, of course.
Don't beat yourself up about it. My tech is what's going to help us get Kasha.
And she's not going to be problematic for just *me.* This demon god thing--Kasha's got world-ruining plans.
Fine. But I'm not doing this for your bad guy gangster aspirations. Which I'm gonna *nip in the bud* by the way.
Right, it's for humanity. Gotcha.

All right. Let's rally the troops.

If the way to Kasha is through tech--you need access to a lab, right?

Ideally.

Don't let this go to your head but I need your help. I need access to all your nerdy science stuff.

Wish I could relish thsi heartfelt plea more. im not exactly available rn. Fihgting ShckQr...

Don't text and fight! Talk later.

Hi, any chance there's an old S.H.I.E.L.D. lab I can use for some world-saving business?

Sure, but you might get your head blown off if I'm not there to disable the security system. And I've got my hands full right now.

So...you're saying there's a chance?

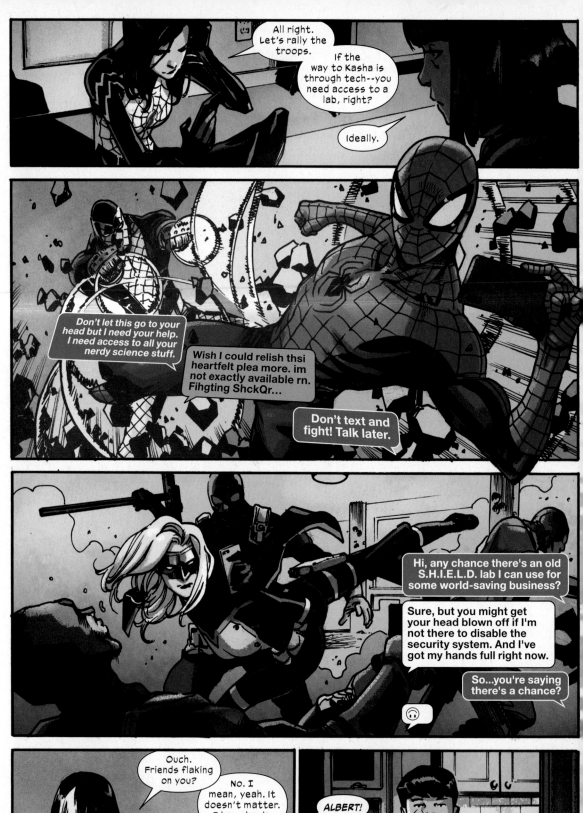

Ouch. Friends flaking on you?

No. I mean, yeah. It doesn't matter. I have back-up.

ALBERT!

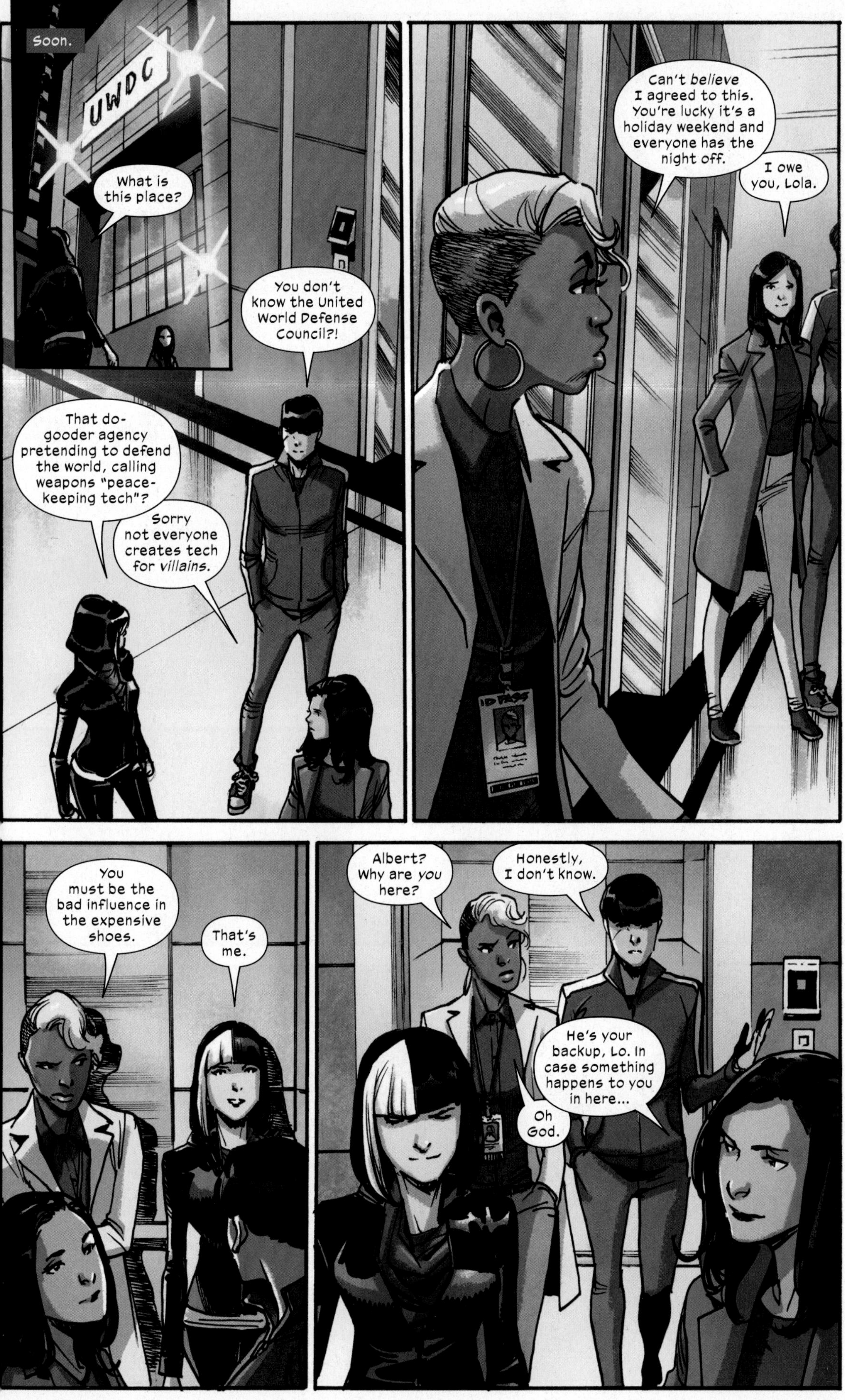
Soon.
UWDC
What is this place?
You don't know the United World Defense Council?!
That do-gooder agency pretending to defend the world, calling weapons "peace-keeping tech"?
Sorry not everyone creates tech for *villains.*
Can't *believe* I agreed to this. You're lucky it's a holiday weekend and everyone has the night off.
I owe you, Lola.
ID PASS
You must be the bad influence in the expensive shoes.
That's me.
Albert? Why are *you* here?
Honestly, I don't know.
He's your backup, Lo. In case something happens to you in here...
Oh God.

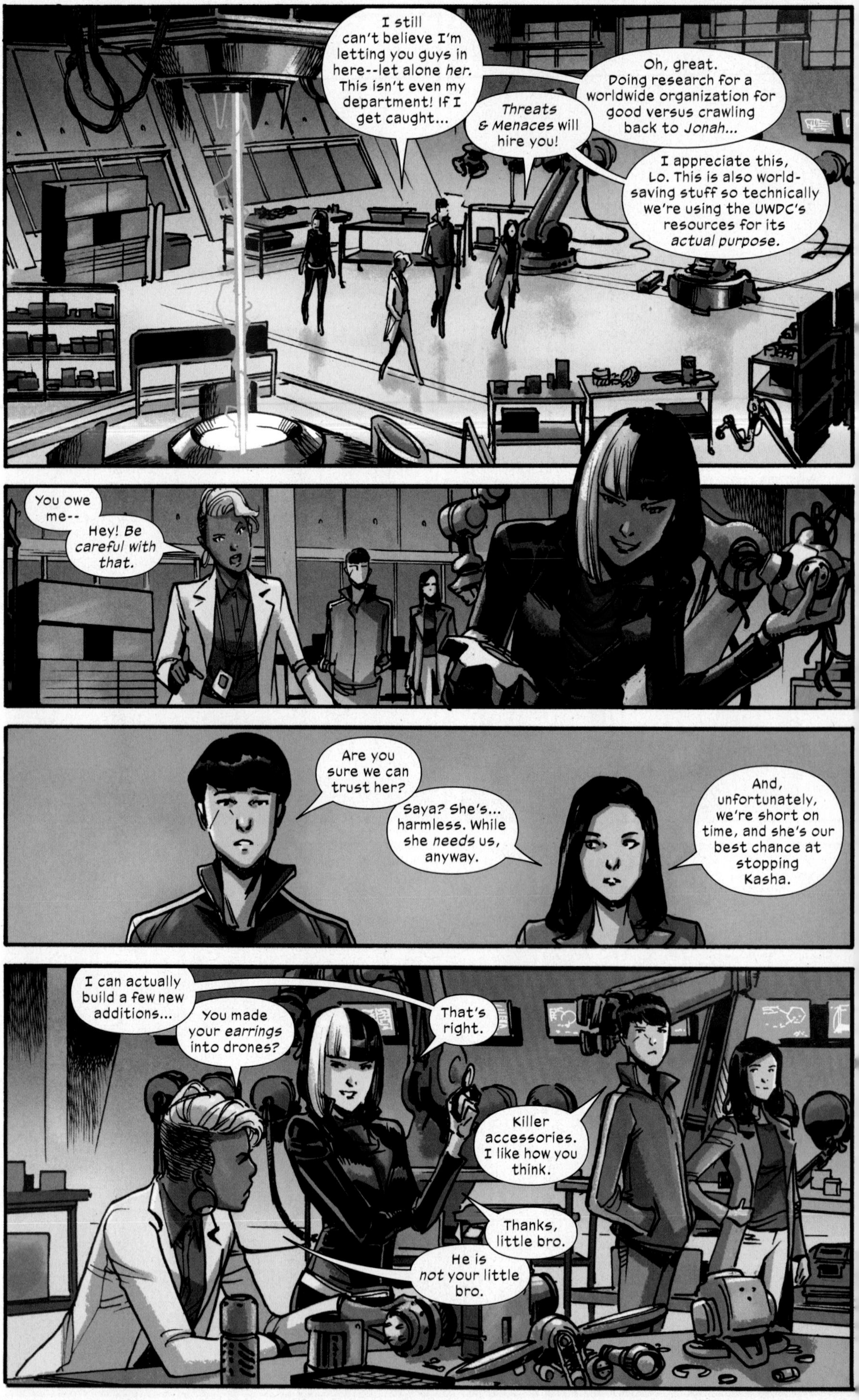
I still can't believe I'm letting you guys in here--let alone *her.* This isn't even my department! If I get caught...
Threats & Menaces will hire you!
Oh, great. Doing research for a worldwide organization for good versus crawling back to *Jonah*...
I appreciate this, Lo. This is also world-saving stuff so technically we're using the UWDC's resources for its *actual purpose.*
You owe me--
Hey! *Be careful with that.*
Are you sure we can trust her?
Saya? She's... harmless. While she *needs* us, anyway.
And, unfortunately, we're short on time, and she's our best chance at stopping Kasha.
I can actually build a few new additions...
You made your *earrings* into drones?
That's right.
Killer accessories. I like how you think.
Thanks, little bro.
He is *not* your little bro.

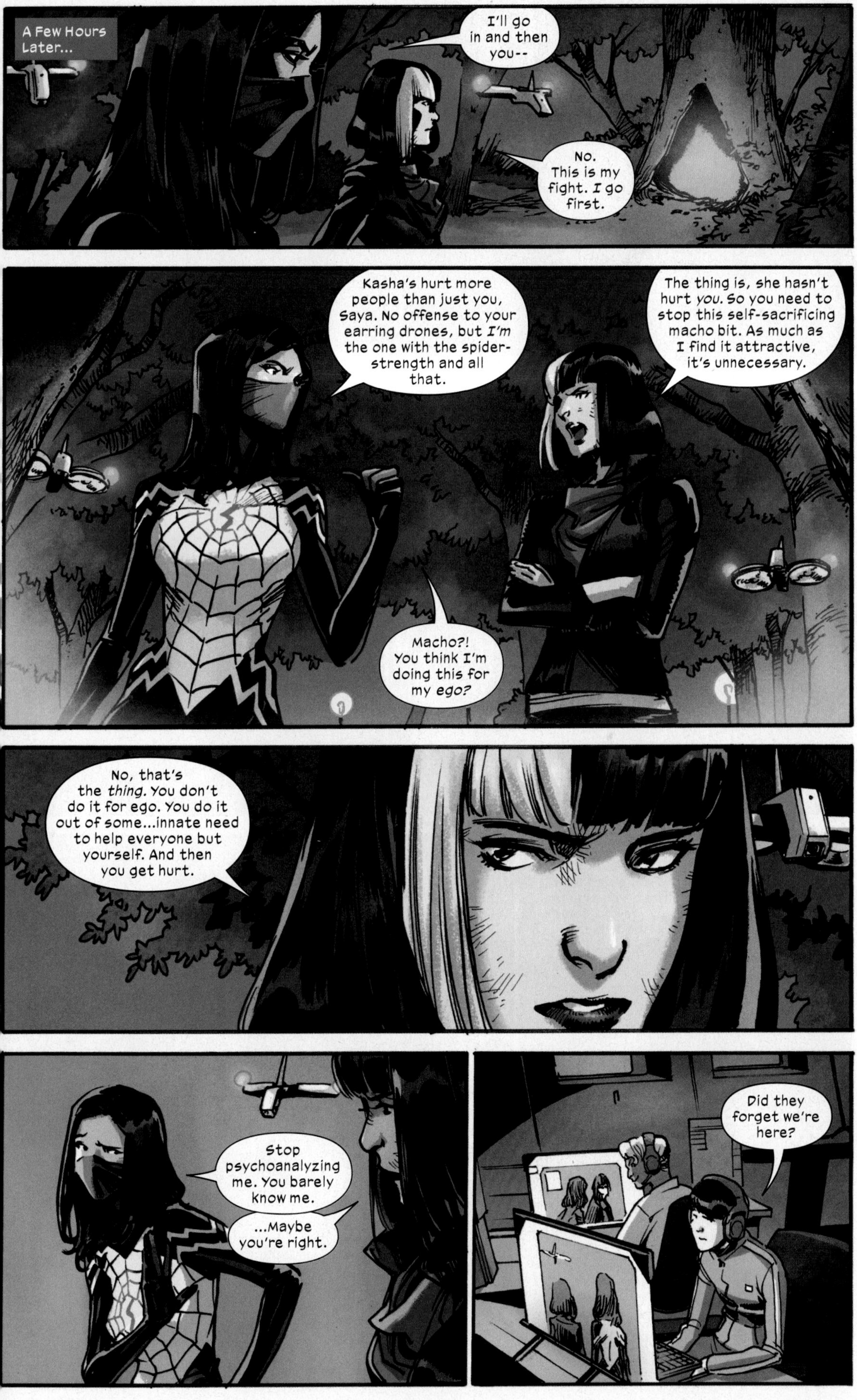
A Few Hours Later...
I'll go in and then you--
No. This is my fight. *I* go first.
Kasha's hurt more people than just you, Saya. No offense to your earring drones, but *I'm* the one with the spider-strength and all that.
The thing is, she hasn't hurt *you*. So you need to stop this self-sacrificing macho bit. As much as I find it attractive, it's unnecessary.
Macho?! You think I'm doing this for my *ego?*
No, that's the *thing*. You don't do it for ego. You do it out of some...innate need to help everyone but yourself. And then you get hurt.
Stop psychoanalyzing me. You barely know me.
...Maybe you're right.
Did they forget we're here?

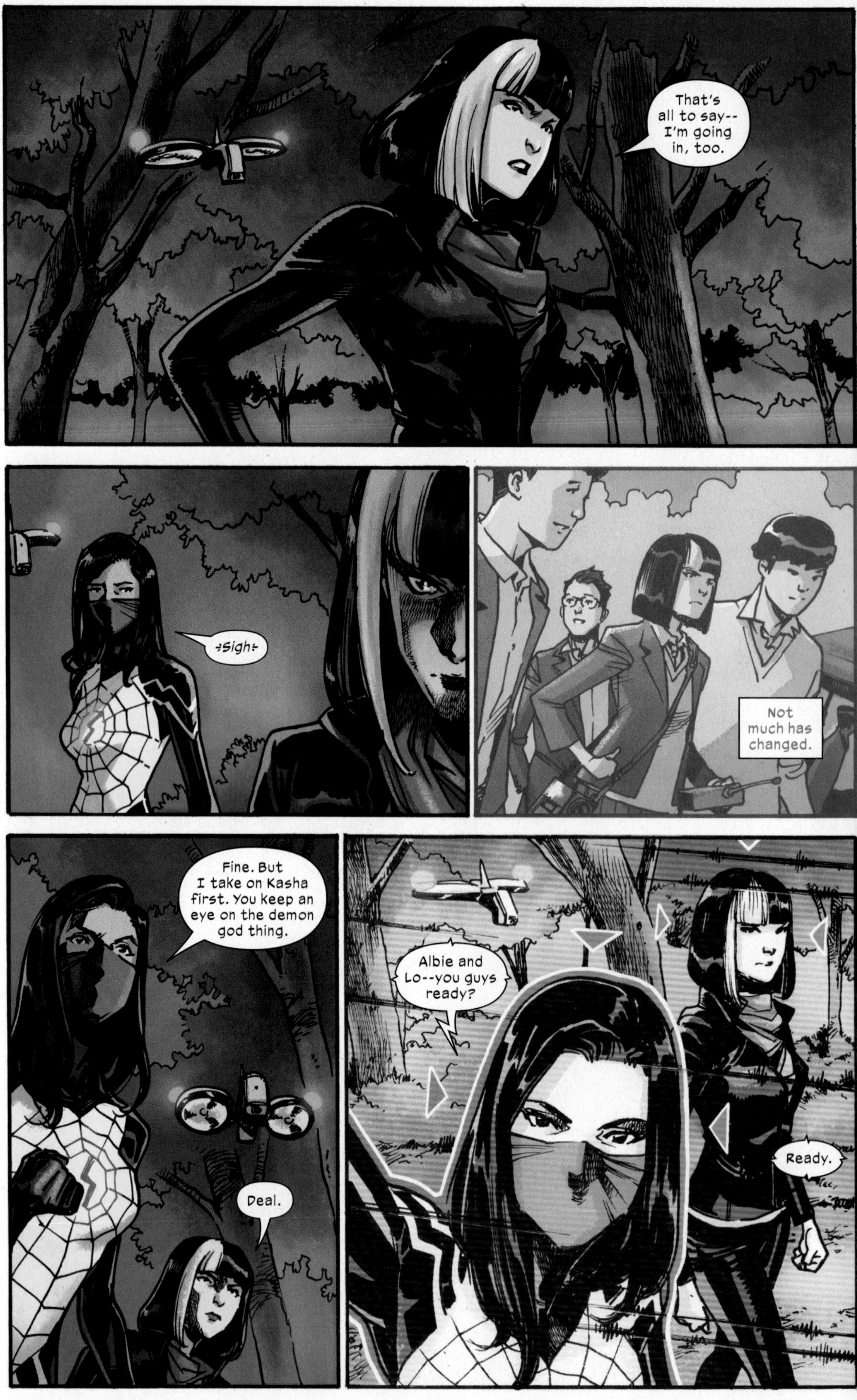

That's all to say-- I'm going in, too.
-Sigh-
Not much has changed.
Fine. But I take on Kasha first. You keep an eye on the demon god thing.
Deal.
Albie and Lo--you guys ready?
Ready.

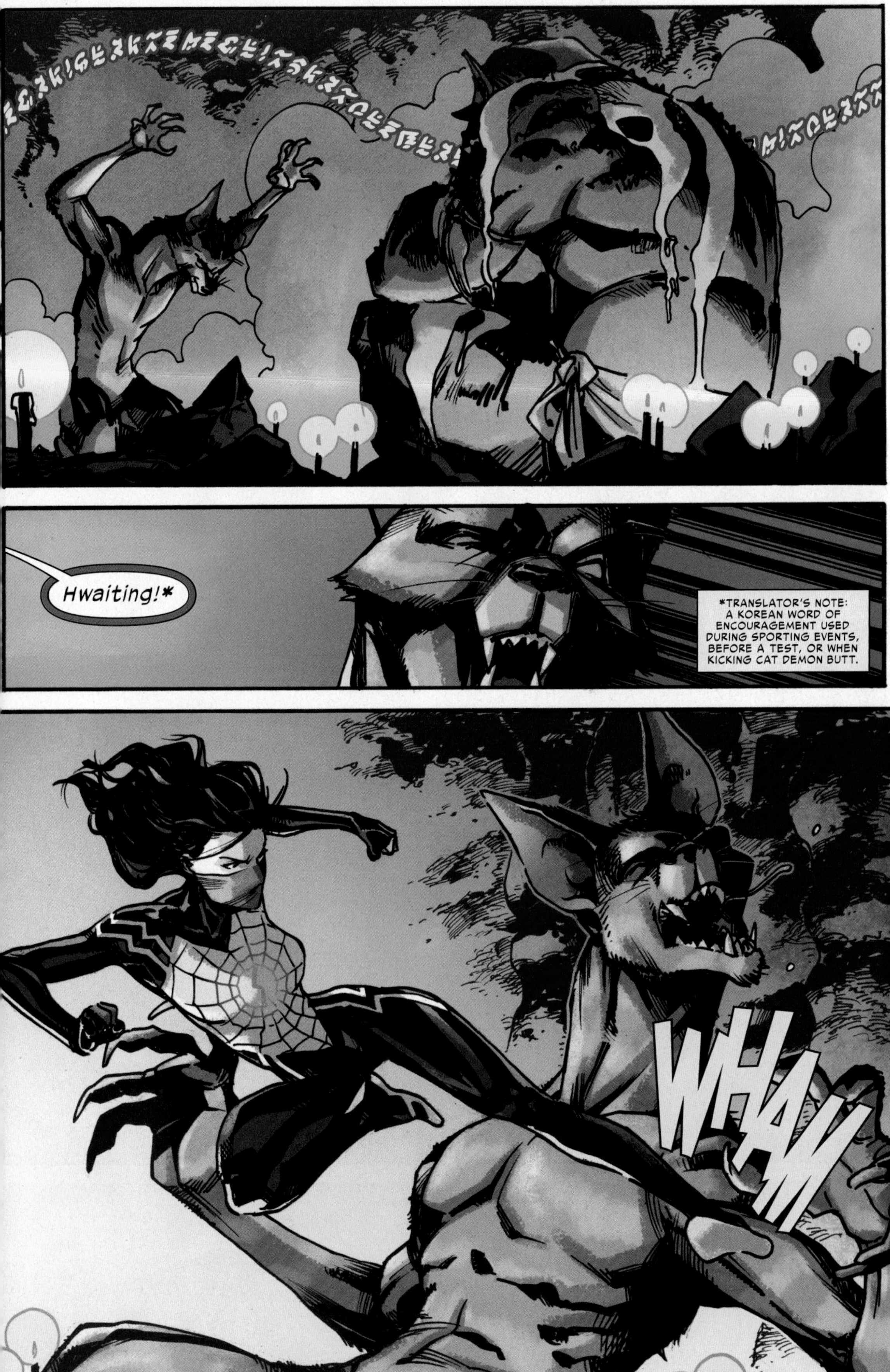
Hwaiting!*
*TRANSLATOR'S NOTE: A KOREAN WORD OF ENCOURAGEMENT USED DURING SPORTING EVENTS, BEFORE A TEST, OR WHEN KICKING CAT DEMON BUTT.
WHAM

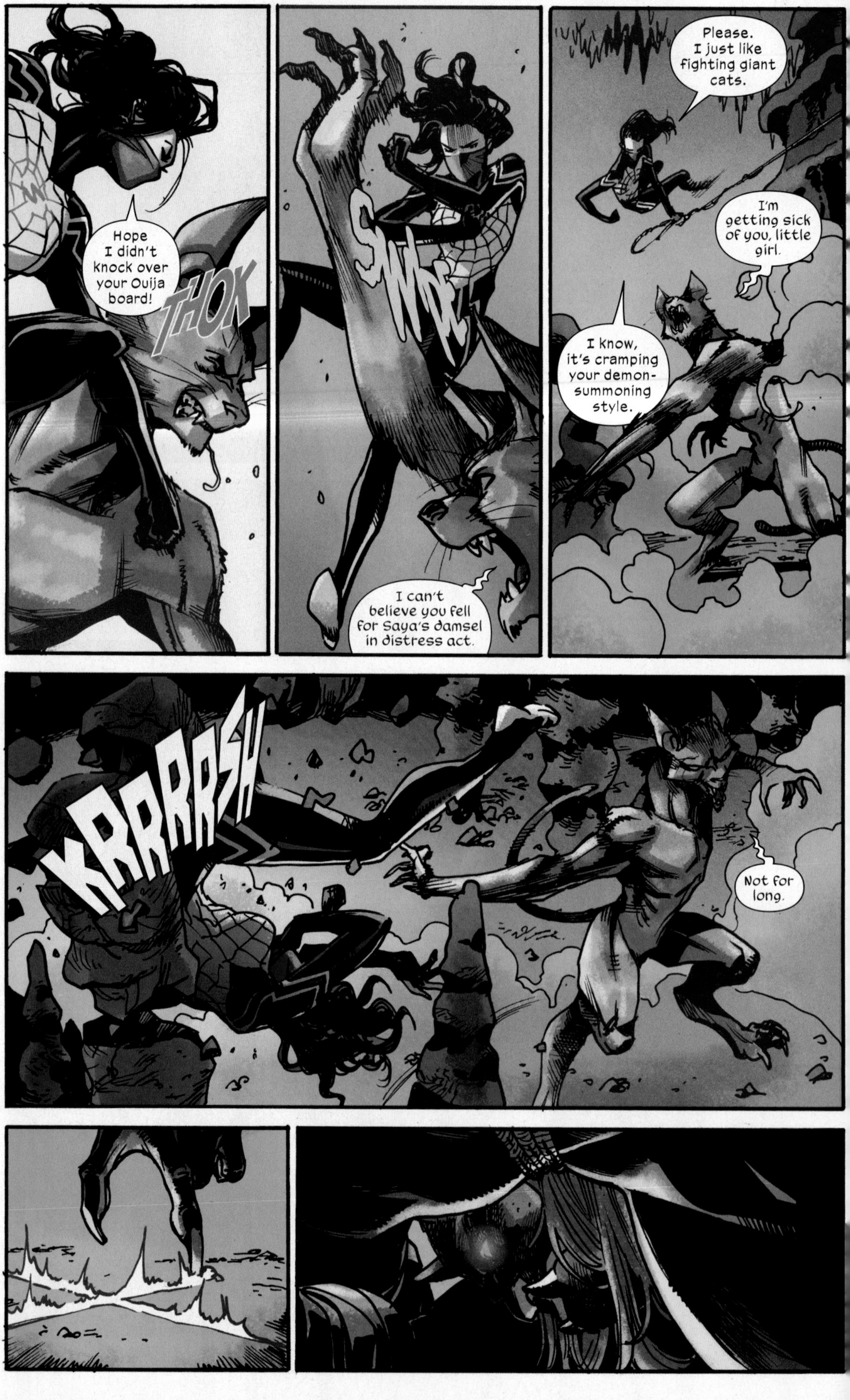
Hope I didn't knock over your Ouija board!
THOK
SWOOP
I can't believe you fell for Saya's damsel in distress act.
Please. I just like fighting giant cats.
I'm getting sick of you, little girl.
I know, it's cramping your demon-summoning style.
KRRRRSH
Not for long.

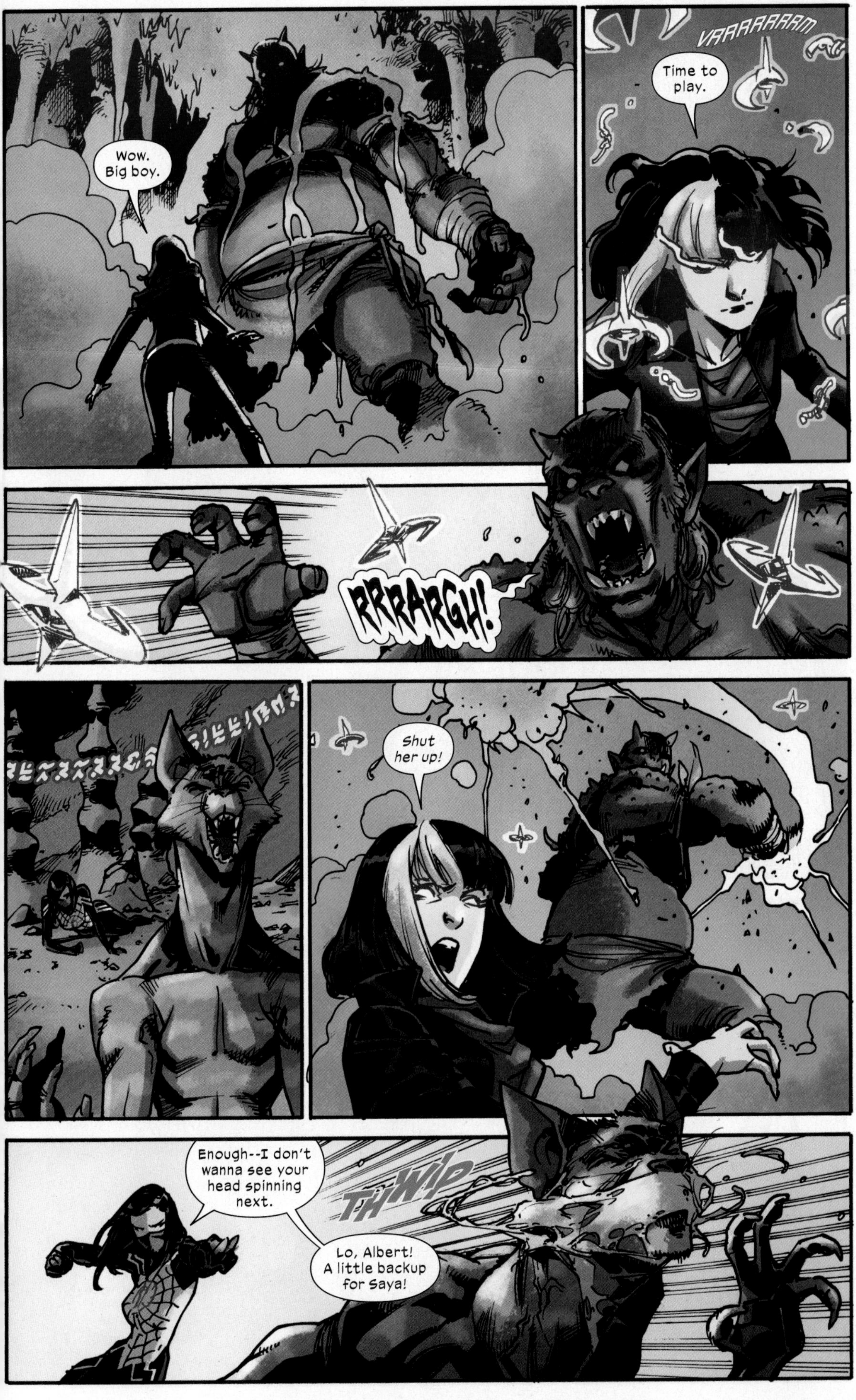
Wow. Big boy.
VRRRRRRRM
Time to play.
RRRARGH!
Shut her up!
Enough--I don't wanna see your head spinning next.
THWIP
Lo, Albert! A little backup for Saya!

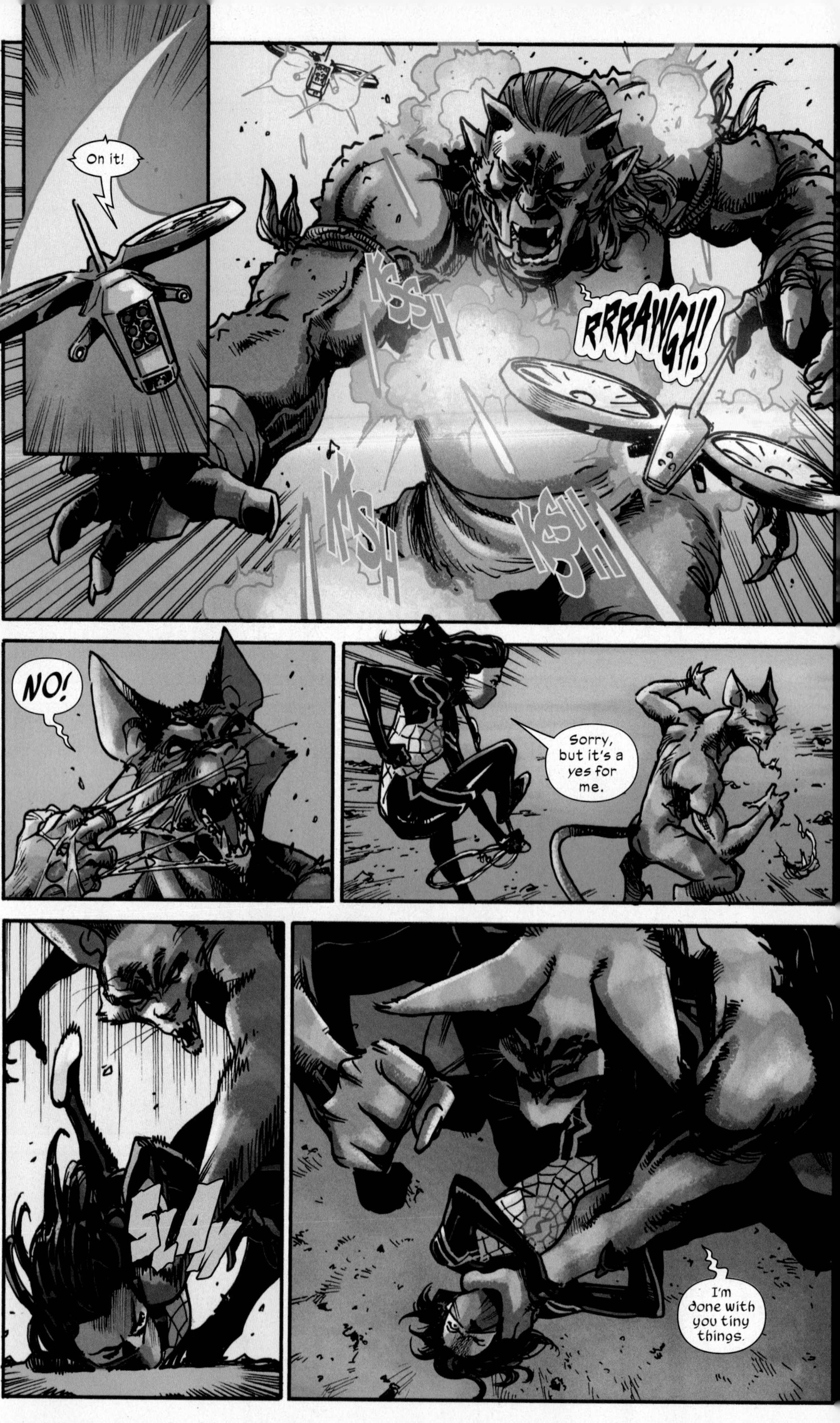

On it!
KSSSH
RRRAWGH!!
KKSH
KSSH
NO!
Sorry, but it's a yes for me.
SLAM
I'm done with you tiny things.

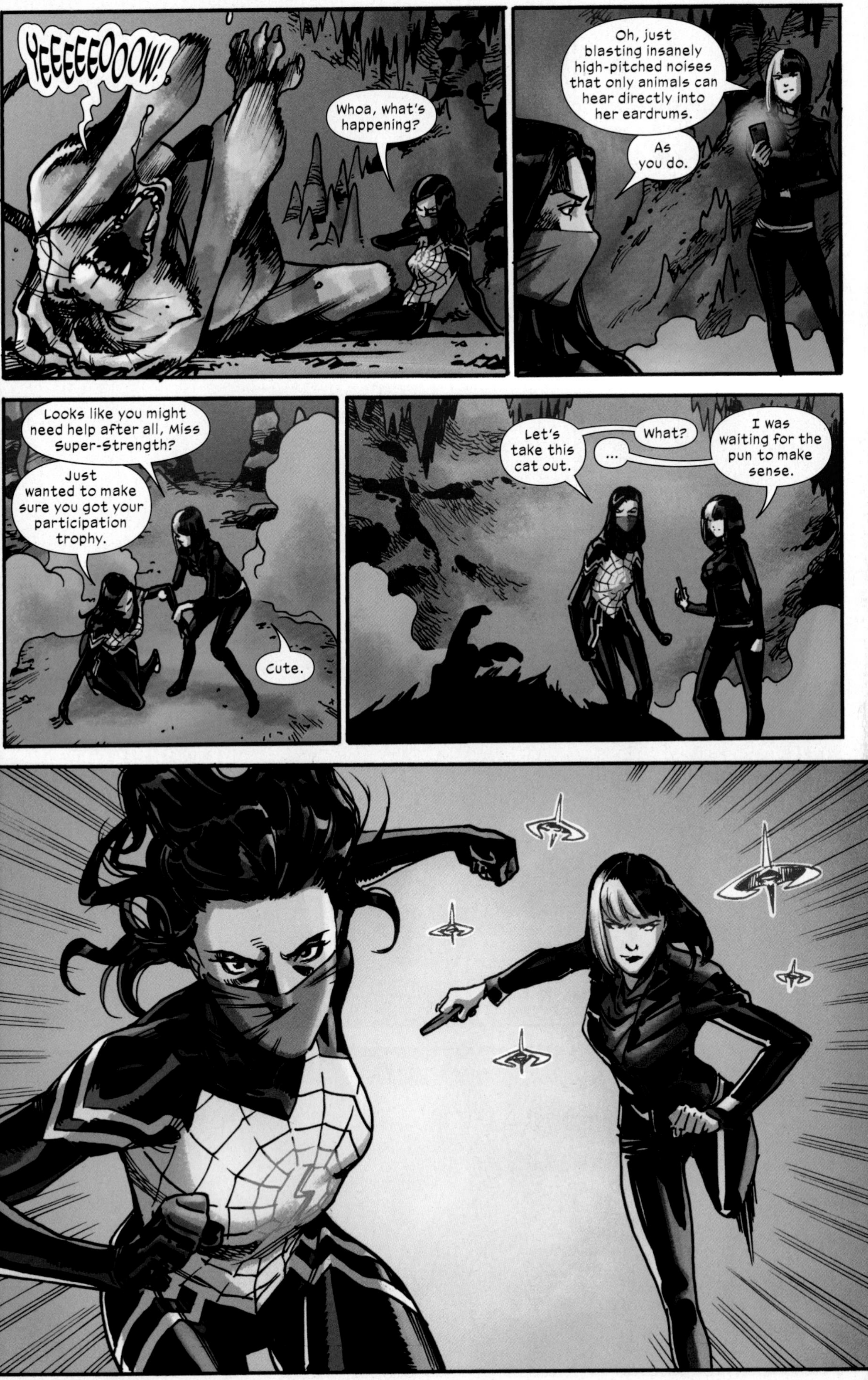
YEEEEEOOOW!
Whoa, what's happening?
Oh, just blasting insanely high-pitched noises that only animals can hear directly into her eardrums.
As you do.
Looks like you might need help after all, Miss Super-Strength?
Just wanted to make sure you got your participation trophy.
Cute.
Let's take this cat out.
What?
...
I was waiting for the pun to make sense.

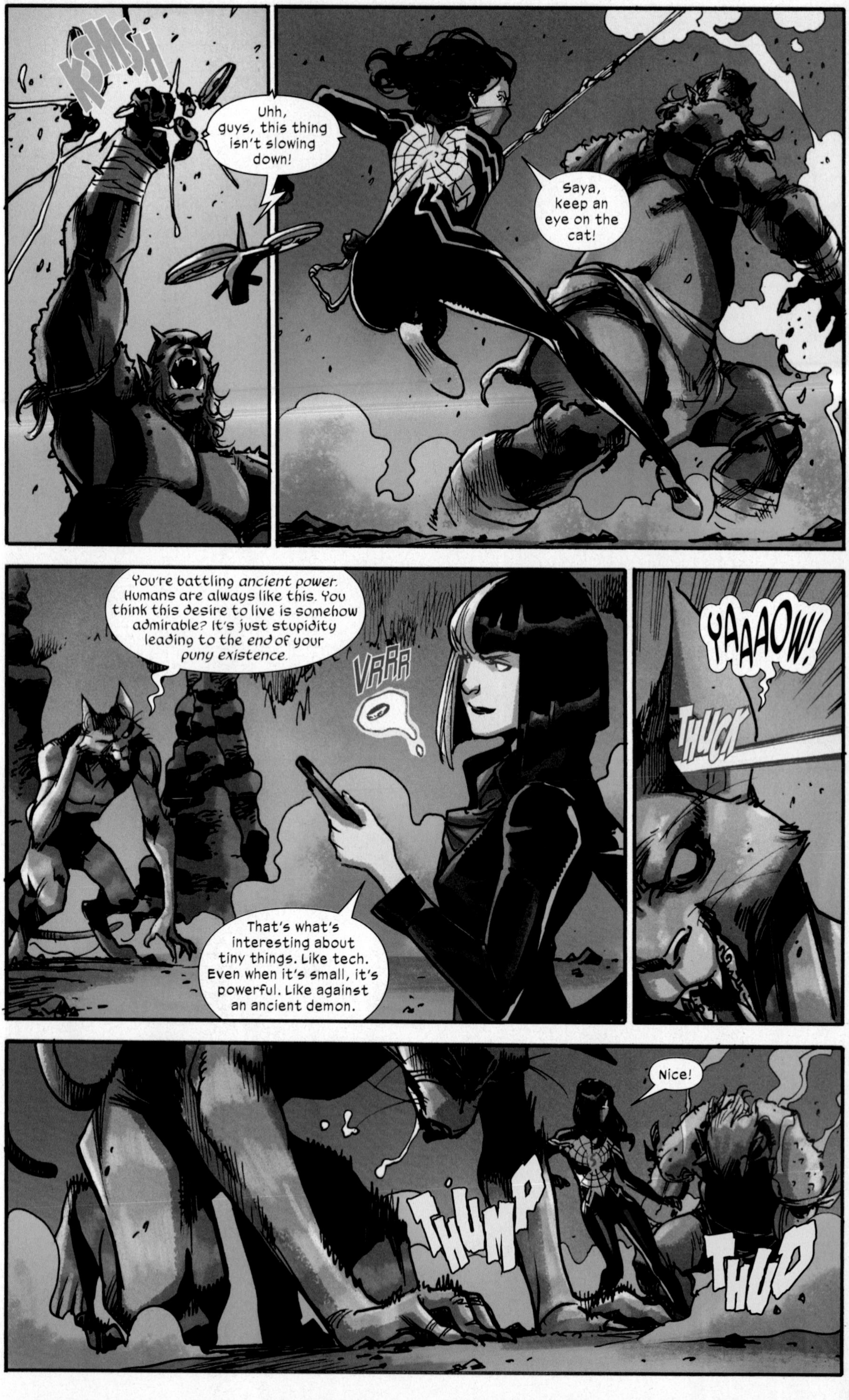
KSMSH
Uhh, guys, this thing isn't slowing down!
Saya, keep an eye on the cat!
You're battling ancient power. Humans are always like this. You think this desire to live is somehow admirable? It's just stupidity leading to the end of your puny existence.
VRRR
That's what's interesting about tiny things. Like tech. Even when it's small, it's powerful. Like against an ancient demon.
YAAAOW!!
THUCK
Nice!
THUMP
THUD

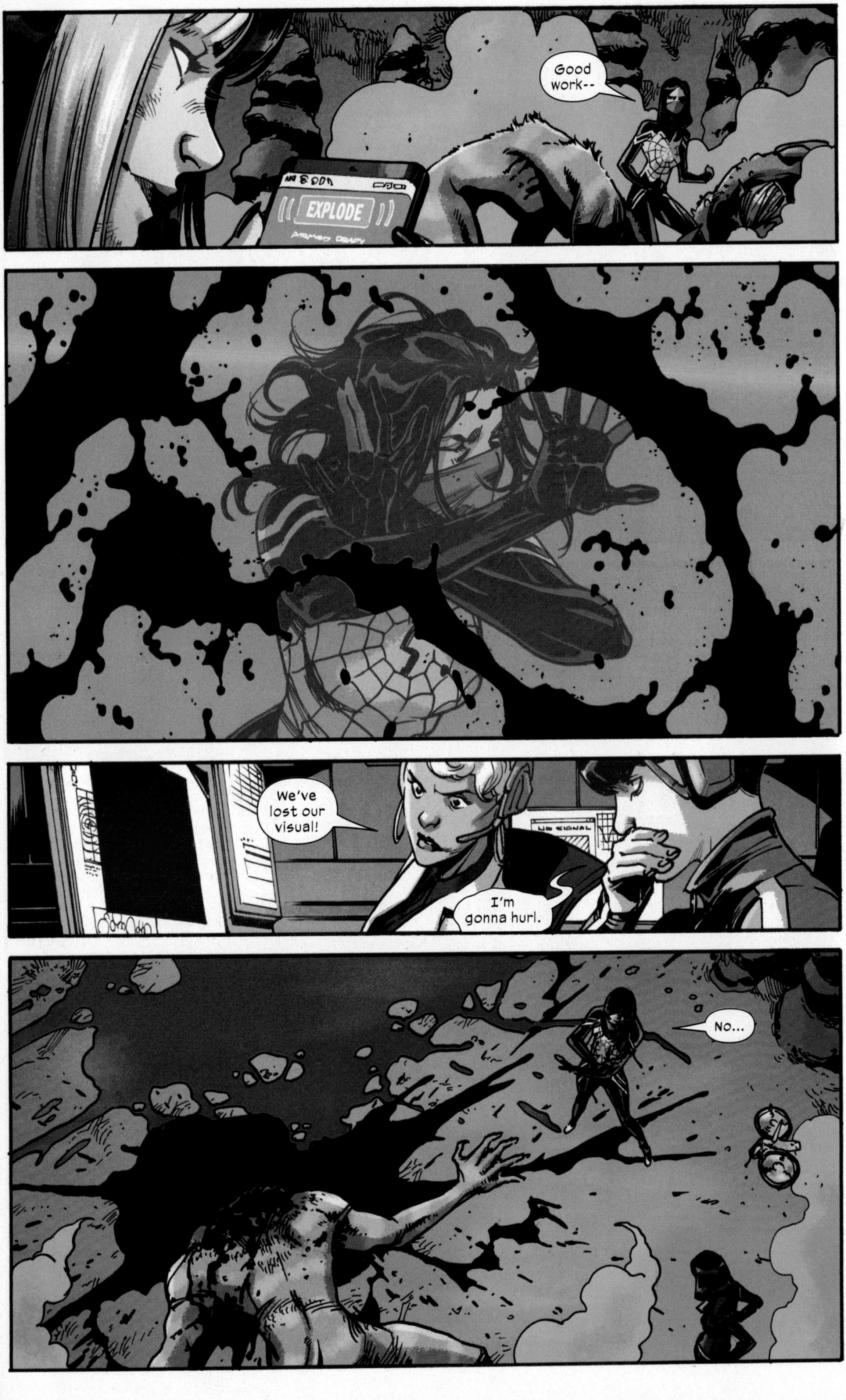
Good work--
EXPLODE
We've lost our visual!
I'm gonna hurl.
No...

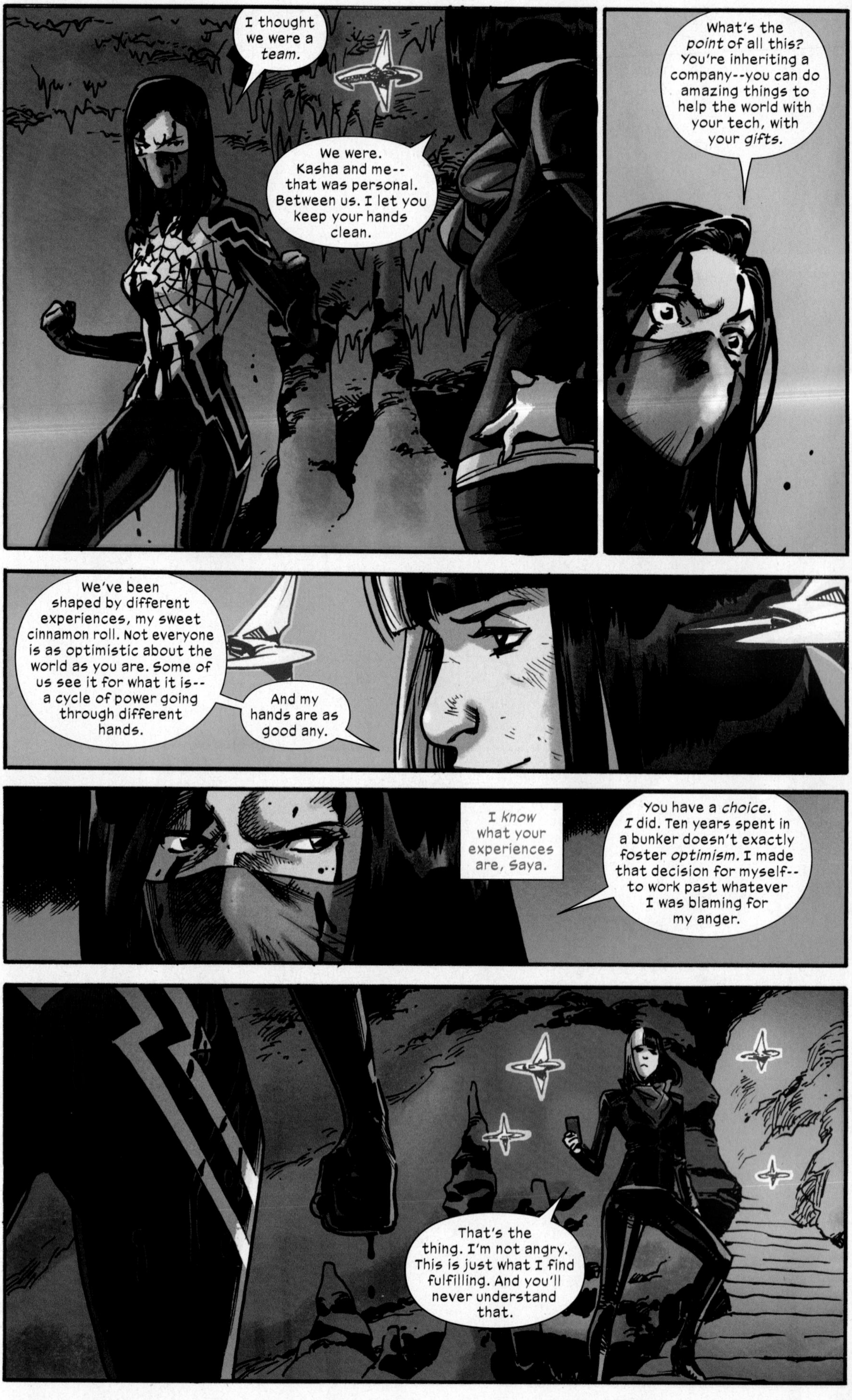
I thought we were a *team.*
We were. Kasha and me-- that was personal. Between us. I let you keep your hands clean.
What's the *point* of all this? You're inheriting a company--you can do amazing things to help the world with your tech, with your *gifts.*
We've been shaped by different experiences, my sweet cinnamon roll. Not everyone is as optimistic about the world as you are. Some of us see it for what it is-- a cycle of power going through different hands.
And my hands are as good any.
I *know* what your experiences are, Saya.
You have a *choice.* *I* did. Ten years spent in a bunker doesn't exactly foster *optimism.* I made that decision for myself-- to work past whatever I was blaming for my anger.
That's the thing. I'm not angry. This is just what I find fulfilling. And you'll never understand that.

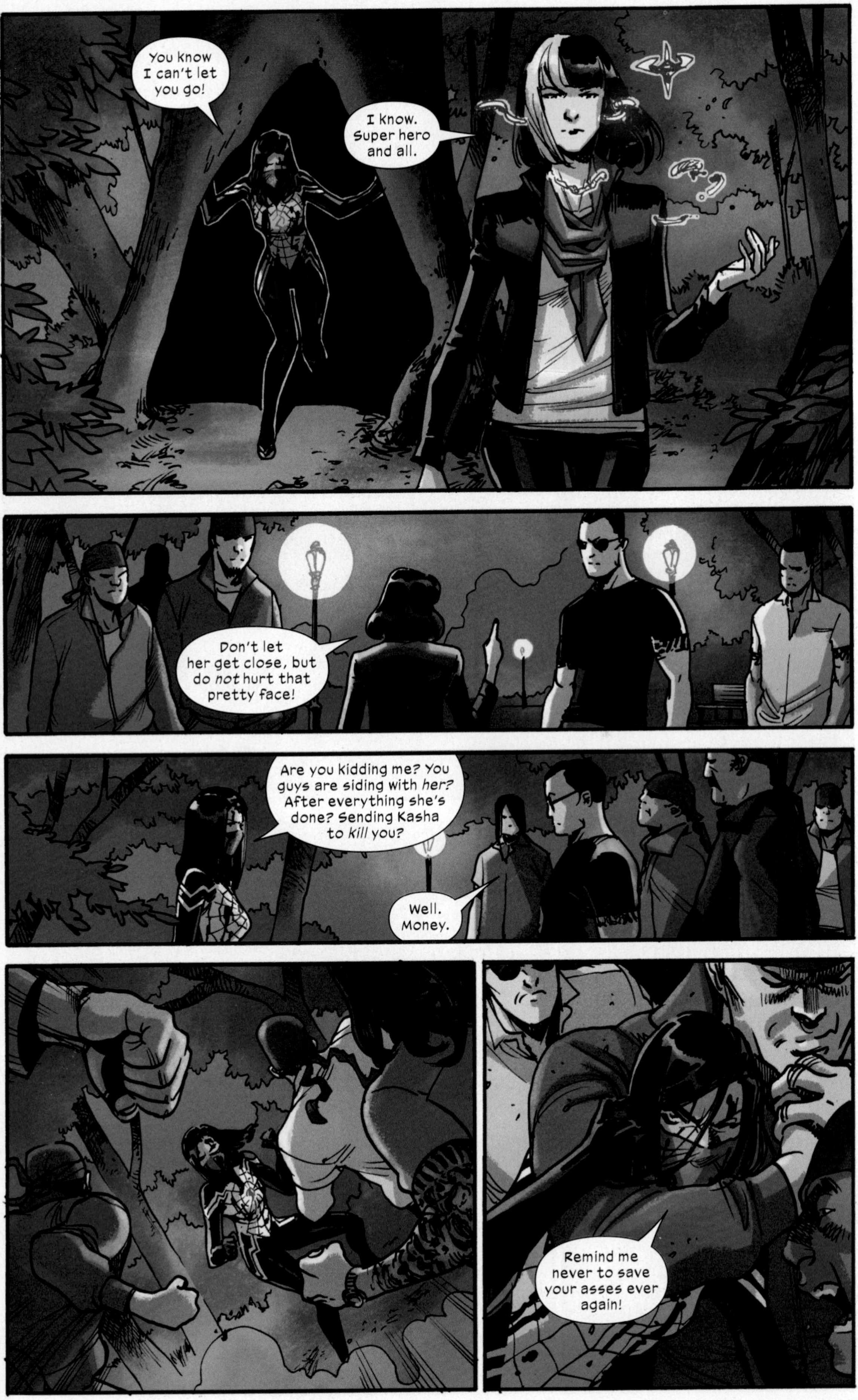
You know I can't let you go!
I know. Super hero and all.
Don't let her get close, but do *not* hurt that pretty face!
Are you kidding me? You guys are siding with *her*? After everything she's done? Sending Kasha to *kill* you?
Well. Money.
Remind me never to save your asses ever again!

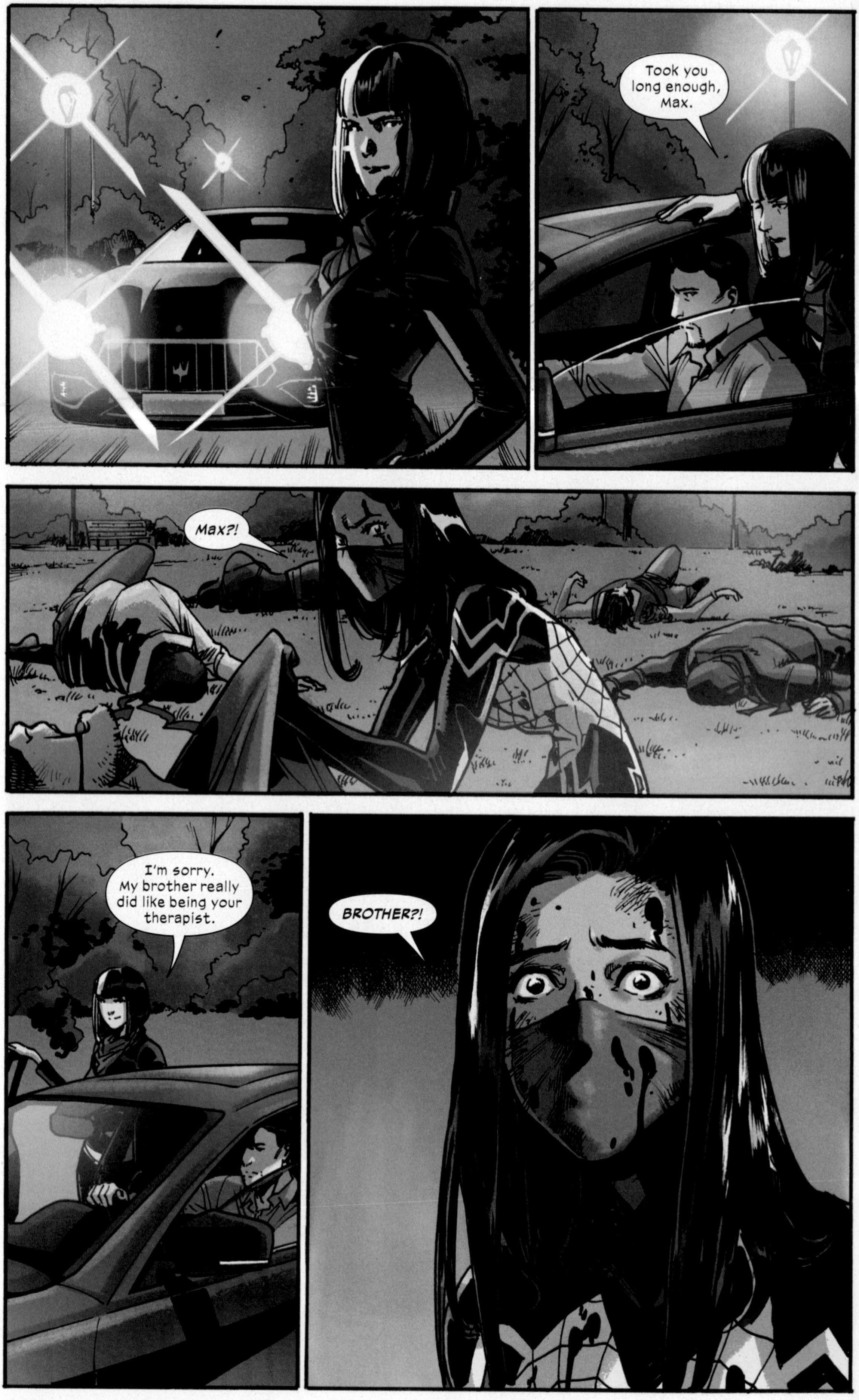
Took you long enough, Max.
Max?!
I'm sorry. My brother really did like being your therapist.
BROTHER?!

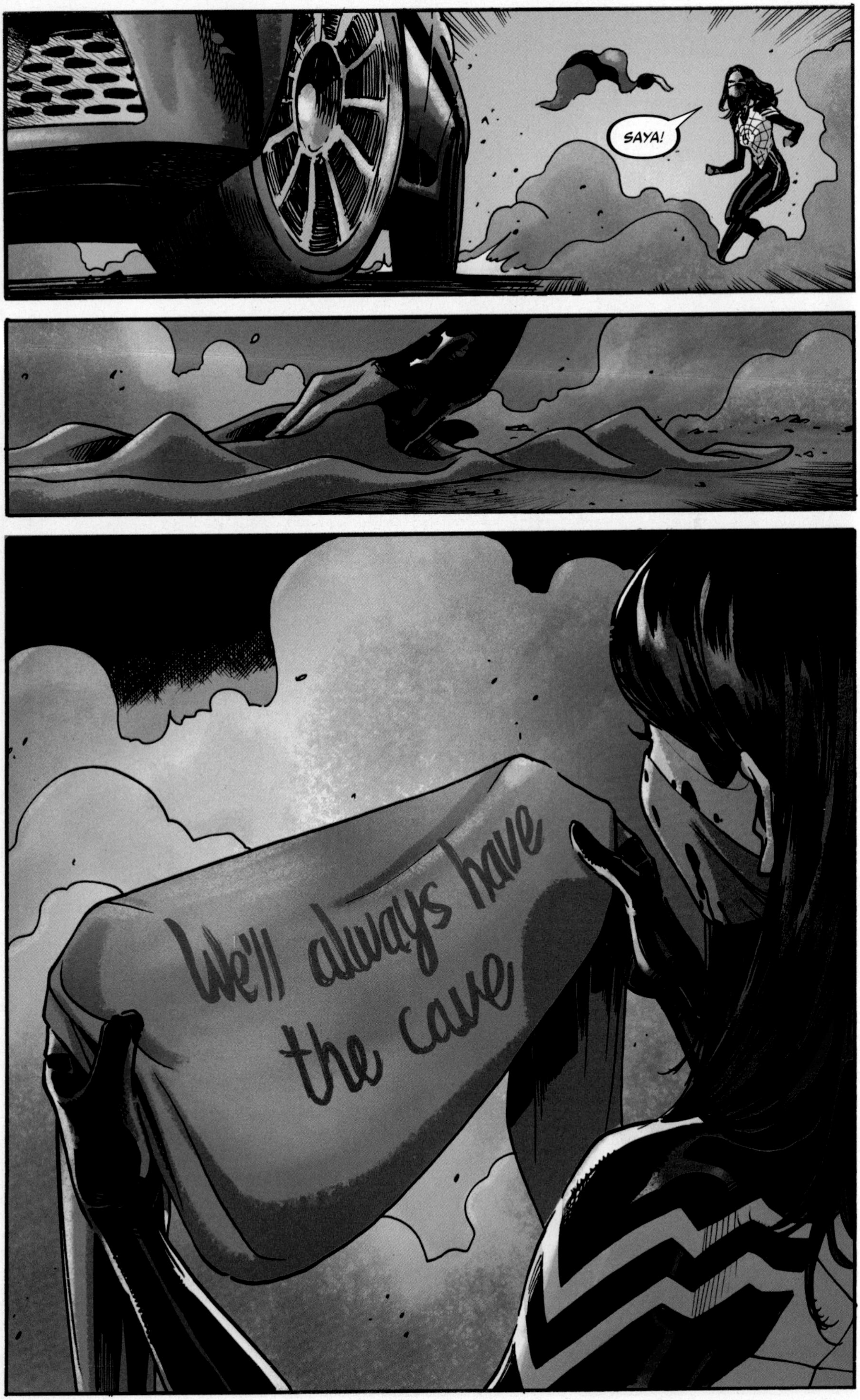
SAYA!
We'll always have the cave

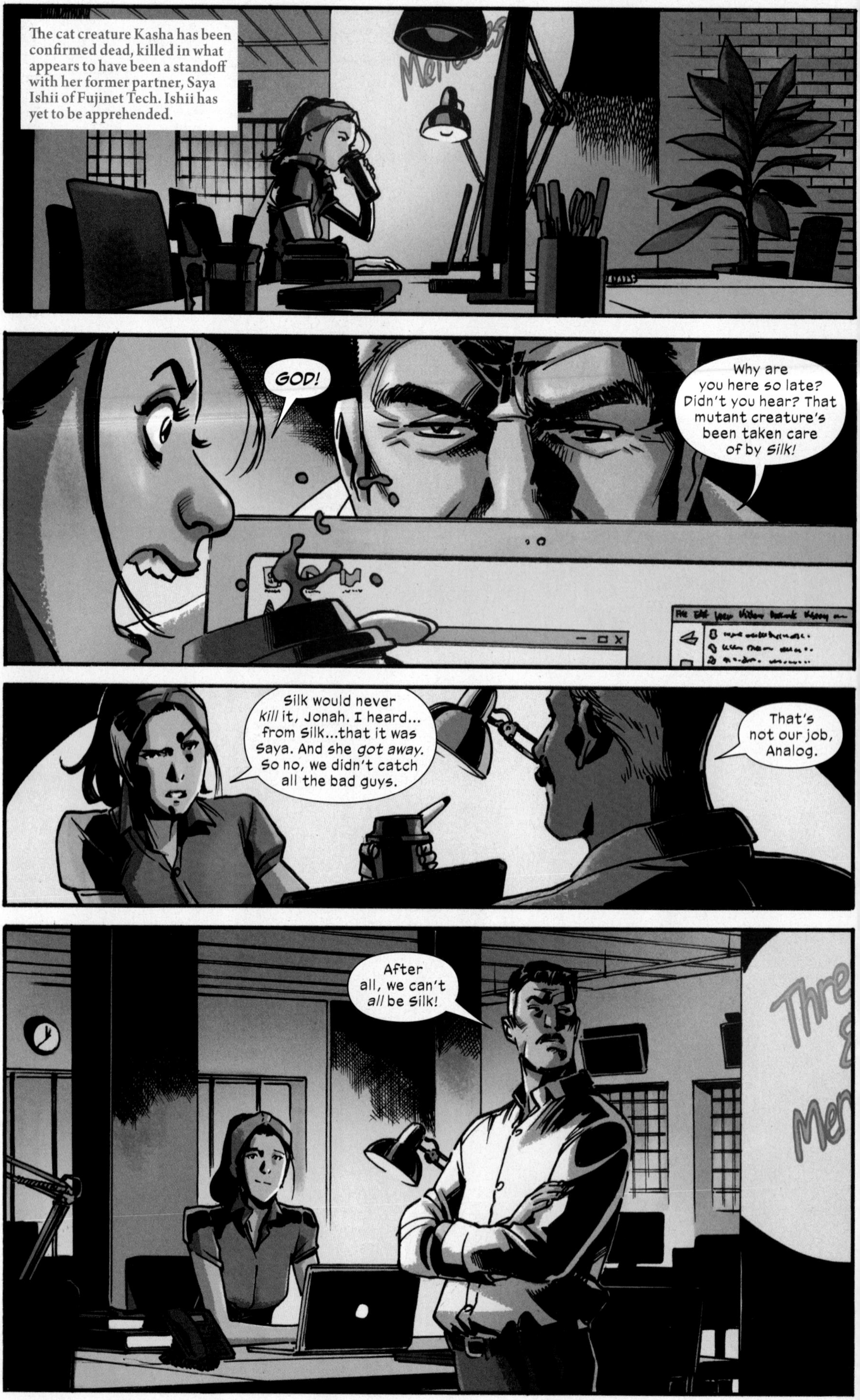
The cat creature Kasha has been confirmed dead, killed in what appears to have been a standoff with her former partner, Saya Ishii of Fujinet Tech. Ishii has yet to be apprehended.
GOD!
Why are you here so late? Didn't you hear? That mutant creature's been taken care of by *Silk!*
Silk would never *kill* it, Jonah. I heard... from Silk...that it was Saya. And she *got away.* So no, we didn't catch all the bad guys.
That's not our job, Analog.
After all, we can't *all* be Silk!

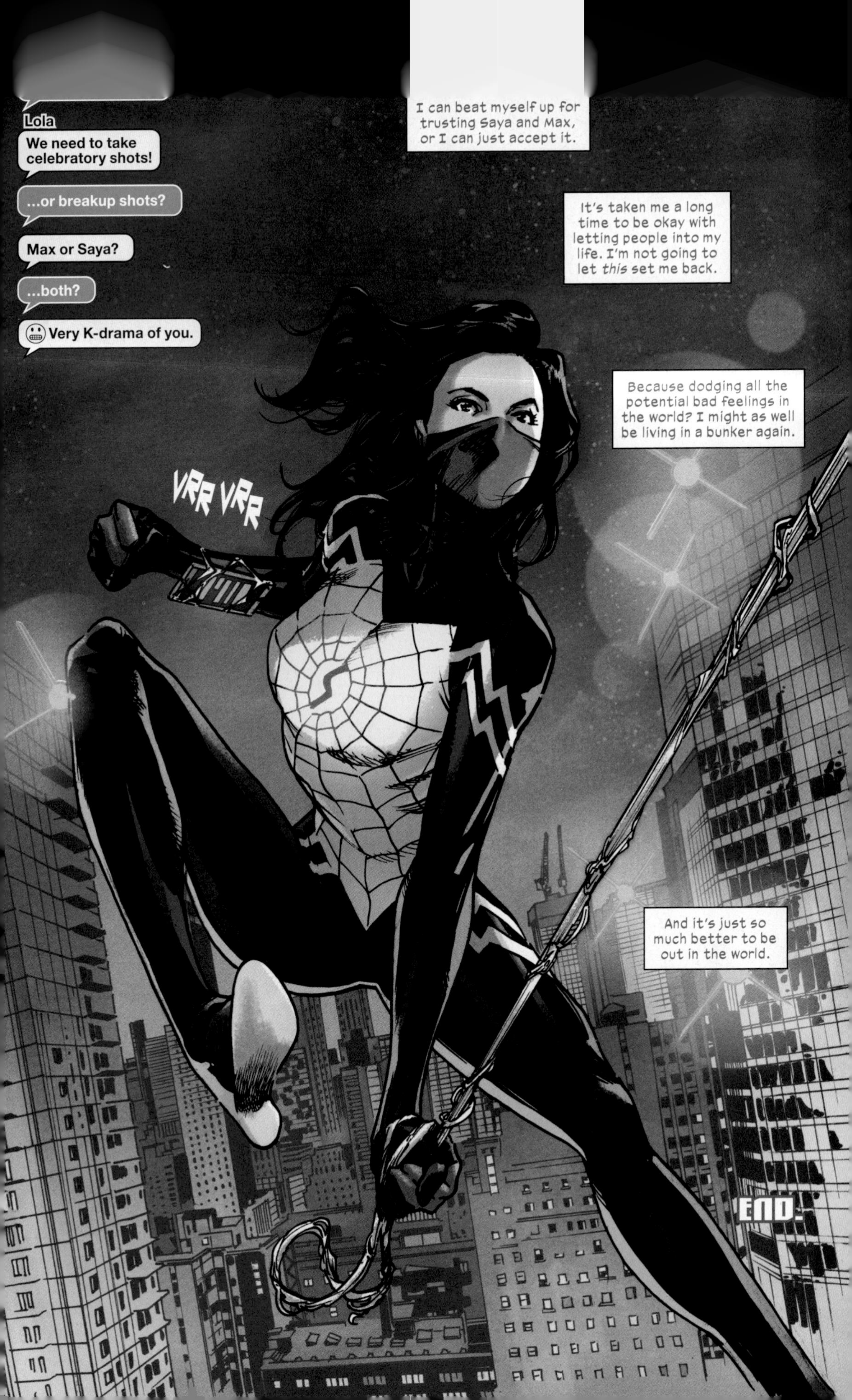

I can beat myself up for trusting Saya and Max, or I can just accept it.
Lola
We need to take celebratory shots!
...or breakup shots?
Max or Saya?
...both?
Very K-drama of you.
It's taken me a long time to be okay with letting people into my life. I'm not going to let *this* set me back.
Because dodging all the potential bad feelings in the world? I might as well be living in a bunker again.
VRR VRR
And it's just so much better to be out in the world.
END.

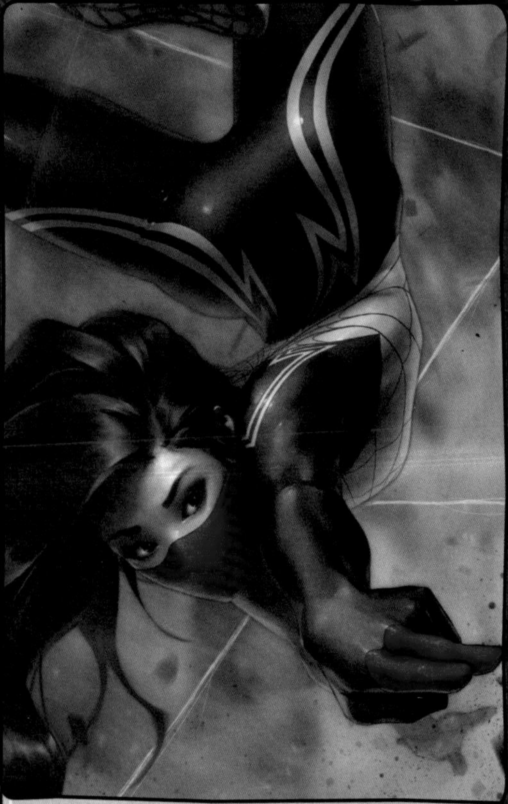

#1 VARIANT by Jeehyung Lee

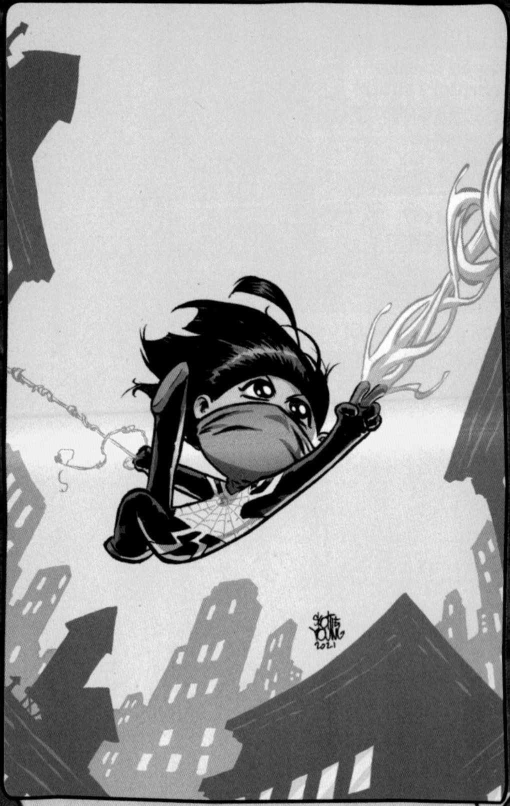

#1 VARIANT by Skottie Young

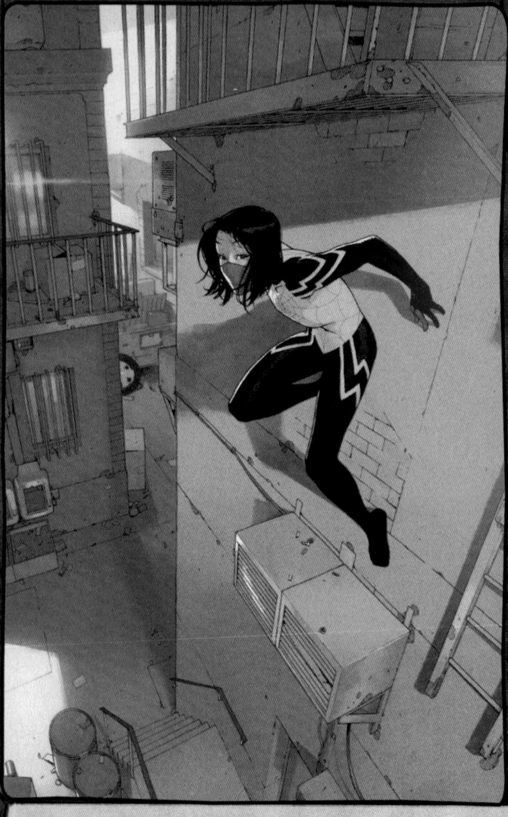

#1 VARIANT by Bengal

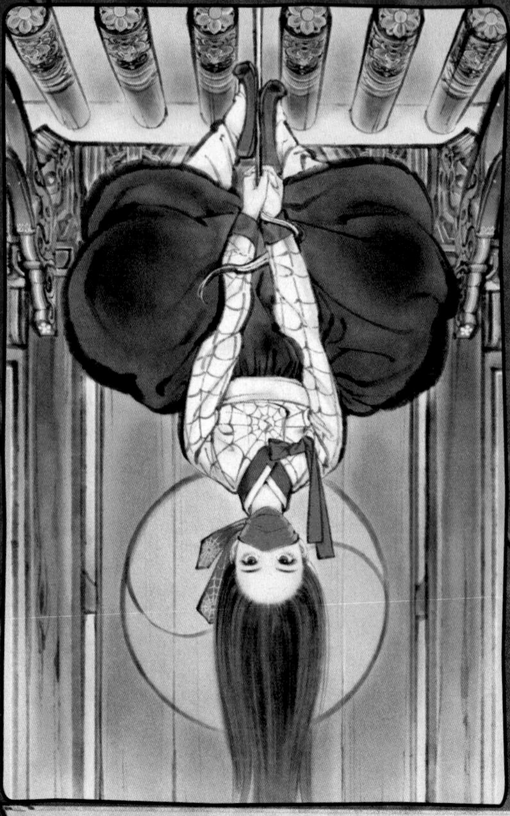

#1 VARIANT by Wooh Nayoung

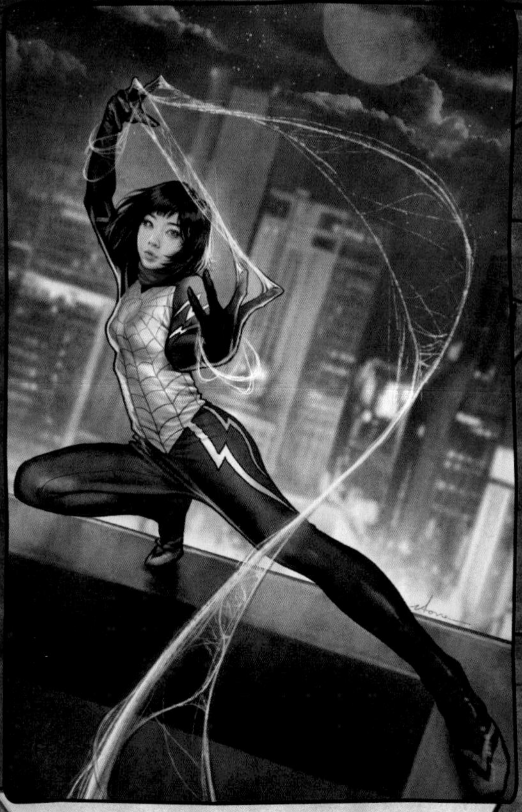

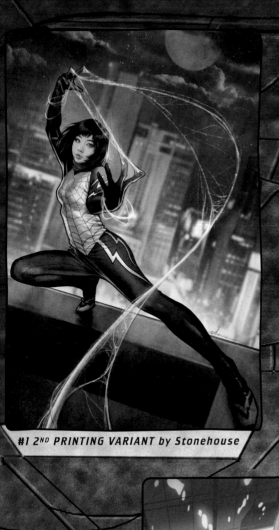

#1 2ND PRINTING VARIANT by Stonehouse

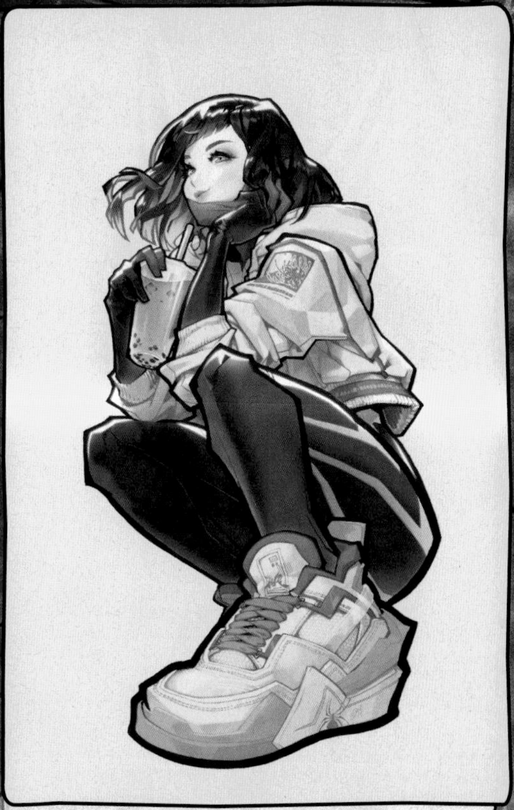

#2 VARIANT by Rose Besch

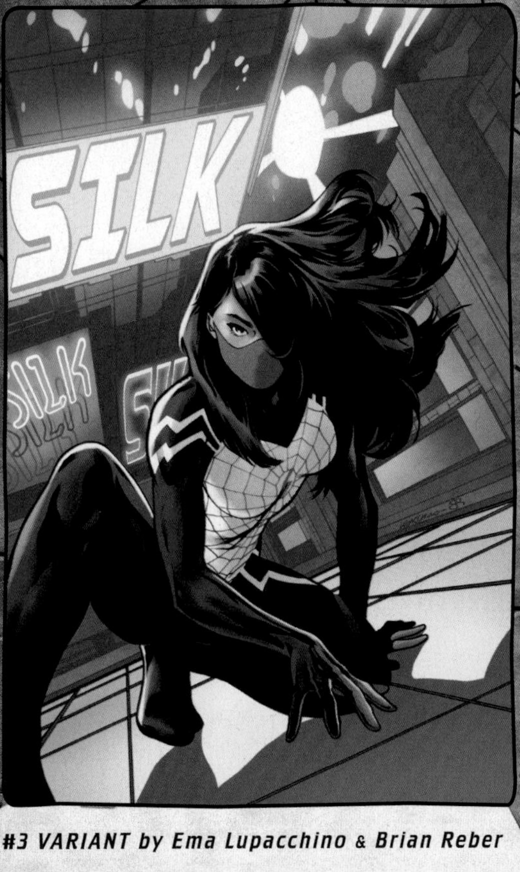
SILK
SILK

#3 VARIANT by Ema Lupacchino & Brian Reber

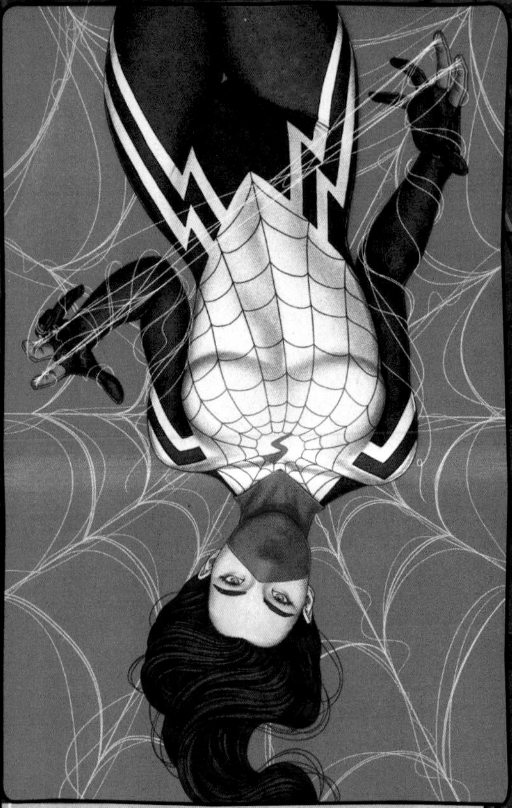

#4 VARIANT by Jenny Frison

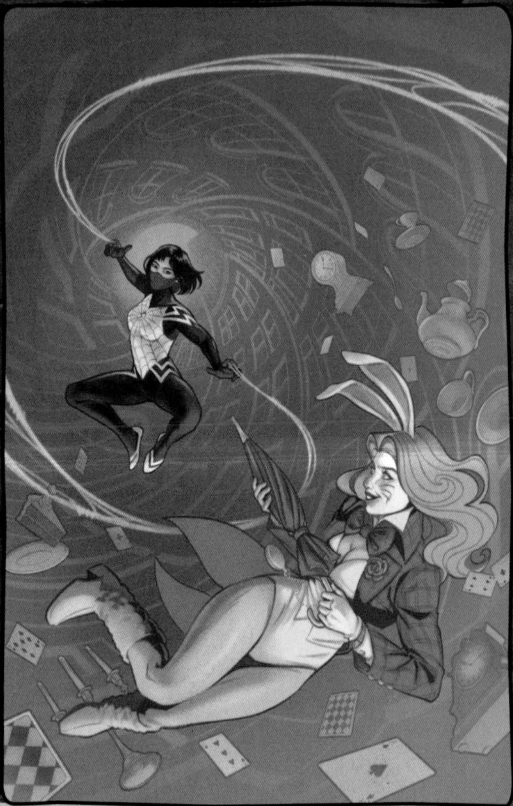

#4 SPIDER-MAN VILLAINS VARIANT
by Betsy Cola

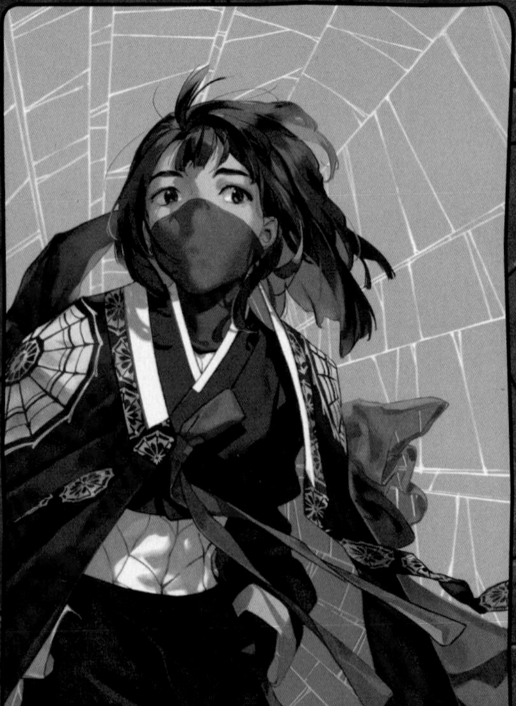

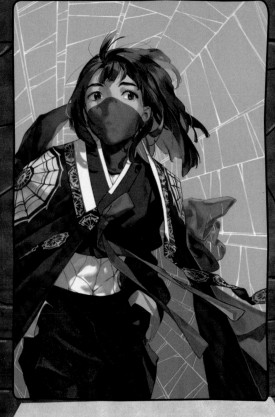

#5 VARIANT by Judy Jong